PLANS OF CHICAGO

PLANS OF CHICAGO

R. SAMUEL ROCHE AND ARIC LASHER

PUBLISHED BY
ARCHITECTS RESEARCH FOUNDATION
DISTRIBUTED BY THE UNIVERSITY OF CHICAGO PRESS

A • R • F

ARCHITECTS RESEARCH FOUNDATION

The Architects Research Foundation is a publicly supported not-for-profit foundation formed to promote the understanding of Chicago's unique architectural, design, and engineering heritage through the commissioning and dissemination of research that will be of practical and educational value to both the profession and the public. DIRECTORS: Gary Ainge, Thomas Beeby, Laurence Booth, James Nagle, Dennis Rupert, John Syvertsen, Daniel Weese.

440 North Wells Street, Suite 200, Chicago, IL 60654

11030 South Langley Avenue, Chicago, IL 60628

ISBN: 978-0-615-28220-6

Cover Illustration: Perspective view of the proposed improvement of Grant Park by Aric Lasher, 2009.

Frontispiece: Satellite view of Chicago, 2001. Image courtesy of NASA/Goddard Space Flight Center Scientific Visualization Studio.

Printed in Germany.

CONTENTS

THE PUBLICATION OF THIS BOOK HAS BEEN MADE
POSSIBLE THROUGH THE GENEROSITY OF THE FOLLOWING

Patrons

The Richard H. Driehaus Charitable Lead Trust
Hammond Beeby Rupert Ainge Architects

Benefactors

David and Juli Grainger
Wendy J. Paulson
J.B. and M.K. Pritzker Family Foundation
The Sanders Foundation
John and Ann Syvertsen

Supporters

Rolf Achilles and Pam Morris
Richard and Jill Almeida
Baldauf Catton von Eckartsberg Architects
Bohlin Cywinski Jackson
Vincent J. Buonanno
John H. and Gail A. Catlin
Clifton Gunderson LLP
Cooper, Robertson & Partners
Judith DiMaio, AIA, Dean, School of
    Architecture & Design, NYIT
John J. George, Partner,
    Daley and George, Ltd.
Edward C. Hirschland
Jeffrey Jahns
Ralph Johnson, Perkins + Will
Helen J. Kessler, FAIA, LEED A.P.
Peter Landon FAIA
Local Initiatives Support Corp. / Chicago
Dirk Lohan, FAIA
Todd Longstaffe-Gowan and Tim Knox
David McConnell
Dietrich Neumann

University of Notre Dame
    School of Architecture
John K. Notz, Jr.
Pelli Clarke Pelli Architects
Steven K. Peterson and Barbara M. Littenberg
Kathryn Quinn, AIA
Rise Group
Robert A. M. Stern Architects, LLP
Dennis E. Rupert and Karen Scott Johnson
Michael and Judith Sawyier
Harold O. Schulz Co., Inc.
Richard W. Shepro and Lindsay E. Roberts
Adele Simmons
Duncan G. Stroik
J. Lawton Thies
36 Foundation, Inc.
Tilton, Kelly + Bell, LLC
James M. Valenti, Valenti Builders
Joseph E. Valenti Jr., Valenti Builders
Burgess and Jennifer Wilson
Yale University

ACKNOWLEDGMENTS

—

Chicago possesses, perhaps to a unique degree, a community of individuals committed to its physical improvement and the cultivation of its legacy of achievement in matters of planning and design.

Without the early support and enthusiasm of Richard Driehaus, *Plans of Chicago* could not have been written. Without the initial endorsement and continuing guidance of Tom Beeby, it would not have developed as a proposal grounded in serious inquiry. Sunny Fischer of the Richard H. Driehaus Foundation encouraged the book at its earliest stages and throughout the process of its publication.

Tom Beeby, Dennis Rupert, and Gary Ainge offered to sponsor this project with resources from the office of Hammond Beeby Rupert Ainge. They saw the need for an organization that would publish books such as this one, and through their efforts, *Plans of Chicago* became the inaugural publication of the Architects Research Foundation, the founding members of which also supported and evaluated the book during its development.

Tom Beeby proposed a clear method of analysis and directed our inquiry toward greater conceptual clarity at a critical point. His foreword focuses general urban planning concerns on the architecture of the city. Dennis Rupert guided this book to completion as the final product of a design process; its coherence and refinement are indebted to his critical vision. Gary Ainge was instrumental in finding a professional audience for the book and encouraged its lavish graphic presentation.

Chicago architect and author Stuart Cohen read an early draft of the manuscript, and his assessment improved its arguments and structure. His afterword addresses urban planning with regard to architectural practice.

Kim Coventry of the Coventry Group brought to this project her formidable skills as an editor and manager and supplied the writing and the publication itself with necessary clarity and directness. Jason Pickleman and Daniel Marsden of the JNL Graphic Design gave the material a fitting and beautiful physical expression.

Teresa Fagan and Laura Andersen at the University of Chicago Press delivered this book to the public. The early encouragement of Adele Simmons of Metropolis 2020, Mary Woolever of the Art Institute of Chicago, Wil Hasbrouck of the Prairie Avenue Bookshop, and John Notz of the Library of American Landscape History helped this project find its footing.

Thanks are also due to those who helped fill the book's pages with illustrations. Jackie Maman and Danielle Kramer of the Art Institute of Chicago and Bryan McDaniel of the Chicago History Museum supplied the archival illustrations of earlier plans. Susan Raposa of the Commission of Fine Arts, Michael Dosch of the Olmsted National Historical Site, Malgosia Myc of the Bentley Historical Library at the University of Michigan, Julia Bachrach of the Chicago Park District, Timo Keinänen of the Museum of Finnish Architecture, and Oskar Muñoz of the Frank Lloyd Wright Foundation provided unfamiliar images of well-known projects. Jason Schifler of the City of Chicago Department of Planning and Development supplied the plans of existing conditions that were the foundations of our own plans. Professor Ray Bromley of the State University of New York at Albany offered guidance on the linear city. Clinton Prior and Sarah Pontius read and commented on drafts of the text. Michael Baumberger helped us complete final drawings.

The support of our subscribers demonstrates Chicago's continuing commitment to planning and design, which is maintained by its citizens as well as admirers from farther afield. Without their support, this project would not have been realized.

– R.S.R. & A.J.L., Chicago, 2009

FOREWORD

VOICES IN THE STREET: THE CITY REMEMBERS

THOMAS H. BEEBY

———

The city is the ultimate artifact of any civilization. For the purpose of discussion, it can be divided into three categories of buildings. Private houses and other structures built for individual use can be considered consumer goods and are not open for social evaluation. Commercial structures where people gather to work, making or exchanging goods and services, are instruments of production and are consumed by their own function. Regardless of their artistic merit, with few exceptions, residential and commercial structures are ultimately expendable over time. Public buildings however are ideological structures and must be judged by the quality of their concrete materiality and their social meaning. The drama of an evolving democratic society made up of a multiplicity of racial, ethnic, and cultural groups rubbing shoulders every day is most apparent in the public realm which extends from the streets into the parks and civic institutions that enrich urban life.

If the city is considered as a work of art, its form is vulnerable for it relies on figuration and history which function through their dialogic capacity and referentiality. Although painting and sculpture can be detached from referentiality and figuration to become abstract, the city in this reductive format has proven incapable of maintaining either legible form or a humane living environment. Art can become literally historicized through installation in a museum; indeed most art today is produced with that end in mind. The city or any of the buildings that aggregate to become its form, when aestheticized or taken out of context, become lifeless and abandoned: a ruin.

Architecture is the spoken word of the city, for it is an understandable communication system employing signs that are ordered in a particular manner. Classical architecture is the most complete extant language of architecture in this country. It is the common ancestor to all of the forms found in a city such as Chicago. Although resisted, opposed, transformed, and trivialized by over 150 years of use and misuse, Classicism

supplies the key to reading the city and its architecture. Classicism in its purest form is a canonic language, an authoritative discourse that attempts to create a world within the world, free of contradiction: perfection. Contradiction is avoided through geometric division and subdivision that order the parts into recognizable patterns. The grid is the most obvious device for creating regularity through repetition. Tripartition creates hierarchy by arranging building plans into three parts, with a dominant central portion. The same division in section as well as elevation creates a base, closely related to the ground, a preferred central portion for occupation, and an upper zone in silhouette against the sky. Classical language relies on a series of fixed and canonic ornamental forms of exact proportion that have evolved from Greek and Roman prototypes. These ornaments are arranged through symmetry to inhabit the ordered and hierarchical space of the structure. Bilateral symmetry is the dominant arrangement of Classical architecture; however, when desired, a vast accumulation of historical precedent allows for a vocabulary of great sophistication.

Through its long use as an ideological language, architecture carries within its forms a complicated and often contradictory set of values that are charged with a heritage that has to do with their past uses and associations. It is exactly this aspect that can give architecture its social meaning, for it carries the past into the present. Much of the architectural thought of the last century has attempted (through abstraction) to avoid the social capacity of architecture to reflect the ideologies of a complex multi-culture.

Chicago is a city of many architectural languages. This condition was driven during its formative growth in the late nineteenth century by the waves of Revival styles emanating from European theory and taste. The last century never fully resolved the battle between Modernism and Traditional architecture, resulting in the current multiplicity of competing ordering patterns. However, the argument for a single authoritative discourse or privileged language unique to Chicago has been a recurring theme for architects, critics, and historians. Architecture suffers from an innate tendency to periodically resist change by raising prevailing norms to the status of a canon. Classicism is the most obvious example of this desire but Modernism in the twentieth century proved equally tendentious. The problem with any privileged language is that it is approached from outside and is therefore distanced. As a monologue it has no exchange with its context or its audience. As a sacred writ, it is recited with great fervor by its proponents but it becomes a dead relic if its power to attract dies.

Chicago has been seen as a center for architectural invention. The Loop, acting as the economic as well as the symbolic heart of the city, has become synonymous with the outside world's view of Chicago. Here the ambition and pride of the business community have built and rebuilt its center at an incredible pace. Private real-estate developers have tested their power in a continuing debate with the public through the filter of government in the form of zoning and building codes. The central business district is the expression of this living dialogue. As with all speculative building, the developer risks financial loss in anticipating the wants of prospective buyers or users. The objective act of construction tempers subjective ambition. Conversely the user evaluates the product subjectively through the act of occupation. Ultimately, the elusive forces of the marketplace establish the life span of a commercial building.

The triumph of Chicago's architecture has been the result of this dialogue between those with money to speculate through building and those who will occupy their buildings. Most of the evolution of the tall building or skyscraper occurred in the Loop at the turn of the last century. The apparent freedom with which architects such as Louis Sullivan, Daniel Burnham, and John Root could remove themselves from the constraints of late-nineteenth-century academic control produced buildings of genuine originality though that was not their primary intent. Individually and as a group, Chicago architects created an internally persuasive discourse that opposed the authoritative discourse of canonic historic style. By allowing themselves to listen to the conflicting voices of their time—which spoke of technical innovation, social advancement, and artistic invention—they found that they could speak in their own words using their own accent and embellishment. They were able to assimilate the languages of the past into a synthesis that freed their discourse from one authoritarian language, as well as from previous convention that was no longer pertinent. These developments coincided with a flowering of literary imagination in Chicago related to the development of the novel; a creative environment that

supported invention based on openness to technical, social, and cultural change had evolved.

It is generally held by critics and historians that the flowering of architectural genius within the First Chicago School was put to an end by the reinstatement of the canon of Classicism by Burnham with the design for the World's Columbian Exposition of 1893. However I do not think the evidence in this case is conclusive. The audacity of the planning and the sheer magnitude of the architectural effort, coupled with an impossible timetable, forced Burnham to consider Classicism for pragmatic reasons alone. His primary intention had to do with the very nature of cities, reflected in his desire to produce a public realm with clear symbolic intent for its constituent buildings. This vast urban complex was envisioned to be clearly civic, not commercial. The remarkable architectural achievement of the tall building had no place in the iconography of the fair. The 'White City' was meant to be a highly charged ideological presence within the city's endless, monotonous grid of blocklike commercial structures designed as instruments of production, or the varied and idiosyncratic residences designed as commodities. It is interesting to note that two of the most paradigmatic, opposing icons of the period—the Reliance Building, a glass office building; and the Palace of Fine Arts, a Classical museum—were designed simultaneously in Burnham's office by the same architect, Charles Atwood. It appears possible that the complexity of practice at the turn of the century has been misunderstood, misconstrued, or forgotten by later critical and historical debate focused on style.

The work of the First Chicago School and subsequently of Frank Lloyd Wright signaled the beginning of the Modern Movement in architecture. Conceptual artistic advances in commercial and residential architecture in Chicago invigorated a new generation of European designers. Ironically, a very different approach to the city arrived with the immigration of Ludwig Mies van der Rohe to Chicago in 1939. On becoming director of the Illinois Institute of Technology's School of Architecture, he imposed a new authoritative discourse onto the architects of Chicago through the influence of his built work and that of his students. A new canon was imposed. The architecture of the Second Chicago School was based on a conception of architecture that would develop as a rational result of technological advancement. Its elegant minimal lines were informed by abstract European art. The use of the structural frame as grid came to represent the new order of land speculation that housed vast corporate bureaucracies. Behind its spare forms lay the decentralized urban vision of Ludwig Hilberseimer, Mies van der Rohe's colleague from Berlin, who had followed him to Chicago. The utopian European linear city proposed by Hilberseimer had no conceptual basis for a dialogue with the past, instead offering the promise of an entirely new city shaped by ostensibly objective planning principles previously untried in practice. The imposition of this vision within the heart of the city in the form of public housing produced sectors that were disconnected from the existing built fabric of Chicago. On the edge of the ever-expanding metropolis however a new linear perimeter was organized according to the precepts of Hilberseimer. Futuristic in the tone of its rhetoric, the Modern City's new suburbs promised the perpetual motion of constant technical advancement through an abstract architectural language. In practice a debased version of traditional houses populated their streets.

The European Modernist architect was an artist by association and practice. As a member of an avant-garde elite, he did not enter into a dialogue beyond the immediate company of fellow artists and architects. The middle class that had supported, both intellectually and financially, the advanced architecture of Burnham, Sullivan, Root, and Wright became a political adversary in the theoretical and political arguments emanating from Europe. These were promoted by the architecture schools in this country. Architecture became the vehicle for the advancement of private artistic visions masquerading as universal truths. The openness to history associated with previous historical convention retreated into the hands of developers in the face of the new authoritarian architectural language of Modernism.

Landmark Preservation as a civic movement was founded in response to the wholesale replacement of historical structures by Modern buildings. Landmark Preservation and Modernism in architecture are reflexive movements that incorporate the same concept of history, isolating the past and all its languages of form from current practice. Landmark Preservation in the name of cultural stewardship aims to save meaningful structures from destruction. Often however there is a sense of covert connoisseurship involved that values certain building styles over others. Guidelines from the federal government for new construction related to existing historic landmarks prohibit the extension of the original language of these buildings into new construction. This directive is based on the concept that architectural languages of the past are dead languages. This practice aestheticizes the landmark structure and decontextualizes it from any future construction, suggesting instead the use of Modern forms as the only appropriate language of our time. The proponents of Modernism eagerly endorse this position by the Landmark Preservation Movement because it reinforces their arguments for a unique canonic architecture for our time.

The characterization of certain buildings and periods of buildings in Chicago as 'masterpieces' or landmarks is an invention of the past forty-five years. In its ardent zeal to save the architectural artifacts of the First Chicago School, the Landmark Preservation Movement has isolated landmark structures from the condition of their production. As with any useful object exhibited in a museum, they suffer from the loss of their reason for being: their economic or social and cultural context. Their openness to life vanishes as the artificial boundaries of historicity are made concrete.

Architectural historians have been interested in the development of building in Chicago since the rise of Modern architecture. They have pursued a reductive theory that suggests that the temporal, social, and cultural separation between the First Chicago School and the Second Chicago School should be collapsed, creating an unassailable authenticity for Chicago architecture based on the simple truths of structural determinacy and the elevation of the technical aspects of architecture. In this formulation, the buildings of the First Chicago School become the direct historical ancestors for the buildings of Mies van der Rohe and his followers. Landmark Preservation then allows structures with approved stylistic attributes to be preserved regardless of their artistic merit, while new over-scaled speculative structures replace the disdained buildings of unorthodox origin. As the new orthodoxy prevails, the immensely rich and varied dialogue of the city that should be represented by its architecture is stilled. The tension that had existed between the entrepreneur seeking personal gain and the city government protecting the public's well-being evaporates as the benefit for all parties is made to appear identical. The psyche of the architect as artist provides the vision that legitimizes this process and public opinion is avoided. True artistic value, however, is the result of the social communication between the architect and society. The artificial intervention of a special interest group to determine the future of buildings within the city subverts that conversation, removing the public from the creative evolutionary process that forms the city.

It has been my belief for some time that an architect's task is to reflect on the city he or she inhabits and to try to determine the historic circumstances that produced its forms. He or she should also attempt to determine the relationship between past times and his or her own. The design and construction of public buildings require sensitivity to the past for these structures must be seen as carrying within their forms a complex and contradictory set of historical elements. All buildings carry with them a history of use and interpretation by which they achieve identity and differentiation. Architecture has the capacity for making present the past and it is this power that gives architecture its social meaning.

Public buildings produce resonance, to reach beyond their literal reality to an extended horizon that involves the user in the complex and ever-changing world of meanings attached to their forms, to surround the observer in the discourse of time. Resonance is a hybrid not a pure experience. Resonance creates an identity for a structure, giving it a cultural context. Wonder is the second characteristic associated with public buildings. It is the primary characteristic of monuments, riveting the attention of the viewer in an elevated sense of expectation through the uniqueness of the physical presence and configuration of the object. The singular difference of the monument, the intensity of its object quality, drowns out all visual interference from competing buildings and the surrounding environment.

These two seemingly contradictory qualities, connection and uniqueness, suggest that hybrid buildings might combine to produce simultaneously a sense of resonant wonder and wonderful resonance for then and only then can both the poetics and the politics of representation be realized. It is easier for our culture to pass from wonder to resonance than from resonance to wonder. Regardless, the goal—difficult but not utopian—should be to press beyond the limits of models, to cross boundaries, to create strong hybrids. This process allows the differing groups within a complex culture to appreciate a building that contains memories of 'others' without supplanting these memories with their own for the experience should be dialogic not monologic.

The significance of a public building should lie in the memories it evokes for only then can the values of a society be represented truly. To achieve this condition requires that the language of the architecture must place context over text, recognizing that at any given time in any given place there will be a set of conditions—social, historical, and cultural—that will ensure that a building built at this time will have a different meaning than it would have under any other conditions. The present and the past collide at this point, as the elements of the emerging design enter into a discourse with their own history. Although the building's overall form is in the control of the architect, the elements that make up this form are drawn from multiple sources, and their combination suggests that they condition one another's meaning. This dialogic imperative, mandated by the preexistence of the languages of architecture in the hand of the architect, should guarantee that there can be no monologue and therefore no privileged language of architecture. The dialogic imperative throws each architectural idea into an arena of conflict, where all the past experiences of those ideas are brought to bear on the architecture of this particular time and place.

In this conceptualization of architectural design, the canonic languages of the past such as Classicism and Modernism can interpenetrate each other. In this conflict, refraction occurs when known architectural elements attain new and unforeseen meaning when placed against one another. However the most potent possibility for discourse lies in the transgression of the ordinary or underestimated 'low' languages related to instruments of production or consumer goods into the heretofore privileged hierarchical rhetoric of 'canonic' architecture. The architecture of the streets and marketplace then struggles to liberate the language of ideological architecture from its prevailing point of view and established truths, even to free clichés from all that is currently accepted.

Architectural language in a city is similar to the language in a novel, which is mutable, reversible, contaminable, and always regenerative. Like all language, it originates in ambivalence, multi-vocality, conflict, incorporation, and transformation. The novel, a form of literature that flowered in the nineteenth century, is one of the triumphs of language. A major device for creative language in the novel involves the mixing of two or more different linguistic consciousnesses often widely separated in time and social space along with the combination of languages and pure dialogues. Novelistic hybrids are intentional; their double voicedness is not meant to be resolved since hybrids can be read simultaneously as belonging to two or more systems. They cannot be isolated by formal grammatical means, by quotation marks. The polyphonic novel has the potential to represent all the social voices of an era through orchestration. I believe architecture has that same potential in its role of providing the language spoken by the city.

INTRODUCTION

The story of the creation and implementation of the *Plan of Chicago* is among its most memorable aspects. Incorporated in 1837, Chicago was less than seventy years old in 1906, but it was the fastest-growing American city and the second-largest city in the country after New York (in Europe, only London, Paris, Berlin, and Vienna were larger). A powerful group of civic-minded businessmen approached Daniel Burnham, the country's foremost urban planner, to design a comprehensive plan for their city. Burnham was also a longtime Chicago resident, and he had made his planning reputation organizing the World's Columbian Exposition in 1893 for some of the same patrons. His plan for Chicago was to be the last and largest in a series of planning commissions that followed from this event. Over the next three years, Burnham, his associate Edward Bennett, and a team of architects, artists, and draftsmen prepared the most comprehensive city plan in

American history. They worked from a specially built studio on the roof of the downtown building where Burnham's architectural practice had its offices, overlooking the city and Lake Michigan, and they presented their progress to their patrons at regular meetings held there over lunch. In 1909 Burnham and his team published their plan in a lavish book full of beautiful, easy-to-understand illustrations of grand, exciting proposals. They also gave a series of illustrated lectures and created a motion picture shown in local theaters to advertise the plan to the public. The Chicago Board of Education adopted a version of the printed plan as a civics textbook for eighth-grade students in the city's public schools. The authority and beauty of the *Plan of Chicago* and the public support it generated persuaded the city to officially adopt it and, over the following decades, to institute many of its boldest proposals.

Just as memorable as the happy convergence of circumstances that enabled the publication of the *Plan of Chicago* is the vision of Chicago's future that is detailed in the plan's pages. Based on the city's phenomenal growth rate, the rising importance of its midwestern hinterland, and the national extent of its transportation connections, the *Plan of Chicago* predicted that over the following fifty years Chicago would become the world's largest and most important city. Burnham and Bennett's proposal gave equal attention to the economic and cultural concerns of the world's rising commercial capital, combining urban and natural public space on an unprecedented scale with improved networks of transportation and circulation that would maintain Chicago's competitive edge over other cities. A radial network of avenues, landscaped parkways, and rail lines connected a central city enriched with public gardens and monuments with a restful natural landscape on the periphery. Many of the plan's proposals, including its circular shape, either already existed or had been proposed in earlier plans; gradual, organic implementation was part of its allure.

The story of the plan's creation and the power of its vision can overwhelm further discussion about it. Both aspects emphasize the plan's place in the past, when urban planners operating under different assumptions practiced different methods of planning. In the years since its publication, other approaches to design have replaced Burnham and Bennett's emphasis on precedent as a source for new proposals. Widespread automobile use and the development of specific and exhaustive methods for gathering data about cities have challenged the relationship between planning and architecture. Today planners ask what the individual driver requires or how the character of a particular neighborhood can be preserved. Insofar as they consider the whole city, they no longer compose it, nor even address it in explicitly visual terms. In a general sense, the *Plan of Chicago* itself is regarded as complete, and this

has further obscured its possible relevance to contemporary planning problems.

It is in this light, however, rather than as an accomplished historical fact, that the *Plan of Chicago* should be considered on the centennial of its publication. As this book shows, contemporary planning problems belong to a larger historical process, a recurring pattern of distinct but related events that includes, but is not limited to, a record of the past. American urbanism fluctuates between periods of uncoordinated growth and those of coordinated planning, and American cities observe the latter only when the collective costs of the former, which are typically stimulated by advancements in transportation technology, outweigh the individual benefits. The early twentieth century marked a turning point between these two types of growth. The railroad remade urban America during the last half of the nineteenth century, concentrating new population growth and new industry in a handful of larger cities and causing these cities to expand drastically. The transforming effects of such dramatic growth were most apparent in Chicago, the country's railroad hub. The congestion created by an exploding population and an expanding periphery obstructed the rail traffic on which the city's economy depended. Continuous peripheral expansion also increased pressure on the center, which was inundated daily with a rising tide of commuting traffic, and caused the natural landscape—the major attraction of peripheral settlement—to recede. Both Chicago's problems and its physical character were typical of other cities in the United States; indeed, with its commercial economy, gridded street plan, dense commercial center, and diffuse residential periphery, Chicago was a larger version of most American cities.

The present significance of the *Plan of Chicago* lies in the resemblance of our own time period to this earlier one and in the typical qualities that Chicago retains, which signal the plan's potential relevance for American cities in general. During the second half of the twentieth century, the automobile remade American cities by fostering peripheral growth on a new scale. This has produced, albeit on a larger scale and through other means, the same congested circulation routes and dwindling natural open space found in the nineteenth-century city. Plans for urban improvement during both periods focused on individual rather than collective requirements: the commuter's need for more-efficient circulation or the resident's requirement for more-convenient access to a natural landscape. Through its second period of uncoordinated peripheral growth, however, Chicago has retained both the concentrated urban center and the open periphery of the past, a physical character it shares with most American cities. By reason of their unique levels of concentration and diffusion, New York and Los Angeles are exceptional in this regard, and Chicago therefore remains the largest typical American city. Its responses to common planning problems can potentially inform other American urban plans.

The *Plan of Chicago* remains the most complete precedent for coordinated urban planning in a typical American city. The appeal of coordinated planning has increased as the collective costs of uncoordinated urban growth have again begun to outweigh the individual convenience it affords. A critical assessment of the plan's strategies for coordinating growth is one goal of this book. This will require an exploration of its role in a national planning movement, where the common strategies of an evolving method can be identified. A complete evaluation will also demand examination of the plan's place in a local context, where those common strategies were directed toward a specific problem, and where we can compare them with strategies from other planning approaches.

Such a critical assessment will also separate recurring planning problems from new ones, allowing us to establish the plan's relevance to contemporary planning problems in Chicago; this is the book's second goal. A plan for future growth that applies the conclusions that have been drawn, both about different planning approaches and about Chicago's persistent character, is its third and final goal. These were also the goals of the *Plan of Chicago*.

This book is neither a comprehensive history nor a comprehensive plan; in both regards, it relates larger ideas selectively, through representative examples of different planning approaches. These examples are specific plans, which convey abstract priorities through concrete proposals, where points of overlap — potential foundations for new plans — are also specific and concrete. Such plans are individual responses to particular circumstances. This book may be read, therefore, as both a continuous narrative and a series of interdependent essays. A comparison of planning approaches through specific proposals will draw on Chicago's uniquely strong and complete planning history, in every stage of which the country's foremost architects and designers are represented. Frederick Law Olmsted designed the prototypical American suburb and peripheral park in Chicago. The American tradition of narrative urban planning was born at the World's Columbian Exposition and achieved its fullest expression in the *Plan of Chicago*. Major Prairie-school architects, including Frank Lloyd Wright, Walter Burley Griffin, and Jens Jensen, tackled the problem of suburban housing in Chicago, where the modern architects Ludwig Mies van der Rohe and Ludwig Hilberseimer also proposed urban plans uniquely suited to the requirements of the automobile-based industrial city. These examples are sources for a new metropolitan plan that coordinates, as did Burnham and Bennett's plan, past precedents with contemporary requirements.

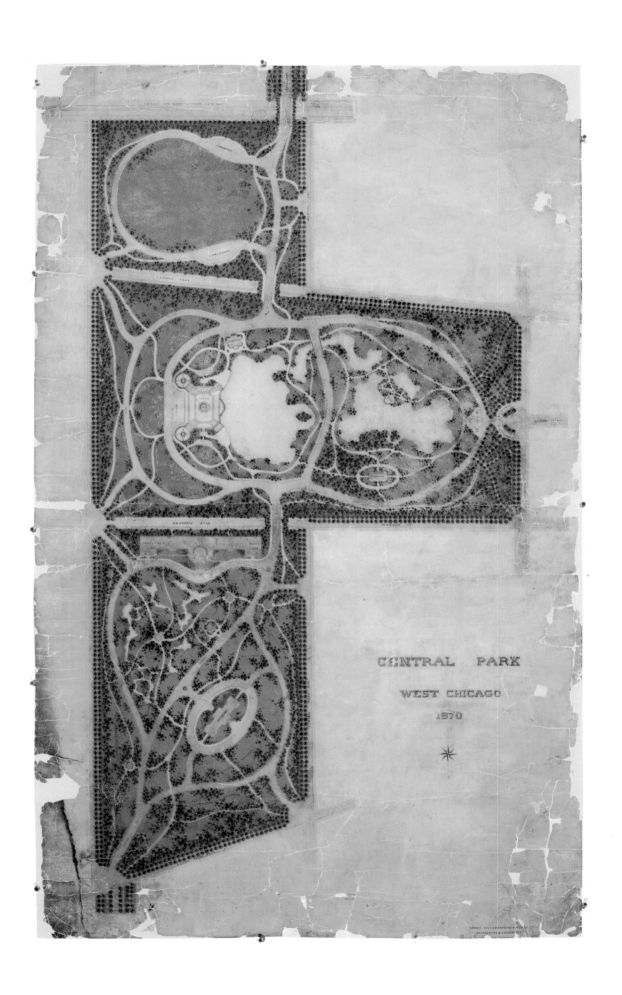

CENTRAL PARK

WEST CHICAGO

1870

CHAPTER 1

EARLY PLANNING IN CHICAGO

COMMERCIAL AND SPECULATIVE ORIGINS · TECHNOLOGICAL
ADVANCES AND THEIR EFFECTS · PERIPHERAL IMPROVEMENTS
TWO APPROACHES TO PARK PLANNING · SUBURBAN HOUSING
SUBURBAN INDUSTRY · CHICAGO IN 1893

COMMERCIAL AND SPECULATIVE ORIGINS

As early as the seventeenth century, potential transportation connections determined that there would be a commercial city on Lake Michigan, at the mouth of the Chicago River, bringing the Great Lakes watershed into close proximity to that of the Mississippi River and its tributaries. The French explorers Jacques Marquette and Louis Joliet, whose canoe was carried by Native Americans across the dry land between the south branch of the Chicago River and the Des Plaines River in 1673, later pointed out that digging a canal across this portage would create a continuous water route between Lake Erie and Florida.[1] A city on the portage would naturally profit from the commerce conveyed along such a route.

On these grounds, the young United States secured Chicago's site in 1795 from a confederation of Native American tribes through the Treaty of Greenville: "one piece of land six miles square at the mouth of Chikago river emptying into the south-west end of Lake Michigan, where a fort formerly stood."[2] An additional clause granted free passage by land and water to United States citizens "from the mouth of Chikago, to the commencement of portage, between that river and the Illinois, and down the Illinois river to the Mississippi."[3] The Treaty of Greenville thereby laid the foundations for a lakeside port at the head of a route for waterborne commerce.

The treaty also ensured that the establishment of the port would conform to existing procedures for adding new territory to the United States. In the years following the Revolutionary War, the federal government assumed the war debts of individual states in exchange for their westward extensions to the Mississippi River, which it surveyed and sold in individual parcels in order to finance the consolidated war debt. The Land Ordinance of 1785 and the Northwest Ordinance of 1787 projected a theoretical surveyor's grid over the entire territory that allowed parcels to be identified and sold without reference to geographical features. This grid was comprised of squares measuring a mile on each side (sections), thirty-six of which made up a township. The square-mile sections of a township could in turn be divided into quarter sections that were half a mile on each side, and from there into streets and building lots (FIGURE 1.2). Through simple subdivision, a system for measuring new territory also became a system for colonizing it. Larger divisions of land contained farms, while smaller divisions contained streets and buildings that could be expanded by subdividing adjacent agricultural sections. This continental grid could accommodate changes in scale and land use over time without disrupting existing conditions. As a part of this system, the city of Chicago was preceded on its site by a plan based on an expandable grid.

The United States government populated this plan with people and buildings by inducing private speculation, or development of land for profit. Such development was encouraged by the creation of a more-ambitious version of the canal originally envisioned by Marquette and Joliet, which would traverse almost one hundred miles, between the Chicago and Illinois rivers. The opening of the Erie Canal in 1825, which gave the Great Lakes access to the eastern seaboard and Europe, made the prospect of an inland canal that would tap potential new markets east and west of Chicago even more appealing. As the original owner of the land along the canal's proposed route, the federal government granted alternate one-mile sections on either side to Illinois, which divided and sold them to finance the canal's construction (FIGURE 1.3). In 1830 Illinois laid out one half section of the Chicago township, which measured one mile by half a mile and was located at the intersection of the Chicago River's three branches, about a mile inland from the lakefront. The state divided it into sixty-six blocks and offered the lots for sale (FIGURE 1.4). Construction of the Illinois and Michigan Canal commenced in 1836.

Figure 1.1 Plan of Central Park, West Chicago Park District, by William Le Baron Jenney, 1870.

5

Figure 1.2 Map showing the principal meridians and base lines in the United States governing U.S. surveys also showing the belts of standard time. Diagram 1: plan of numbering townships; diagram 2: plan of a township divided into thirty-six sections; diagram 3: possible subdivisions of a section; diagram 4: fractional part of a section.

Figure 1.3 Map showing land grants along the Illinois and Michigan Canal, 1956. As noted, "the shaded sections indicate the lands along the canal route certified to the state of Illinois under the provisions of the Act of Congress approved March 2, 1827." The two other maps represent additional land grants, approved in 1842 and 1854.

Figure 1.2
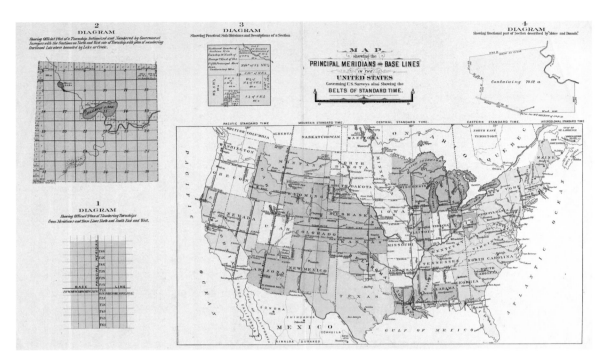

Figure 1.3
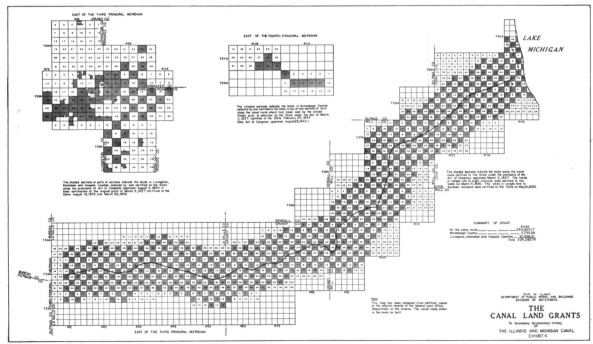

Figure 1.4 Map of Chicago and additions by Edward Benton Talcott, 1836. The original settlement is outlined in pink. The projected Fort Dearborn Addition is directly below this, to the east.

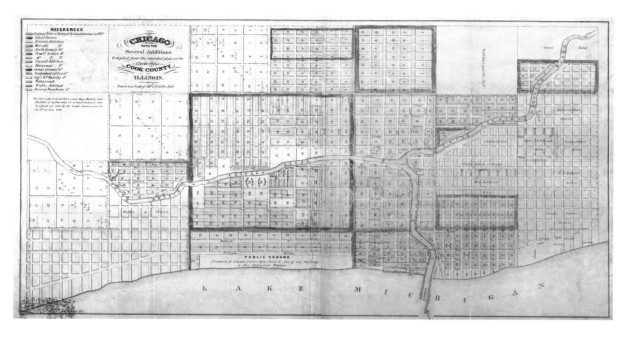

Figure 1.4

From the outset, the federal and state governments tied Chicago's urban development to that of its transportation connections.[4] These connections, however, were potential rather than actual during the first two decades of the city's growth, and the value of land therefore remained largely theoretical, which only intensified speculation in real estate. Transactions began to concentrate along the route to the proposed canal, on the northern and western edges of the southeast portion of the original settlement, today defined by Wacker Drive on the north and west, State Street on the East, and Madison Street on the south. The northern boundary of this area was the main branch of the Chicago River, which offered a protected harbor and was thus developed as the city's port. To the east, the federal government retained a lakefront parcel occupied by Fort Dearborn, which had been built in 1803 at the river's mouth to secure the outcome of the Treaty of Greenville. Bounded on two sides by water and on the third by Fort Dearborn, the southeastern section could only expand southward, away from the port. Better access to transportation routes, the resulting commercial pressure to concentrate trade, and federal prerogative together laid the foundation for a compact urban precinct in an open landscape.

The earliest residents of Chicago had settled outside this zone, either north or west of the river, or around Forth Dearborn. Commercial concentration, together with the early port-related industry that clung to all three branches of the Chicago River, pushed new residential development beyond the center of commercial speculation to the north, west, and south, where land use took on a larger scale and a less-urban character. Speculation in housing thrived on this periphery, where proximity to the center was balanced by the availability of larger parcels farther away. In this way, a primarily residential periphery, dependent on convenient connections to the center and without clearly defined limits, developed as soon as Chicago expanded beyond its original settlement in the 1840s.

Public space also appeared outside the commercial center, on the lakefront parcel to the east, where it evolved as another inducement to speculation. As this intensified in the adjacent southeast portion of the city, the federal government found the option of developing its holdings increasingly attractive. In 1839 it added its lakefront property to the existing grid and divided it into building lots on two new streets parallel to the shoreline, Wabash and Michigan avenues (FIGURES 1.4 and 1.5). The lots along the river to the north were highly desirable additions to the harbor, but those in the southern portion lacked obvious commercial appeal. The federal government designated one block of southern lots as public land. The prospect that this area would remain undeveloped underscored its scenic potential and raised the value of surrounding lots. This new public space also adjoined a larger lakefront parcel to the east, which the canal commissioners had designated "a public ground . . . free and clear of any building" in a previous addition to the town.[5] The federal and state governments had found a place for scenic public space within the established process of speculative urban development.

Figure 1.5 Map of Chicago and vicinity by William Clogher, 1849. The Fort Dearborn addition is shown as realized.

Figure 1.5

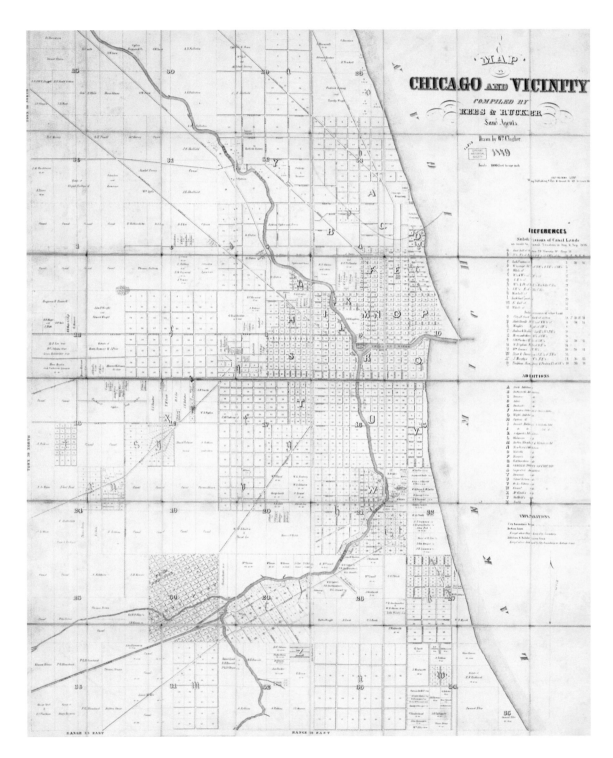

Government initiative founded Chicago and stimulated its development by private interests with the promise of profitable returns on investment. This process created the beginnings of a city that had two parts with complementary uses and contrasting physical characters. One of these was urban; the other was a middle ground between town and country. Together they described a simple radial arrangement with concentric zones laid over a neutral gridiron plan. Settlement decreased in density and increased in scale as it extended away from the lake, but the governing lines of the grid remained constant. This dual physical character, the city's larger radial pattern, and its local orthogonal one were already evident when Chicago's nominal reason for being, the Illinois and Michigan Canal, was completed in 1848 (FIGURE 1.5).

TECHNOLOGICAL ADVANCES AND THEIR EFFECTS

Advances in transportation and building technology transformed Chicago while further entrenching its established character. The railroad made the city the national transportation hub that its water connections had long suggested it could become. Together with new construction techniques, it fueled and serviced an unprecedented growth rate in Chicago, making the youngest major city in the United States the second largest by 1890.[6] New modes of transportation and building further developed the complementary characters of the center and the periphery.

The first railroad from Chicago opened the same year that the Illinois and Michigan Canal was completed. Chicago mayor and real-estate developer William Ogden, together with Illinois farmers and investors from Chicago and the East Coast, developed the Galena and Chicago Union Railroad as a better way to move agricultural products to market.[7] During the rainy season, when this traffic was heaviest, horse-drawn carts became bogged down in the low, flat land around Chicago. The same terrain could easily accommodate railroad tracks, which functioned without regard to weather or climate. For this reason, the railroad possessed advantages over the water transportation that it had been envisioned to serve. Moreover, waterborne commerce was confined to existing watercourses, which did not always follow the shortest distance between two points. New rail lines using the shortest courses, on the other hand, could draw raw materials quickly, cheaply, and consistently from previously inaccessible territory. Better access to these raw materials created new markets for them. The railroad, together with the mechanical reaper (manufactured in Chicago by Cyrus McCormick beginning in 1847), increased agricultural production on the farms south and west

of Chicago. It also opened up forests in Wisconsin and Michigan to lumber production. Railroad development made Chicago a center of grain and lumber distribution. Railroad connections also attracted more-intensive industry to Chicago. Beginning in 1869, when the refrigerated railcar was invented, meat processed in Chicago at the consolidated Union Stock Yards (opened in 1865) could be shipped anywhere in the country. Steel manufacturing gathered raw materials from a wide area that was also centered on Chicago. These new industries created a demand for more railroad routes, which in turn attracted more industry. In 1861 seven routes converged on Chicago; by 1873 there were fourteen.[8]

If Chicago was at the center of a web of raw materials, it was also at one end of a direct line that delivered them to eastern markets. Trunk lines from Chicago through Buffalo to New York and Boston, and through Pittsburgh to Philadelphia, established the midwestern city as a critical entrepôt, the major transfer point for raw goods moving from west to east and for manufactured goods moving from east to west. Trains traveling across the country could not bypass Chicago—the western terminus for lines originating on the East Coast and the eastern terminus for those originating on the West Coast—because they had to change lines there.[9]

Locally, this rail activity converged on the central city, where it serviced the port and the related industry that congregated there through the end of the nineteenth century. By 1871 it further isolated the port and commercial core behind a ring of rail yards, which began to close around the South Side—the primary path for commercial expansion—when a passenger station opened on Van Buren Street in 1867 (FIGURE 1.6). A larger, more-efficient system for delivering freight created commercial growth and a demand for new office space at its more-constrained hub. The opportunity to rebuild this hub at a scale and density appropriate to those demands presented itself in 1871, when the Great Chicago Fire destroyed much of the center and the surrounding city while leaving the rail lines untouched.

A new type of steel-frame construction and the invention of the elevator made this possible beginning in the 1880s. Debuting at around ten stories and assembled from locally manufactured steel, the steel-frame tall office building was cheaper to build and more profitable to rent than its masonry predecessor. Because the load-bearing walls of masonry buildings had to be thicker at the bottom than at the top, they necessarily contained small, dark offices on their lower floors.[10] The exterior walls of steel-frame buildings, on the other hand, were merely the interstices of a frame supported by rigid joint connections. They could therefore be opened up to an unprecedented degree, and even tall buildings right next to one another could have offices with adequate lighting and ventilation.

Figure 1.6 Map showing property of railroads in the business center of Chicago, 1898. The Van Buren Street station is shown in peach.

As the product of an industry that mass-produced standard parts for basic configurations, the steel-frame tall office building exhibited a standard character, with one example fundamentally resembling the next in plan, section, and elevation. Only the specific requirements of a given site distorted the ideal model of this three-dimensional grid. In Chicago this distortion was minimal because the sites that received tall buildings also belonged to a standard grid. There the tall office building extended the continental grid into three dimensions and further divided it into floors and offices. On smaller lots, tall buildings were slabs, with two rows of offices on either side of a hallway; on the larger half-block and, occasionally, full-block lots, they were courtyard buildings with offices facing both inward and outward (FIGURE 1.7). A burgeoning market for office space concentrated in a privileged, standardized precinct, combined with local steel production and the pragmatic attitudes of speculators and architects, yielded a process of conservative experimentation that wrought from each parcel its most intensive and efficient use, remaking Chicago's commercial center on a larger scale and at a higher density. These conditions ensured that the basic structural, organizational, and expressive possibilities of the steel-frame tall building were first and most thoroughly worked out in Chicago.

Population growth kept pace with growth in commerce and industry. From 1850 to 1870, Chicago's population grew tenfold, from 30,000 to 300,000; by 1890 it had more than tripled again, and Chicago overtook Philadelphia as the nation's second-largest city. During the same period, Chicago's

area increased fivefold, from 36 square miles to about 169 (FIGURE 1.8).[11] New populations settled diffusely on a drastically expanded periphery, to which the railroad and its local counterparts gave easy access. Beginning in 1858, horses pulling cars on tracks brought peripheral residents to the city center. The cable car, powered by a constantly moving buried cable that it gripped and released, conveyed residents from even farther away by 1882. Later in the same decade, the electric streetcar, which moved along a raised guideline, flourished still farther into the periphery. In 1893 Chicago's first section of elevated rail opened in time to take visitors to the World's Columbian Exposition on the far southern periphery, seven miles from the center.

New modes of transportation served new settlement farther out more readily than they replaced old modes in existing neighborhoods. Each one moved faster and stopped less frequently than its predecessors, fostering a larger and more-diffuse pattern of settlement. With land always available beyond the existing periphery for new settlement, peripheral expansion remained the most attractive option for residential growth. Thus, horsecar lines continued to serve the old periphery within a few miles of the center until 1900.

Together, old and new modes of transportation forged a coordinated network. The faster modes utilized major peripheral streets, which were either the half-mile divisions of the quarter sections or old arterial roads that had been subsumed into the expanding city and now cut diagonally through the grid. Residents traveling from the far periphery typically changed

Figure 1.6

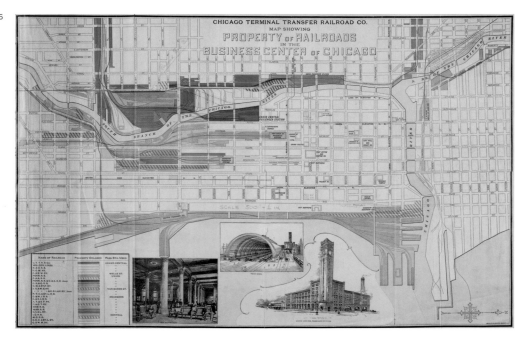

Figure 1.7
Left: Monadnock Block, plan of the second and fourteenth floors, by Burnham and Root, 1889.
Right: Rand-McNally Building, plan of the fourth floor, by Burnham and Root, 1888.

Figure 1.8 Map showing territorial growth of the city of Chicago by Charles Müller and Roderick Manstein, 1891.

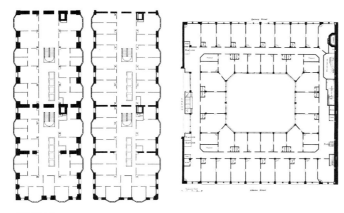

Figure 1.7

Figure 1.8

transportation type as they approached the center, which was serviced on nearly every street by cable cars or horsecars.

Converging passenger traffic thus added to the pressures of freight and commerce concentrated on the city center. This traffic only increased when the means of processing it improved. In 1897 the Union Elevated Railroad built a continuous elevated track in the city center that allowed trains from three separate existing lines to turn around without stopping. This loop further circumscribed the commercial core and gave it the name by which it is still known.[12] Beyond it a ring of passenger railroad terminals was put in place by 1893 (FIGURE 1.6).

During the 1890s, a second generation of steel-frame buildings, twice as tall as their predecessors, was under construction within the Loop. Another Chicago innovation in frame construction, which predated the steel frame by fifty years, had by then created another uniform physical environment on the periphery. Balloon framing transformed home construction from the work of skilled craftsmen into an industry, populating the peripheral landscape with single-family homes built cheaply and quickly.[13] Workers without specialized skills could lay out walls of vertical and horizontal supports on the ground, nail them together, raise them into place, and cover them with clapboards. Like steel-frame construction, balloon framing utilized mass-produced standard parts—in this case, nails and lumber—which were processed locally and were therefore readily available. A burgeoning market for new housing, convenient transportation connections, and available open land together produced a peripheral environment that was as standard as its central-city counterpart.

PERIPHERAL IMPROVEMENTS

Conditions in the commercial center and on the residential periphery produced distinct approaches to improvement, undertaken by local government in concert with relevant private interests. Central city improvements targeted infrastructure to induce private investment and enhance overall economic performance. Developers were responsible for upgrading their own buildings and lots. In 1855 the Chicago City Council mandated that the city's streets be raised to improve drainage and accommodate the first comprehensive sewerage system in the United States, a process that was largely complete by 1858 (FIGURE 1.9).[14] Ten years later, a two-mile long tunnel beneath Lake Michigan was built to supply Chicago with fresh water, and it was supplemented in 1880 by a longer tunnel that served residents farther from the lake.

Peripheral conditions called for comprehensive rather than targeted improvements. The pollution, congestion, and noise of the central city might threaten workers' health or

Figure 1.9   Plan of the Chicago sewerage system by the Chicago Board of Sewerage Commissioners, 1858.

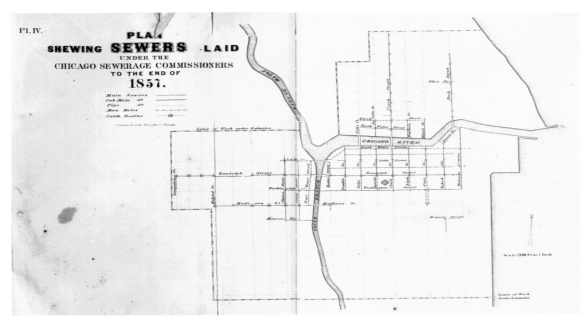

nerves, but as it was confined by geography and transportation lines, these problems could be escaped. The peripheral environment, on the other hand, was both uniform and pervasive. As a result, it consumed the natural landscape that was supposedly the periphery's main attraction and created a monotonous sprawl that had none of the restful qualities that housing in a natural landscape should have.

The periphery's complementary functional relationship to the central city, its range of uses, and its broad extent further encouraged comprehensive improvements there. As the counterpart to a working center, and the home of its commercial and industrial leaders, the periphery was a logical place to address the issues of recreation and culture. The complexity of the overall peripheral program—the collection of purposes it served—which included housing, recreation, circulation, and access to a natural landscape, also invited planners to experiment with these elements. Unlike the center, the periphery provided them with the room, and therefore the freedom, to do so.

Beginning in the 1860s, peripheral improvements focused on creating parks to address all these elements (including housing on occasion) at once. As reclaimed or improved natural landscapes, parks could reestablish the main draw of the periphery and thereby lure new residents to the surrounding neighborhoods. In Chicago the development of a metropolitan park system that serviced both local residents and the larger region (with its pool of prospective buyers) was not merely, or even primarily, a shared civic enterprise. Separate park districts on the north, south, and west sides of the city, each granted its own charter by the state legislature in 1869, competed for the same affluent residents.[15] Parcels that were large enough to draw

crowds and had easy access to transportation were therefore essential to these plans, and the separate districts emerged on the far periphery in a wide arc, through which the spokes of the radiating transportation network passed (FIGURE 1.10).

The park parcels' local interaction with the existing urban pattern, their size and configuration, and their existing natural features determined the complementary characters of the larger districts. The most remote park district was also the largest and most ambitious in terms of its program.

TWO APPROACHES TO PARK PLANNING

Frederick Law Olmsted was already recognized as the foremost American landscape architect when the South Park Commission asked him to design its park system in 1869. A decade earlier, his winning design for Central Park in New York City—submitted with his design partner, the English architect Calbert Vaux—had made his reputation and established landscape architecture as a profession.[16] Olmsted and Vaux's plan built on an English tradition of romantic planning that emphasized the inherent "natural" properties of landscape, in contrast to a classical tradition of garden design that treated a building's natural setting as a rational extension of its architecture. Romantic planning emphasized the aesthetic effects of the landscape in its own right, and its extension beyond private estates into the realm of public improvement coincided with a growing awareness of the costs of industrial urbanization.[17] Olmsted and Vaux had designed romantic plans for an equally ambitious park in Brooklyn and the beginnings of a unified park system for Buffalo. They had also extended their planning

Figure 1.10 Chicago boulevard and park system, 1879–80. From *History of Chicago from the Earliest Period to the Present Time* by A. T. Andreas, 1886.

beyond parks, with proposals for urban parkways, suburban and rural institutional campuses, a cemetery, and a residential community, all of which evolved from the natural landscape rather than the urban grid.[18] Olmsted and Vaux's 1871 plan for the South Park District represented their largest park plan and, with its pendant housing program, their most ambitious foray into planning to date.[19] In integrating recreation, circulation, and housing into an enhanced natural landscape, it proposed a distinct physical order for suburban settlement.[20]

The Chicago real-estate magnate Paul Cornell had initially conceived the South Park District as a joint venture between Chicago and the independent town of Hyde Park, seven miles to the south, which he had founded in 1853.[21] He was an original member of the South Park Commission, which in 1869 acquired three parcels next to Hyde Park, considerably beyond the city limits: a six-hundred-acre tract on Lake Michigan, another parcel about two thirds as large a mile to the west, and a connecting strip six hundred feet wide.

Olmsted and Vaux sought to forge from these separate parcels a single landscape that would unify and focus the natural surroundings.[22] In contrast to the enhanced landscapes of their Manhattan and Brooklyn parks, which offered natural

Figure 1.10

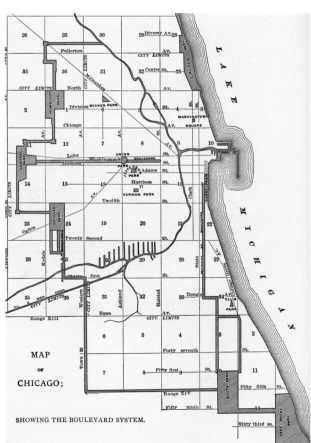

escapes from urban surroundings, the Chicago parks were intended to endow the residential neighborhoods of the Chicago periphery with their own romantic character.

Taking Lake Michigan, the only impressive geographic feature in Chicago, as a point of departure, Olmsted and Vaux constructed a plan around the concept of constant water connections (FIGURE I.II).[23] They imagined the three parcels as the site of a watercourse, which would originate in the inland parcel, called the Upper Park; flow along the connector, called the Midway Plaisance; and empty into Lake Michigan by a series of lagoons in the so-called Lower Park. A "river" with a source and a mouth imposed a simple and dramatic unity on separate parcels, which Olmsted and Vaux described as divisions of a larger South Park, further unifying the system with a single name.

Lake Michigan connected the South Park to the city center. Olmsted wrote that regular ferry service, utilizing a pier in the Lower Park, would allow the South Park "to practically begin at the mouth of the Chicago River."[24] Even the inland Upper Park would be accessible to the larger city by water. The watercourse also arranged the other elements of the park and the local activities within each section. Extensive lagoons in the Lower Park precluded a single, large open space there, and so a meadow called the South Open became the dominant feature of the Upper Park, which in any case was already an inland prairie. By occupying the interior of each park parcel, these large features freed the edges for daily neighborhood use.

This simple arrangement would bring area residents into direct, regular contact with the park. Public natural space would mingle with private natural space around individual homes, which would occupy the curving streets that continued the park drives.[25] These drives provided access to park activities and offered leisurely alternatives to other transportation routes in this part of the city. Park drives would continue farther afield as boulevards, routes for leisure circulation enriched with landscape elements from which commercial and public transportation were excluded.[26] The park district charters had already provided for the necessary connections between these three systems, but boulevards were also established elements of Olmsted and Vaux's repertoire, having been included in the park plans for Brooklyn and Buffalo.[27] Endowed with some of the naturalistic character of their destinations, boulevards supplied urban neighborhoods remote from actual parks with some of their sense of repose.

The South Park's large size, remote location, and expansive character allowed, and even encouraged, Olmsted and Vaux to propose a comprehensive suburban order that complemented rather than extended the existing peripheral settlement pattern. None of these qualities, however, prevented the park planners

Figure 1.11   Plan of the proposed Chicago South Park District by Olmsted, Vaux and Co. Landscape Architects, 1871.

Figure 1.11

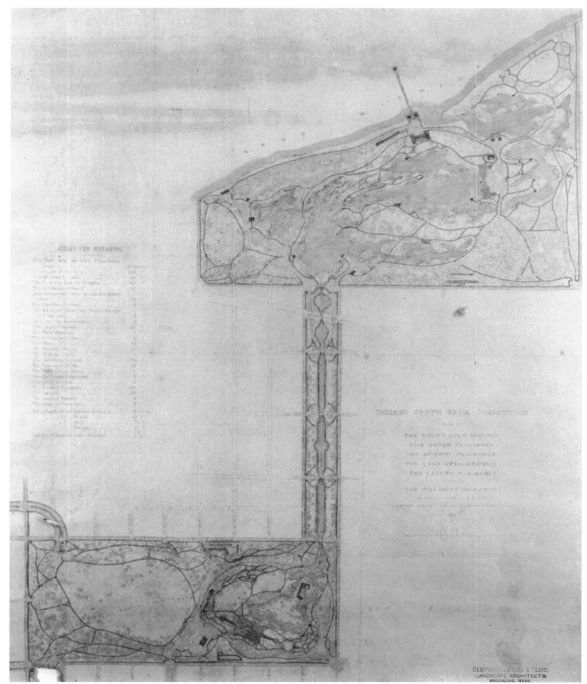

from presenting their designs as parts of the larger city. The South Park was easily accessible by rail, and Olmsted detailed plans for connecting it to the central city by ferry. This alternate connection, the park's romantic character, and its seamlessly integrated program, in which one element could not be easily separated from the others, all confirmed the ambitiously planned park system as an equal counterpart to the commercial core and no less a part of the larger city.[28]

The West Park District, closer to the city than the South Park and further entangled with existing patterns of transportation and settlement, more fully engaged the existing street grid and accepted its established terms. In this context, the West Parks emerged with an urbane character that emphasized the improving effects of culture as much as the restorative effects of landscape. Existing transportation lines, the price of available land, and the state legislature's stipulation that three parks be evenly distributed within Chicago's city limits set the parameters for planning the West Park District. The park commissioners procured three parcels with boulevard connections that described a shallow concentric arc about four miles from the central city; together, these totaled about six hundred acres, the size of the Lower Park division of the South Park. This smaller system, spread across a larger segment of the periphery, was closer to the city center and therefore crossed by many more lines of transportation. The South Park's upper and lower divisions were separated by two major through streets and one rail line, while a total of six major through streets (four half-mile streets and two diagonal streets) and two rail lines traversed the West Park District, with three of those streets dividing two of the parcels. Nor did these parcels violate the existing divisions of the grid; each either occupied an available subdivision of a quarter section or was assembled from subdivisions in adjacent quarter sections. These conditions did not favor rethinking the existing pattern of residential settlement in the surrounding neighborhoods, which in 1869 had already begun to develop along the established course of orthogonal subdivision (SEE FIGURE 5.2).

Such constraints limited effective romantic planning because they could not be convincingly escaped. In 1870 the West Park Commission hired the architect and engineer William Le Baron Jenney, who brought to park planning a rational rather than romantic emphasis.[29] He graduated in 1856 from the École Centrale des Arts et Manufactures in Paris, which established technical expertise through a holistic approach to design that reconciled a range of practical requirements. Among Jenney's student projects were a water system, grading and drainage improvements to a site, and a country house. A varied practical curriculum produced a rational design approach that might integrate elements of a complementary

character but, unlike romantic planning, would resist subordinating one to the other.[30] Jenney therefore designed the West Park District as an ensemble that preserved distinct functional and compositional divisions. He made each park—or, as necessary, park division—a contained landscape arranged around a central tableau, which often included a lake or a pond that also drained the low sites and provided the scenic value supplied by Lake Michigan in the other park districts.

The dividing lines of circulation and the overall irregular outlines of the parcels further arranged the complementary components of these contained landscapes. In Humboldt Park, an open meadow for sport occupied a projection of the park's main square, which was largely filled by a picturesque lake. Central Park's three divisions corresponded to three distinct zones: a large open field, a water landscape further subdivided into two ponds by a park drive, and a wood with zoological and botanical exhibits (FIGURE 1.1).[31] Douglas Park, the southernmost of the three parks, was a larger version of this central section, with a lake divided into two parts by a diagonal through street that took on a leisurely curve where it ran through the park.

Adopting a romantic character was one way circulation routes helped maintain and negotiate the transition between the urban street grid and the parks' contained landscapes. Placed along park edges, they set off those landscapes and received and redirected the orthogonal streets of the surrounding blocks. Where it was impossible for their romantic character to extend outward into adjacent neighborhoods, Jenney elaborated the transition between one street type and another with formal plazas or *rond pointes*. These sometimes extended beyond the confines of the park to create points of departure for the park boulevards that, as in the South Park District, combined the straight lines of the grid with the softening effects of landscape elements. A graduated relationship between urban and natural order, the presentation of natural landscapes as contained sites, and didactic elements such as botanical and zoological gardens identified the West Parks as places where one could imbibe culture in a natural setting rather than romantic natural escapes from urban conditions. As sites with visible boundaries, the parks were gardens as well as landscapes; and with their prominent buildings, public terraces, and planted axes, they were natural extensions of the built order. They took cues from their surroundings and thus enriched the grid rather than proposing an alternative to it. Olmsted's parks suggested that nature was a form of culture; Jenney's situated urban culture in a natural setting.

These distinct approaches were influenced by the size, configuration, and distance of the South and West park districts from the central city. In the North Park District, comprised

Figure 1.12   Plan of Riverside, Illinois, by Olmsted, Vaux and Co. Landscape Architects, 1869.

Figure 1.12

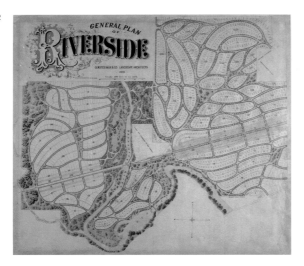

largely of the lakefront and extending northward from a vacated cemetery, closer proximity to the central city and a narrow depth, combined with a scenic natural edge, suggested a combination of these approaches.[32] Both romantic and cultural parks established a clear and constant relationship between the transportation connections on which they depended and the natural landscape they were designed to revive and improve, thus satisfying the practical and aesthetic requirements of the periphery.

Access and composition were therefore entwined. Where existing or proposed routes of through circulation penetrated the parks, as in the proposed South Park watercourse, or passed through them, as in the subdivided West Parks, they determined the parks' basic arrangement and suggested an appropriate character. Internal park drives not only provided access to park interiors and supplementary routes for through traffic, but they also defined their basic divisions and negotiated between natural and urban surroundings. As boulevards extended beyond park boundaries, they offered the same leisurely alternative for traffic moving through the city.

Parks and boulevards exposed peripheral residents to the natural landscape with a minimum appropriation of dedicated parkland. A common desire for natural exposure had to be negotiated with the city's primary mission of housing its population. Boulevards constituted the most practical way to enclose a periphery with a large circumference with continuous park space. They introduced natural enrichment into even the most monotonous neighborhoods, connected them to larger parks, and provided natural points for dividing responsibility for improvements between separate park districts. Thus, they allowed a competitive method of implementation to produce a unified whole.

SUBURBAN HOUSING

The railroad existed before the local transportation innovations on which peripheral improvements relied. Railroads moved faster than other forms of transportation and made fewer stops, and they allowed residents who chose to—largely the wealthy, who could afford annual train passes—to bypass the periphery altogether without cutting their ties to the center. Many well-to-do Chicagoans settled in the ring of suburbs that evolved along the radiating rail network or in once-independent towns with new rail connections. Separated from the periphery by unsettled land, these were exclusively or largely devoted to housing commuters in a natural landscape. Openness combined with exclusivity appealed to residents with means and therefore to developers, who by controlling larger parcels of cheaper land could combine circulation, housing, and recreation even more freely than they did on the periphery.

This was the goal of Riverside, a suburb that was established by the developer Emery Childs and a group of East Coast investors in 1868. It was located on a bend in the Des Plaines River, at the first suburban stop on the Chicago, Burlington, and Quincy Railroad, about ten miles southwest of the central city. Designed by Olmsted and Vaux in 1869, it was one of the first suburbs in the world and the major precedent for the residential component of the South Park, which was designed two years later, in 1871.[33]

At Riverside, however, the architects succeeded in realizing a distinct suburban order that, in Olmsted's view, combined urban amenities with a rural character.[34] Among the former were paved and well-drained roads, generous public space, and a relatively high density of residential settlement. A shared natural landscape was the key to establishing a rural character, and the Des Plaines River suggested its specific quality. Olmsted lined the riverbank with public open space, which continued along routes of circulation through neighborhoods not on the river (FIGURE 1.12). Streets and residential blocks conformed to the serpentine lines of this threaded landscape, which could not be distinguished from the private natural space around individual homes. Olmsted and Vaux pulled homes back thirty feet from the street and screened them with irregularly planted trees. The architects also provided private driveways that kept carriages off the street. In Riverside the enhanced natural landscape served as a shared continuum and a unified and unifying setting for housing, circulation, and park space.

As in their South Park proposal, Olmsted and Vaux characterized this alternative order as a complement rather than an antithesis to the existing urban pattern, and to that end, they also sought complementary connections to the city. They

Figure 1.13 Top: View from the roof of the Pullman Arcade, looking northeast to the Hotel Florence, 1895.
Bottom: View from the roof of the Pullman Arcade, looking north to the Pullman Works, 1895.

Figure 1.14 Plan of Pullman, Illinois, by Solon Beman and Nathan Barrett, 1879. The northern section, to the left of the Pullman factories, was not built.
The town center is located in the southern section, to the right of the factories.

planned a parkway between Riverside and Chicago that, in its range of program and leisurely character, would convey suburban qualities to Chicago just as the railroad conveyed its urban efficiency to the suburbs. Continuous rows of trees would separate traffic by type, punctuated by roadside parks with shelters where travelers could stop and rest. Commerce would be banned along the parkway, and a continuous hedge would preserve suburban privacy.

The Great Fire of 1871 not only prevented Childs from realizing this parkway but also threatened the viability of Riverside. Subsequent transportation developments largely disproved Olmsted's assertion that the suburban businessman would enjoy "taking air and exercise . . . incidentally to his necessary communication with his store or office."[35] Instead, they demonstrated that suburban residents wanted to reach their destinations as quickly as possible. Convenience remained the essential goal of regional circulation.

SUBURBAN INDUSTRY

The railroad also allowed industry to move out of the central city, where acquiring land for expansion was expensive. As long as it was built close to railroad lines, industry was better suited to land beyond the periphery, which was cheap and close to alternate water connections. The Calumet River, which emptied into Lake Michigan twelve miles south of the city center (also that much closer to southern markets and the Illinois and Michigan Canal), began to attract industry in the 1870s with a series of harbor improvements. Following an established pattern, Calumet Harbor lured industry by promising to create a connection to the canal. By the time the Calumet-Saganashkee Channel was completed in 1922, Calumet Harbor was already the center of Chicago's heavy industry.

Figure 1.13

Bypassing the periphery gave industrialists the same freedom in planning their factories as speculative developers had in planning suburbs. Limited housing opportunities so far from the periphery, and the promise of reduced travel time and a more stable workforce, encouraged them to combine factories with housing and recreation. The private railcar manufacturer George Pullman established the town of Pullman in 1880 on the western shore of Lake Calumet, southwest of Calumet Harbor, not so much to escape urban conditions as to reconstitute them around manufacturing (FIGURE 1.8). He hired the architect Solon Beman and the landscape architect Nathan Barrett to lay out a community that would include the Pullman factories, housing for workers, parks and public spaces, shops, a market, and a hotel.

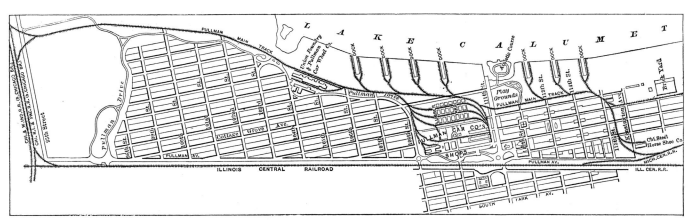

Figure 1.14

Their plan arranged these elements on the continental grid, which could be imposed on the open landscape and absorbed later when the periphery reached Pullman. The architects thereby re-created Chicago's physical pattern of distinct zones on a smaller scale (FIGURE 1.14). Maximum access to transportation dictated that the Pullman factories must occupy the town's center (located at the narrowest point between Lake Calumet and the Illinois Central rail line). These were accessible by rail from both sides and arranged along rail spurs rather than streets.

Beman and Barrett projected residential neighborhoods to the north and south, on which they planned attached houses uniformly set back from the street. The fact that Pullman residents walked to work concentrated residential settlement and endowed the entire town with a more-urban aspect than most of Chicago.[36] The planners located public space along the southern boundary of the factory buildings, where it negotiated between their large scale and the smaller scale of the residential blocks to the south. They carved a public square out of this dense residential fabric; to the north, they set off the factory buildings as objects in a landscaped park with a pond (FIGURE 1.13). Rational and romantic public spaces mingled across a boulevard that connected them to recreation grounds on Lake Calumet.

Pullman's subsequent history demonstrated the potential hazards of imposing such comprehensive planning on an essentially captive workforce. Eliminating the need for transportation deprived workers of freedom of movement and established a precedent for more overt attempts to control their actions. The Pullman strike of 1894, the repercussions of which forced George Pullman to cede ownership of the town, began when the company cut wages by thirty percent without adjusting workers' rents. As a result of this historical context, the value of Pullman as a prototype for self-sufficient towns planned on a grid around transportation requirements has been overlooked.

Riverside and Pullman shared a target audience, culled either by class or occupation, and a self-contained physical order that was functionally dependent on the larger city. Residents of Riverside worked in Chicago, though they lived outside it; the suburb merely extended an existing separation between work and home. Though its residents need not travel as far to get from home to work, Pullman still depended on Chicago's rail connections to receive raw materials and deliver its products, and on its labor source to assemble them.

CHICAGO IN 1893

In Chicago efforts to improve housing, recreation, circulation, and industry by combining them—what might be termed comprehensive planning—originated on or beyond the periphery, where a complex program coincided with a freedom to experiment. Comprehensive plans evolved in a context of spatial segregation, where transportation advances and seemingly limitless room to expand preserved the functional relations between different zones while also pulling them apart. Housing, commerce, and industry therefore pursued improvement in their own locations, according to their own particular requirements. These improvements could not be applied to the city as a whole. Olmsted's efforts to forge a romantic suburban order, for example, depended on the assumption that the American city was composed of equal and opposite parts rather than a single overarching order. In this context, the grid was an urban emissary, and in rejecting it, picturesque peripheral planning also discarded the only established tool for relating the city's disparate parts. How could a picturesque order be expanded without sacrificing its overall legibility? How could it accommodate changes in scale or use over time? In theory and in practice, the grid could supply workable answers to those questions, but the evolution of romantic peripheral plans proved that the grid could not satisfy all the requirements of the residential periphery on its own.

A rational center and an (ideally) picturesque periphery nevertheless described a larger radial pattern, to which the individually implemented, competing elements of the transportation network, the peripheral housing program, and the metropolitan park system all conformed (FIGURE 1.15). The railroad had entrenched this pattern while increasing the separation of its parts, exposing in the process the potential monotony of Chicago's uniform street grid. The city lacked a unified planning approach that could negotiate a compact core, a diffuse periphery, and a natural landscape.

Figure 1.15 Grand view of Chicago by Th. Treutlin, 1893.

Figure 1.15

CHAPTER 2

PLANNING FROM THE CENTER AT
THE WORLD'S COLUMBIAN EXPOSITION

NEEDS AND DESIRES FOR URBAN IMPROVEMENT

THE WORLD'S COLUMBIAN EXPOSITION AS A PLANNING PROBLEM

INFLUENCES AND PRECEDENTS · A SYNTHESIZED PLANNING APPROACH

AN OBJECT LESSON IN PLANNING

NEEDS AND DESIRES FOR URBAN IMPROVEMENT

The American city had to be imagined as a whole before it could be improved comprehensively. Prior to 1890, the transportation network that allowed zones of housing, commerce, and industry to develop separately in Chicago was their only common element. All three zones, however, had the same requirements for water supply, drainage, and waste disposal. The 1855 water-carriage sewerage plan and Olmsted's 1869 plan for Riverside, which included water service and storm drains, thus represented different approaches to the same problem. Demands for basic services increased along with population growth and dispersion, though they did not necessarily correspond to existing political boundaries. The regional pattern of settlement produced by the transportation network eventually necessitated regional coordination of infrastructure and thus promoted a common regional identity.

The railroad also forged a common identity that was based on civic pride. By creating a new scale of exchange between cities, and by imposing standard units of time and measurement on their transactions, the national rail network brought them into constant contact, fostering interdependence and thus competition. The ambitious cultural and physical embellishments financed directly or indirectly by new private industrial wealth serviced national aspirations as well as local requirements. In hiring the designer of Central Park for an even larger park in Chicago, the South Park Commissioners were challenging New York in a national competition for cultural prestige.

American civic leaders and designers typically looked to European precedents as models for improvement, not merely because their shared cultural and ethnic roots were European,

but also because European cities, which had embarked on the process of urban industrialization earlier than American cities, were also further along in the related program of urban embellishment.[1] To varying degrees across the Old World, a rising commercial class used urban improvements to accommodate middle-class housing and shopping on a new scale. Even while pulling down the walls that for centuries had given European cities clear boundaries, the middle class continued to seek better living conditions within the city; thus, the improvements they effected retained an urban character.[2]

In American cities, on the other hand, the separate zones that existed for working and living presented two viable sites for cultural improvement. As the city's historical point of origin and the only zone used by everyone, the commercial center also attracted government buildings, hotels, and stores. Even in Chicago, where commercial pressures were especially acute, other equally intensive or highly symbolic uses shared space with commercial buildings. But the identification of culture as a leisure pursuit distinct from work generally located cultural improvements on the residential periphery, a tendency fostered by a perception that waves of immigration made the central city vulnerable to corrupting foreign influences.[3] In Chicago, therefore, peripheral park improvements preceded the construction of new homes for the leading cultural institutions on the edge of the central city by about twenty years.[4]

In late-nineteenth-century America, concrete requirements for coordinated infrastructure emerged alongside an idealistic desire to enrich urban life. New industry and transportation, explosive population growth, and unprecedented physical expansion called for a new scale of improvement.

Figure 2.2 Five world's fair plans, 1893.

THE WORLD'S COLUMBIAN
EXPOSITION AS A PLANNING PROBLEM

By coincidence, the most physically dispersed major American city gained the first opportunity to address infrastructure and cultural enrichment together as one undertaking. In 1890 the United States Congress and President Benjamin Harrison awarded Chicago the honor of hosting the World's Fair of 1892, despite stiff competition from New York, Washington, D.C., and St. Louis.[5] A world's fair was a national display of technological and cultural achievement for an international audience. The fact that the 1892 fair would fall on the four hundredth anniversary of Christopher Columbus's discovery of the New World imbued it with further significance for the United States. It was also an occasion to mark America's transition from an agricultural to an industrial economy and to announce its new international prominence. To that end, the federal government raised expectations for the fair when, in designating Chicago as its site, it renamed the event the World's Columbian Exposition and postponed the opening until 1893 to give Chicago more time to prepare an impressive display. During its six-month run, from May through October 1893, the exposition emerged as a commercial success, a national cultural phenomenon, an implicit critique of American cities, and a model for coordinated urban planning.

The fair's program was a concentrated version of that of the American city. Its daily attendance was comparable to the daytime population of central Chicago, which required basic services and convenient internal and external connections.[6] The fair's cultural impact, public prestige, and financial viability depended on its ability to draw, educate, and entertain this population. A limited site on which a single actor or group could impose a specific plan recalled peripheral and suburban improvements in Chicago, in which developers, park commissioners, and industrialists implemented specific programs for targeted audiences on clearly defined sites under their centralized control. Thus, in circulating and servicing a daily population, the fair functioned like the central city. Its designers enjoyed the freedom to impose a vision that in Chicago was reserved for projects on or beyond the periphery. As a design problem, the fair contained the seeds of a functional work of art.

INFLUENCES AND PRECEDENTS

The process and implications of site selection, and the decision that the Chicago exposition should display a national character, determined the fair's basic plan and the composition of its design team. Fair organizers scrapped an early proposal to divide the exhibits between the central-city lakefront and

Olmsted's Lower Park when agricultural interests complained that their displays would be ignored if consigned to a site on the periphery. As the central lakefront could not accommodate the entire fair program, the organizers, acting on Olmsted's advice, moved the combined exhibits to the Lower Park and expanded the exposition site along the Midway Plaisance (SEE FIGURE 1.11). Vestiges of the original separation between different types of exhibits persisted in the fair's final plan (though distinct zones can also be discerned in plans for earlier fairs; FIGURE 2.2).

Figure 2.2

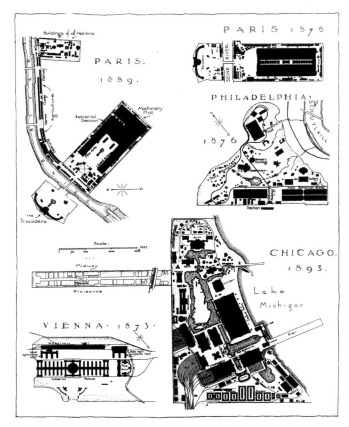

In Olmsted's original park proposal, only fitfully implemented, the fair's organizers had a completed plan for their site already in hand. An exposition might equally well rely on water connections that supplied both circulation routes and scenic value, and Olmsted's plan provided a crucial head start on a project already behind schedule.[7] By utilizing it, the fair organizers also ensured that the exposition site could be converted to park use after it closed. The fact that Olmsted's intentions for the Lower Park had gone largely unrealized in the intervening twenty years made it an even more attractive site. Jackson Park (renamed in 1881, along with the Upper Park, which became Washington Park) was available, convenient to rail and ferry connections, and clear of buildings. The

Figure 2.3 The Eiffel Tower and Champ de Mars seen from Trocadéro Palace, Exposition Universelle, 1889.
Figure 2.4 Interior view of the Galerie des Machines, Exposition Universelle, 1889.

fair organizers hired Olmsted and his associate Henry Codman to oversee revisions to his original plan. They also hired Daniel Burnham and his partner John Root, prolific and established architects of commercial buildings in central Chicago, to oversee construction of the fair's buildings; Burnham in turn invited a team of ten architects to design them.

The composition of this team reconciled conflicting views of the fair as a local undertaking and a national enterprise. Five eastern architects and five western (or Chicago) architects would design the fair together. The former were graduates of the École des Beaux-Arts in Paris, which was regarded in Europe and the United States as the world's leading institution for professional training in art and architecture.[8] Richard Morris Hunt, the first American graduate, was considered the dean of American architecture. George B. Post and Henry Van Brunt had been pupils in Hunt's New York atelier. Robert Swain Peabody was Van Brunt's former protégé, and Charles McKim had worked for the second American graduate of the school, Henry Hobson Richardson, before designing the country's first major public monument in the French academic classical style, the Boston Public Library, in 1888. Together these five architects constituted a tight-knit professional group with a common approach based on shared experience.

The five western architects were not as strongly identified with a single design tradition. Jenney had designed the major prototype for the steel-framed tall office building, as well as the West Parks System.[9] Louis Sullivan was a commercial architect who was already emerging as the leading innovator of a skyscraper style. Root, as Burnham's partner, was responsible for most of the firm's design work.[10] Henry Ives Cobb was perhaps the leading institutional architect in Chicago, though his position was being challenged by Beman, the architect of Pullman. Between them, these architects had dealt with all aspects of the

typical American city, and together they had designed a wider range of buildings in more styles than their eastern counterparts.

The multiple parts of the fair's program, the existing plan for its site, and the varied composition of its team of designers dictated that the final result be comprised of distinct parts. The imported principles of academic planning held the key to relating these parts; a unified composition that preserved the individuality of its elements was in fact their ideal. The École viewed a building's plan as a composition whose parts were the specialized rooms that served its particular function, together with more general spaces for circulation, service, and ceremony. The art of Beaux-Arts planning lay in composing a hierarchical arrangement that would demonstrate a building's function and its place in a larger hierarchy of building types. As an official academy, the École was concerned with the public role of architecture and hence with the upper reaches of this hierarchy. Through plans symmetrically organized along formal axes, it sought the simple, stable imagery that French official taste required. Axes established a clear visual relationship between the elements at either end, while also implying a narrative progression from one end to the other. Movement along an axis — from vestibule to rotunda, for example, or from rotunda to courtroom — described both a literal journey and a demonstration of function. Axes also encouraged an even distribution of reinforcing elements, and thus a basic bilateral symmetry.

The principle of a hierarchical arrangement of partially autonomous parts, however, transcended a specific arrangement, design method, or building type. In providing a sympathetic setting for enriching elements of painting and sculpture, it even transcended the medium of architecture. It established a clear relationship between functional efficiency and visual order, and thus an ordering system on which any functional work of art might rely.

Figure 2.3

Figure 2.4

Figure 2.5 Central dome, Exposition Universelle, 1889.
Figure 2.6 View of the Court of Honor, looking west, 1893.

Figure 2.6

Earlier world's fairs offered specific examples for arranging an exposition program (FIGURE 2.2). The Centennial Exposition held in Philadelphia in 1876 also celebrated a significant anniversary, the centennial of the signing of the Declaration of Independence. However, it lacked a coherent physical plan, which may partly explain why it failed to establish the resonant public image that culturally prestigious, commercially successful fairs seemed to require. London's Great Exhibition, which under royal sponsorship gathered all the products of an industrial empire under one roof in the enormous greenhouse known as the Crystal Palace, had attained both cultural and financial success in 1851.[11] But the French, who hosted world's fairs in Paris in 1855, 1867, 1878, and 1889, had set a new standard with the most recent fair. The Exposition Universelle of 1889 included multiple zones connected by water and rail, rational planning reminiscent of Beaux-Arts practice, and examples of iron and glass construction that equaled the Crystal Palace's scale and surpassed it in the public imagination. Matching exhibition halls enclosed the axial main court, which was terminated at either end by ambitious examples of the newest metal-frame building technology. The Eiffel Tower was the world's tallest structure, and the Galerie des Machines had the longest interior span (FIGURES 2.3 and 2.4).[12] This rational arrangement exhibited a decorative rather than classical style of architecture, in keeping with its festive function (FIGURE 2.5). Nor was the fair's arrangement an implicit urban plan; through the earlier efforts of Napoleon III and Baron Haussmann, Paris in 1889 had already been realized as the most ambitious, complete, and physically unified urban improvement of the nineteenth century.[13] In this context, the Exposition Universelle appealed unabashedly to the excitement of new technology.

Figure 2.5

A SYNTHESIZED PLANNING APPROACH

For Chicago the plan of the Exposition Universelle provided a point of departure for another vision, one that enlisted new technology in a broader program of urban improvement (FIGURE 2.6). The fair's designers expanded the Paris plan into a flexible narrative that related all types of exhibits and incorporated the romantic landscape tradition represented by Olmsted's original plan. This narrative was composed of two main parts, a central ensemble that recast a Beaux-Arts design exercise in "urban" surroundings, and a romantic landscape that evoked existing peripheral parks. The designers arranged these complementary zones around Olmsted's proposed lagoons. By varying the character of this constant water connection, they described a simple and obvious transition from an "urban" ensemble to a "suburban" landscape. Simultaneous attention to the arranging connections and the arranged elements imposed simplicity and unity on their design (FIGURE 2.7).

The "urban" Court of Honor occupied the fair's literal, functional, and metaphorical center. Its plan reproduced that of the main court of the Exposition Universelle, but it also reflected its function as the primary point of arrival and departure for visitors. An enclosed axial plaza ran from east to west across the long axis of the fair—from a rail station at one end to a lakefront pier at the other—collecting visitors arriving at either end and distributing them to the adjacent exhibits north and south. The hub of circulation also housed exhibits devoted to technological advancement, the most exciting and broadly appealing part of the fair's program. Exhibition halls for electricity, machinery, manufactures and liberal arts, and agriculture showcased the United States' technological leadership in the fair's most heavily trafficked space.

Figure 2.7 Souvenir map of the World's Columbian Exposition, 1893.

Figure 2.7

Figure 2.8 Elevation of the Agriculture Building by McKim, Mead, and White, 1893.

Figure 2.9 View of the lagoon and Wooded Island from the Manufactures and Liberal Arts Building, 1893. In the center is the Illinois Building, to its right the Palace of Fine Arts. The United States Government Building is in the foreground, with the Fisheries Building beyond.

Figure 2.8

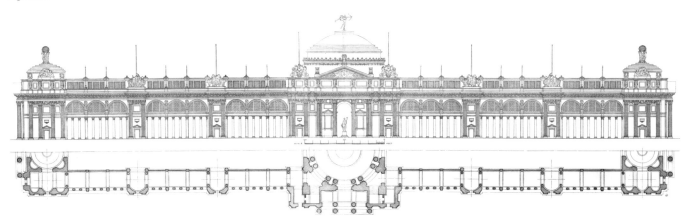

This integrated program received a unified architectural expression that departed completely from that of its precedent. The eastern architects created a Beaux-Arts ensemble on a scale not yet realized elsewhere. A central water basin—a formalized Olmsted lagoon—which entered from Lake Michigan by an arched water gate at the court's eastern end, accentuated the east-west axis of circulation, which was further reinforced by the parallel facades of the four exhibition halls rising from behind broad terraces. These also directed attention to the ends of the court, where focal elements marked the points of arrival and departure. To the east, a screen of columns above the water gate carried the enclosing walls across the court's open end. To the west, the domed Administration Building, which recalled the Eiffel Tower in plan and placement, served as a covered, open-air vestibule to the court and fair. It anchored the entire composition with a characteristic

Figure 2.9

Beaux-Arts form that recalled a national capitol or patriotic shrine (FIGURE 2.1).[14] All of these buildings were individual compositions as well as participants in the larger ensemble. They shared a basic planning module of twenty-five feet, a common cornice height of sixty feet, a covered portico along the rear edge of the basin terrace, and a characteristically French tripartite plan (FIGURE 2.8). All of them employed a classical vocabulary and sported monumental sculptural embellishments. These qualities contrasted with a physical flimsiness that was apparent on close inspection, for they were temporary structures built of plaster and lathe. All were painted white, which enhanced both the monumental character of the design and the insubstantial character of its realization. The Court of Honor was a privileged precinct with the character of a paper design realized in three dimensions, and this chimerical quality, combined with the near-total absence of an American precedent for urban ensemble planning, endowed the central ensemble and the entire fair with that resonant public image that conferred cultural prestige and commercial success.[15]

A transverse canal following the fair's long axis passed out of one corner of the court and into an idealized suburban landscape that recalled Olmsted's earlier park plan. This canal gradually took on a less-formal character, widening into a lagoon with irregular edges and then dividing into a smaller pond and a serpentine canal that returned to Lake Michigan. A series of exhibit pavilions gathered freely on the banks. In accordance with standard practice, these were occupied by national and state delegations, as well as the artistic and cultural enterprises that identified with nature in the actual American city. A context of freely arranged objects suggested looser formal relations between buildings; thus, the eclectic western architects designed these pavilions in a variety of architectural styles. If the exhibition halls that defined the Court of Honor were self-contained urban blocks shaping a common space,

Figure 2.10 Palace of Fine Arts by Charles Atwood, 1893. View from across the North Pond.
Figure 2.11 View of the train station, Administration Building, and Court of Honor, looking east, 1893.

these buildings were extroverted villas that occupied their own territory. Their tripartite plans were composed of wings and porticoes that reached outward to maximize exposure to light and air. A wooded island occupying most of the irregular lagoon lent these varied, free-standing objects a unifying pastoral character (FIGURE 2.9).

The Palace of Fine Arts expressed most succinctly and compellingly the complementary relationship between a high-minded cultural enterprise and its picturesque surroundings. This tripartite villa, with a more delicate and refined version of the Court of Honor's classical architecture, descended by steps and terraces directly to the waters of the irregular North Pond (FIGURE 2.10).[16] One could alight there from a boat that had passed from the Court of Honor through idealized urban and peripheral conditions, which emerged as equal and opposite poles in a continuous narrative.

A livestock exhibit south of the Court of Honor and a carnival section west of the pastoral landscape exhibited "low" versions of the elevated themes found elsewhere in the exposition. Both eschewed elaborate planning in favor of the most economical arrangement of exhibit stalls. The livestock exhibit occupied a series of open, rectangular pens, serviced from the rear by a spur railroad line. The carnival was set up in the original boulevard link between Olmsted's parks, the Midway Plaisance, which was initially designed as a canal but never excavated. Pivotal connections between these areas and the rest of the fair and exhibits with overlapping themes established these "lower" sections of the exposition as extensions of the Court of Honor and the pastoral landscape. The livestock exhibit was joined to the rest of the fair by the Agriculture Building on the Court of Honor and a pavilion for showing livestock modeled on a Roman amphitheater. Vending booths on the Midway proffered amusements in exotic environments— a street in Cairo or Old Vienna—based on the building arrangement and program in the adjacent zone of the fair. Each of the four zones—the Court of Honor, the pastoral landscape, the Midway Plaisance, and the livestock exhibit—was either a

Figure 2.10

version of or a complement to the others. Those of high culture abutted those of low culture; a formal basin led to an irregular lagoon, and urban space to a romantic landscape. A matrix of simple relationships provided a place for every program component.

AN OBJECT LESSON IN PLANNING

In its coordinated approach to planning, the fair did not adopt a single style or attitude; rather, it accommodated multiple styles and attitudes (FIGURE 2.11). The Court of Honor was only the most vivid example of a composition grounded in mediation. Its tone struck a balance between two purer attitudes toward the role of new technology in a civilized society. The French enthusiasm on display at the Exposition Universelle had a counterpart in English reservations about the corrupting effects of industrialization, which were expressed by a school of thinkers and artists centered on John Ruskin.[17] In this context, the court's classical architecture not only softened the potentially jarring effects of new technology, but also ennobled it by presenting it in the context of a classical heritage. Despite Sullivan's subsequent condemnation, the fair's architecture cannot be characterized as a conservative revival.[18] At the time

Figure 2.11

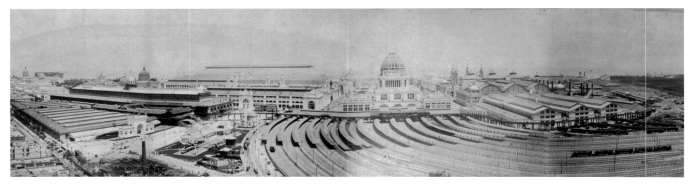

of the fair, the methods of the École des Beaux-Arts represented the most up-to-date architectural practice, and its American practitioners were considered to be at the leading edge of the architectural profession.[19] In any case, the ensemble that critics later disparaged as too faithful was without either European or American precedent, not merely in its scale and scope but also in its shared authorship and thrilling effect.[20] Not since the Renaissance had multiple authors in multiple media collaborated to this extent to produce public architecture.[21] The presentation of a Beaux-Arts design exercise as a full-size architectural model was nothing short of inspired, reconciling the fair's temporary nature with its didactic character as an object lesson.

The Court of Honor's individual buildings struck the same balance between precedent and innovation. The basic form of the Administration Building, for example, might recall Renaissance and Enlightenment prototypes, but its open-air interior and its function as a covered outdoor vestibule brought to mind the more-recent covered arcades of Italy.[22] Though the Manufactures and Liberal Arts Building, the fair's largest, replaced the Galerie des Machines as the world's largest single-span structure, its enlistment as one wall of the Court of Honor required that it play no greater role than its counterparts.[23] Innovation and precedent were most thrillingly reconciled on each night of the fair's run, when a program of electric night lighting was concentrated on the Court of Honor, reversing the role of classical architecture as a frame for technology by putting it on display.

This pragmatic and opportunistic moderation was typical of the larger enterprise. Almost insurmountable time constraints forced the fair's designers to utilize a ready method and a prepared site plan. Their design emerged as a simple negotiation between these elements, one that required them to extend their use of the classical vocabulary beyond official public architecture and to expand the accepted terms of rational and romantic planning. The fair as a building type did not traditionally merit the attention of the École; nor was a program of amusement traditionally conceived as an object lesson in composition. As they were implemented in the real world, in sometimes unsympathetic existing conditions, both French rational planning and romantic planning produced closed, internally logical systems that related to their surroundings by juxtaposition. The fair's planners introduced the idea of a gradual transition from one approach to the other by placing two closed systems in an open and reciprocal relationship.

In coordinating rational planning with romantic planning, vernacular exhibit architecture with elevated public architecture, and a program of amusement with broader planning ambitions, the fair's designers tailored European centralized planning to the special circumstances of American cities, where the appeal of a rational urban order was always complemented by the allure of an "unsettled" natural landscape. The Chicago fair was planned from the center, with program spreading outward from a "central" concentration of circulation and program on the Court of Honor, but this center had an equal and opposite counterpart in the adjacent pastoral landscape (FIGURE 2.12). Centralized planning typically situates all given elements in a single order, but the breadth and flexibility of the fair's centralizing order were uniquely American. In America planning from the center included an equal and complementary emphasis on the periphery.

The fair's planners presented these ideas to the public in an understated and moderating fashion. Van Brunt, the architect of the Electricity Building and the author of a series of popular articles on the fair published in 1892, argued even before it opened that the fair's architecture was exactly that—fair architecture—an "insubstantial pageant of . . . vast covered inclosures [sic] faced with a decorative mask of plaster composition."[24] He located the "living and progressive art" of modern architecture "in the latest commercial, educational, and domestic structures in and near our largest cities."[25] Nor did the fair's designers specifically claim it as an urban critique, instead emphasizing fundamental ordering principles on which all kinds of planning might rely.[26]

Such subtleties may have been lost on the fair's twenty-one million visitors, for whom the implicit rebuke of existing central cities must have been clear enough. But the unprecedented coordination on display in the Court of Honor cannot be separated from that of the larger enterprise. The fair demonstrated the flexibility and complexity that a general principle of order could produce. A newly rich and culturally ambitious United States, which both required and desired that its physically sprawling and uncoordinated cities be improved, was bound to discover in the fair's architecture the seeds of a broader application. The World's Columbian Exposition was therefore, in Burnham's words, "the beginning, in our day and in this country, of the orderly arrangement of extensive public grounds and buildings."[27]

Figure 2.12 Bird's-eye view of the World's Columbian Exposition, 1893.

BIRD'S-EYE VIEW OF THE WORLD'S COLUMBIAN EXPOSITION, CHICAGO, 1893.

Figure 2.12

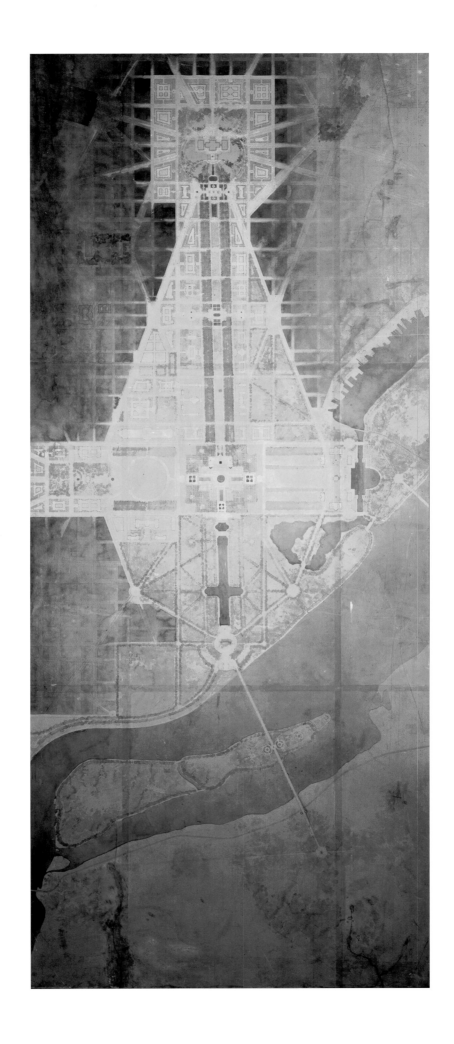

CHAPTER 3

PLANNING FROM THE
CENTER IN WASHINGTON, D.C.

OPPORTUNITY FOR METROPOLITAN IMPROVEMENT · EXISTING

CONDITIONS AND INFLUENCES · EXPANSION OF

NARRATIVE PLANNING · PRESENTATION AND IMPLEMENTATION

OPPORTUNITY FOR METROPOLITAN IMPROVEMENT

The prestige conferred on Burnham, McKim, and the other planners of the Chicago World's Fair demonstrated that, whatever their specific intentions, they had planned and executed a transformative cultural event with real implications for architecture and urban planning. In 1894 Burnham served as president of the American Institute of Architects, a position four other fair planners subsequently held in unbroken succession.[1] In the same year, Burnham and McKim helped found the American Academy in Rome, modeled on the existing Académie de France à Rome, which provided the country's most promising artists and architects with the opportunity to study classical works of art intensively. Burnham's firm became the preeminent architectural practice in Chicago, while McKim, with his partners William Mead and Stanford White, lead a national revival of classical architecture from his office in New York. In a series of prestigious commissions for state capitols, college campuses, country houses, and private clubs, McKim, Mead and White extended the Court of Honor's axial planning and academic character into the real world of public architecture. Opportunities to create larger urban ensembles or to coordinate monumental classical architecture with romantic landscape planning, however, remained limited.

For Olmsted, who was a generation older than his collaborators, the Chicago fair was a capstone rather than a springboard. Parks that he had already designed and were now being completed continued to set the tone for regional park planning. The Boston Municipal Park System, called the Emerald Necklace, comprised existing parks and boulevards designed by Olmsted and his younger colleague Charles Eliot beginning in 1881, and at Olmsted's retirement in 1895, it was the most ambitious, varied, and conceptually succinct metropolitan park system in the United States (FIGURE 3.2). A series of parks and boulevards shaped around watercourses and catchment ponds connected Boston Common in the central city to Franklin Park on the suburban periphery and reconciled drainage requirements with recreation and landscape preservation. Becoming larger in size and more romantic in character as it moved toward the periphery, the Emerald Necklace endowed the primary peripheral planning tool with the narrative qualities of the Chicago fair.[2]

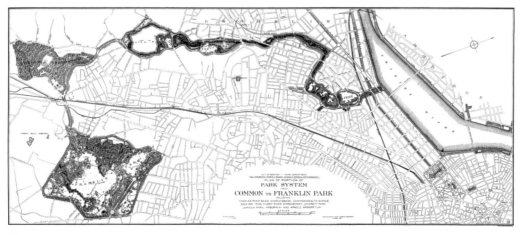

Figure 3.2

Figure 3.1 *General plan of the Mall system*. Illustration 19 from Senate Report No. 166 by the Senate Park Commission, 1902.

Figure 3.2 Plan of a portion of the Boston Municipal Park System, from Boston Common to Franklin Park, including the Charles River Basin, Charlesbank, Commonwealth Avenue, Back Bay Fens, Muddy River Improvement, Leverett Park, Jamaica Park, Arborway, and Arnold Arboretum, by Olmsted, Olmsted and Eliot, Landscape Architects, 1894.

Figure 3.3 Detail of a plan of the city intended for the permanent seat of the government of the United States by Pierre-Charles L'Enfant, 1791 (computer-assisted reproduction produced by the United States Geological Survey for the Library of Congress, 1991).

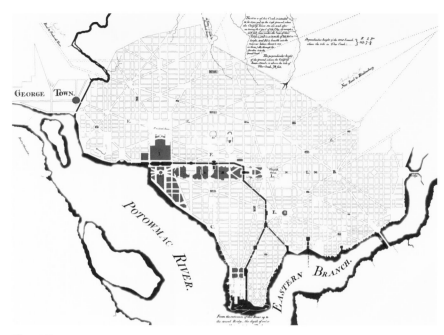

Figure 3.3

Classical public buildings and metropolitan park systems were separately pursued aspects of the Chicago fair's comprehensive program. Neither addressed the city's whole range of functions, scales, and uses. A proper application of the fair's object lesson in planning required a real metropolitan planning program, one that called for improving the central city and the periphery together. The World's Columbian Exposition fostered an appetite for a planning approach that was too ambitious to find an immediate outlet.

A metropolitan improvement program of this kind eventually arose from circumstances that were reminiscent of those that had produced the Chicago fair. In 1901 Washington, D.C., proposed a comprehensive parks program that reconciled sweeping urban improvements with a peripheral park system. Up to that point, the national capital had lagged far behind other American cities in these areas. Though its population increased fourfold between 1860 and 1900, as a planned city owned by the federal government, Washington lacked the system of private speculation and patronage that implemented urban improvements in other American cities.[3] But as the national capital, Washington had the country's largest collection of monumental public architecture and, in what had been realized of its original plan, its only urban ensemble conceived around public park space.[4] The author of this plan, the French engineer Pierre-Charles L'Enfant, had elaborated a grand and subtle vision that combined monumental architecture with a natural landscape in 1791. His plan had been fitfully implemented and then, during rapid growth in the decades following the Civil War, actively undermined.

The lack of peripheral parks to service new growth and the opportunity to preserve and improve a compromised ensemble led the United States government to implement the nation's first comprehensive metropolitan improvement. As in Chicago, a desire to express the United States' growing international stature coincided with a significant anniversary to provide the immediate impetus. The end of the Spanish-American War in 1898 left the United States in possession of Cuba, Puerto Rico, the Philippines, and Guam, making it a colonial power. The year 1900 marked the centennial of Washington's founding as the nation's capital. These circumstances allowed Senator James McMillan of Michigan, head of the Senate committee on the District of Columbia, to assemble a comprehensive program of improvements from a number of separate proposals in 1901.[5] The central aims of this program were to revive L'Enfant's plan for what was now the central city and to connect it to a peripheral park system that would make Washington competitive with other large cities. Owing to the special character of a central city conceived around public park space, this proposal remained in name a park-system improvement, and it would re-create, on a larger scale, the natural setting that L'Enfant had envisioned for the capital.[6]

This sympathetic extension of L'Enfant's vision was also a real-world analogue to the fair's program. As a setting for the public display of shared achievements, Washington's monumental core functioned as a national Court of Honor. As a respite from the city and an enhanced natural landscape, the proposed peripheral park system recalled both the fair's idealized suburban landscape and contemporary metropolitan park systems.

Figure 3.4 View of Washington by E. Sachse and Co., 1852.

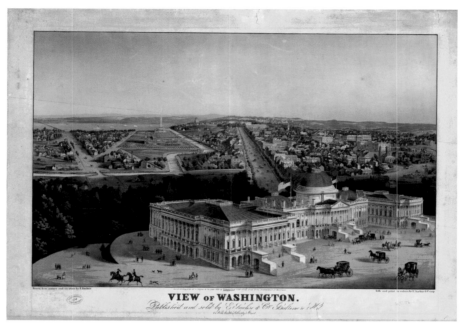

Figure 3.4

The Chicago fair's main planners were obvious choices to carry out the proposal. Burnham and Frederick Law Olmsted, Jr., who carried on his father's work after his death in 1903, were approached first. They invited McKim and the sculptor Augustus Saint-Gaudens, who had also collaborated on the fair's design, to join them.[7] Together, they constituted the Senate Park Commission and reported directly to McMillan's committee. As in Chicago, the team charged with the final design answered to the body responsible for implementing it.[8]

EXISTING CONDITIONS AND INFLUENCES

Washington, D.C., presented the commissioners with a site sympathetic to centralized planning and a precedent consonant with their experience in Chicago. As a federal district, the capital was as close to a controlled site as an actual city could be. L'Enfant's 1791 plan belonged to a tradition of rational French planning that was largely consistent with subsequent developments at the École des Beaux-Arts, exhibiting the same axial planning and hierarchical composition. By engaging these with natural surroundings, L'Enfant produced an arcadian landscape studded with monuments that also represented an earlier synthesis of the rational and romantic qualities of the 1901 Washington parks program.

More narrowly, as a scheme for organizing an ensemble of classical buildings in a natural landscape, L'Enfant's plan provided a specific precedent for "the orderly arrangement of extensive public grounds and buildings."[9] The engineer related the central government buildings to one another both directly,

by formal axes, and indirectly, by shared exposure to a natural landscape (FIGURE 3.3). The Capitol and the President's House, as the respective seats of the legislative and executive branches, anchored two corners of a right triangle laid on its side on the eastern bank of the Potomac River.[10] They were connected directly by Pennsylvania Avenue, which formed the triangle's hypotenuse, but each also faced down its own natural axis on the second and third arms of the triangle. One of these axes was the Mall, which L'Enfant described as "an avenue a mile long and four hundred feet wide;"[11] the other was the President's Park. They converged on the triangle's third point, an equestrian statue of George Washington on the riverbank, which was framed by the natural landscape beyond. L'Enfant thus opened a rational arrangement of buildings to its surroundings and balanced their relations to one another with their independent relations to the landscape. His triangular composition also exploited the site's existing topography by placing the Capitol and President's House on its most significant elevations (FIGURE 3.4).

Other elements of his plan recalled improvement strategies already familiar to the Senate Park Commissioners. By combining a street and lawn in the design of the Mall, L'Enfant identified circulation with natural repose. By channeling a canal from the Potomac along this linear park, he enlisted another natural element in a formal sequence while draining unhealthy low land.[12]

Though L'Enfant's city plan was largely implemented, his arcadian vision for the capital was not realized. The federal government adopted his arrangement of the Capitol and the

Figure 3.5 Plans of Versailles, Washington, D.C. (proposed), and Paris (1901), at a common scale.

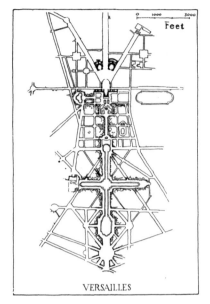
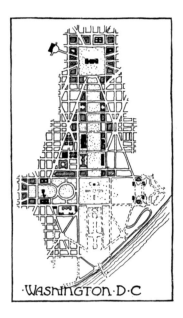
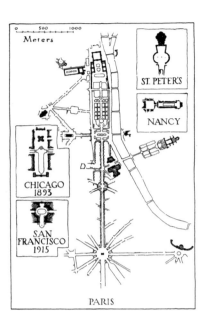

Figure 3.5

President's House around the Mall, segments of his canal system, and his street plan, which combined a diagonal web with a grid, but initially these were too grand for a young republic whose individual states resisted federal coordination.[13] When Washington did assume a national role in the post–Civil War decades, the idea of an arcadian metropolis in an unspoiled landscape was no longer feasible. The new rail-based transportation pattern, which further developed the existing character of mercantile cities like Chicago, actively undermined L'Enfant's plan for Washington.[14] A railroad depot athwart the Mall blocked its axis and violated its character. In 1900 the Pennsylvania Railroad was preparing to enlarge this depot in return for eliminating grade crossings on its lines. A railroad line had also filled in the segment of L'Enfant's canal along the Mall.

Violations of L'Enfant's plan were not limited to the railroad. The completion of the south wing of the Department of the Treasury in 1861 had blocked the axis along Pennsylvania Avenue between the Capitol and the White House.[15] The triangular area between the avenue and the Mall had become a notorious slum. Andrew Jackson Downing's 1851 plan for the Mall reconfigured L'Enfant's avenue as a romantic landscape, across which were scattered the main building of the Smithsonian Institution, the Arts and Industries Building, and the Department of Agriculture.[16] In 1885 the Washington Monument was completed at the crossing of the Mall and the President's Park, replacing L'Enfant's proposed equestrian statue with a colossal obelisk and transforming the

natural corridors he envisioned between the Capitol, the President's House, and the Potomac River into clearly terminated axes. The Washington Monument's effectiveness as a terminal marker, however, was undermined when poor soil conditions forced its relocation to a site east and slightly south of the actual crossing. The crossing itself was also no longer adjacent to the Potomac River, which had been partly filled in by the Army Corps of Engineers to combat poor drainage and accommodate demands for more recreational space.

In 1901 Washington could no longer be made to conform to L'Enfant's original intentions. Relating a central ensemble that now occupied an urban setting to a natural landscape required a change in scale. The park commissioners therefore proposed to treat the rational and romantic qualities that were reconciled in L'Enfant's plan as the complementary poles of a metropolitan narrative with central and peripheral parts. They envisioned a rational urban ensemble in the central city as contiguous with a much-larger natural periphery. This was a more-ambitious version of the Chicago fair's narrative plan.

As in Chicago, the central portion of this plan relied on European precedent (FIGURE 3.5). Capitals and country palaces, some of which had also been sources for L'Enfant's plan, provided examples of individual buildings and larger ensembles rationally related to natural and urban surroundings, and in 1901 Burnham, McKim, and Olmsted crossed the Atlantic Ocean to study them. At Versailles, outside Paris, and Hampton Court Palace, outside London, they observed how

Figure 3.6 Bird's-eye view of the McMillan Plan for central Washington, D.C. Illustration 20 from Senate Report No. 166 by the Senate Park Commission, 1902.
Figure 3.7 *View of the Lincoln Memorial site from the old Naval Observatory.* Illustration 51 from Senate Report No. 166 by the Senate Park Commission, 1902.
Figure 3.8 View of the proposed southern memorial from the shore of the Potomac River. Illustration 54 from Senate Report No. 166 by the Senate Park Commission, 1902.

Figure 3.6

regular axes defined by trees or water established buildings as focal points and extended their presence into the natural surroundings. In Rome the commissioners absorbed the ancient capital's timeless and standard permanence, but more specifically, they studied the use of public fountains to combat the torpor of a hot climate (FIGURE 3.11). In Paris the Tuileries axis, which ran westward from the Louvre, the old city palace of the French monarchs, to the Arc de Triomphe, demonstrated how a narrative arrangement of public monuments could also function as a circulation route between the central city and the periphery.

EXPANSION OF NARRATIVE PLANNING

In Washington the park commissioners modeled a rational reconfiguration of L'Enfant's central ensemble on these precedents (FIGURE 3.6). They extended the axes of the Mall and the President's Park beyond the Washington Monument to terminal points on the new riverfront, marked by two memorials to great statesmen. L'Enfant's open triangle became an array of four closed axes around the Washington Monument. Together they described a gradual transition from the urban surroundings of the Capitol and the White House in the east and north, to a garden landscape around the two new monuments to the west and south.

Individual buildings and axial connections conformed to this larger narrative. Like the Chicago fair's Court of Honor, the Capitol and the White House were each framed by a formal ensemble that defined a clear precinct around them. The new memorials, like the Palace of Fine Arts, were garden pavilions in a natural landscape. The park commissioners projected these as elemental architectural forms in white marble. The western memorial, intended for Abraham Lincoln, was an open Greek temple; the southern one, which became the Jefferson Memorial, was a Roman rotunda (FIGURES 3.7 and 3.8).[17]

Figure 3.7

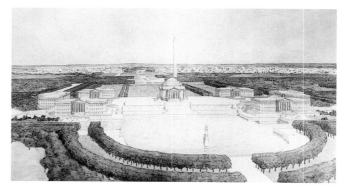

Figure 3.8

Figure 3.9 *View showing the proposed development of the Lincoln Memorial site, seen from the canal.* Illustration 49 from Senate Report No. 166 by the Senate Park Commission, 1902.

Figure 3.10
Top: *Model of the Mall showing the present conditions, looking east.* Illustration 34 from Senate Report No. 166 by the Senate Park Commission, 1902.
Bottom: *Model of the Mall showing the proposed treatment, looking east.* Illustration 35 from Senate Report No. 166 by the Senate Park Commission, 1902.

Figure 3.9

Figure 3.10

The two arms of the extended Mall were "urban" and "natural" counterparts. The Mall proper, between the Capitol and the Washington Monument, was a semi-enclosed court, defined by rows of linden trees and, beyond them, a uniform wall of buildings housing the national institutions of science and culture. The Mall's westward extension, with an axial canal to the Lincoln Memorial set amidst tree-lined allées, was a garden landscape modeled on Versailles (FIGURE 3.9). The President's Park was a drill and parade ground, where the president could review military exercises from the White House. Its southern extension was a public equivalent, which the park commissioners called the Washington Common, with a stadium or a field for public gatherings along the axis between the Washington Monument and the future Jefferson Memorial,[18] around which were loosely grouped athletic and cultural buildings and grounds (FIGURE 3.8).

Almost at the juncture of these four zones, the Washington Monument mediated between them. The park commissioners planned a cross-shaped sunken garden at the crossing, the eastern arm of which was a stepped terrace supporting the Washington Monument. This sympathetic setting emphasized the monument as part of the crossing and created a plausible explanation for its misalignment (FIGURES 3.1 and 3.12).[19]

The landscape elements that connected all of these zones also carried circulation routes for traffic moving through the urban core and beyond it to the periphery. Though the park commissioners had transformed the Mall itself from an avenue into an axial lawn, the streets on either side constituted — like the Tuileries axis from the Louvre to the Arc de Triomphe — a direct connection between the central city and the periphery. The park commissioners envisioned the Lincoln Memorial in the role of the Arc de Triomphe, as the hub of a web that concentrated inbound traffic and distributed outbound traffic around the periphery.

Public improvements that were not explicitly part of this monumental ensemble were designed to enhance it. Improvements to urban neighborhoods and transportation infrastructure tested the limits of a metropolitan improvement that was officially designated as a parks plan. The Pennsylvania Railroad terminal was relocated from the Mall to a site northeast of the Capitol, at the end of an existing diagonal street.[20] The park commissioners designated the triangular slum area between the Mall and Pennsylvania Avenue — what would become the Federal Triangle — as the municipal seat of government. A memorial bridge over the Potomac (the kernel from which McMillan's comprehensive program had developed) was pulled into the Lincoln Memorial ensemble, from which it extended as a radial connection on axis with Arlington National Cemetery (FIGURE 3.1).[21]

Figure 3.11
Left: *Fountain in front of Villa Medici, Rome, suggesting the public value of hilltops wisely treated.* Illustration 175 from Senate Report No. 166 by the Senate Park Commission, 1902.
Right: View from the Washington Monument terrace, looking toward Arlington. Illustration 45 from Senate Report No. 166 by the Senate Park Commission, 1902.

Figure 3.11

The Lincoln Memorial was the logical point of connection between a rationally landscaped monumental center and a romantically landscaped peripheral park system (FIGURE 3.7). This system described an irregular ring around the central city and included every aspect of Washington's varied topography (FIGURE 3.13). By claiming hilltops, many of which were capped by Civil War forts, as public parks of historic import, the park commissioners would preserve the most visible elements of the natural landscape, confine development to the valleys between, and raise the value of surrounding real estate. They proposed improving existing watercourses and marshes, many of them malarial, with raised public promenades that controlled drainage and incorporated quays and warehouses for waterborne commerce on their lower levels. A series of parkways connected these improvements with one another, and a proposed scenic drive to Mount Vernon extended the concept of the boulevard beyond the district to suburban Virginia, recalling the senior Olmsted's proposed parkway between Riverside and Chicago. A program of local playgrounds augmented the boulevards as a means of bringing park amenities to neighborhoods that were remote from the park system.

The regional parks plan proposed by the park commissioners revived the L'Enfant plan's engagement with a natural setting by enlarging its scale. By treating this setting as a preserved landscape belt, it allowed for the possibility of urban expansion beyond the existing periphery, in which case the natural belt, which included a range of hills, could preserve the fiction that Washington occupied a natural landscape. By identifying this belt with the requirements of peripheral circulation, the parks plan provided access to it and an impetus for setting it aside.

PRESENTATION AND IMPLEMENTATION

The McMillan Plan was publicly exhibited at the Corcoran Gallery of Art in early 1902 and collected officially into Senate Report 166.[22] Utilizing a full repertory of representational techniques, the park commissioners set forth a vision for the national capital that appealed largely to sentiment and imagination. Two models of central Washington showed existing and proposed conditions side by side (FIGURE 3.10). Lavishly rendered drawings depicted the plan from above, as a simple and legible pattern on the landscape, or placed viewers on the ground next to buildings and monuments. Equally impressive plans, sections, and elevations emphasized these proposals as feasible designs. Photographs of European precedents were interspersed with realistically rendered proposals based on them (FIGURE 3.11), and photographs of existing conditions appeared alongside those of analogous, successfully implemented American improvements. The plan's presentation exhibited the broad and inclusive character of the plan itself. The unified result portrayed a possible outcome as an achievable goal.

Washington as we know it today, particularly its central monumental ensemble, is a product of the park commissioners' plan (FIGURE 3.12). Despite early setbacks, the McMillan Plan established a framework for central Washington that later developments have adhered to, both in broad conception and in specific detail.[23] L'Enfant's original plan remains recognizable within a sympathetic transformation. Union Station, the Federal Triangle, Union Square at the foot of Capitol Hill, the Arlington Memorial Bridge, and the national museums along the Mall were all realized according to the plan's specifications in the decades following its public presentation. The plan's enduring potency at the scale of architecture is best demonstrated by the fact that the Lincoln and Jefferson memorials, completed

Figure 3.12 *General view of the Monument Garden and Mall, looking toward the Capitol.* Illustration 58 from Senate Report No. 166 by the Senate Park Commission, 1902.

in 1922 and 1937, respectively, were built just as the park commissioners imagined them.

The McMillan Plan's proposed peripheral park system was not as faithfully implemented. A few elements were realized along the lines indicated by the plan. The Rock Creek and Potomac Parkway, George Washington Memorial Parkway, and Baltimore-Washington Memorial Parkway connect the District of Columbia with a regional periphery, though they are as much circulators of commuting traffic as recreational drives. Rock Creek Park, which predated the plan, was subsequently improved by Olmsted according to its recommendations. The lowlands around the Anacostia River, envisioned as a water park, were fitfully improved. Today Washington's peripheral sprawl is indistinguishable from that of other American cities, and its natural periphery continues to retreat.

A narrative plan for the national capital suggested both the possibilities and the limits of planning from the center in American cities. While the Chicago fair had intimated that comprehensive metropolitan improvements must address zones of different scale and character, its small, clearly defined site and limited (or implicit) ambitions as an urban plan curtailed a full demonstration. The McMillan Plan tested and resolved the spatial implications of the fair's narrative planning in the real world, where a large, typical, and indistinct periphery usually surrounded a relatively small, privileged, and unique central city.[24] But a more-ambitious application was limited by its specific program and by the special circumstances of improving a national capital. In a government city endowed from the beginning with a central park space — which was viewed as contiguous with, or at least related to, its major public buildings — the potential reach of a plan for improvement based on parks was greater than elsewhere. Washington's unique character also gave the fullest possible expression to a strategy of circulation enriched with landscape elements. The Mall's function as a forum of public monuments, derived solely from its special status, made it a more clearly defined park and connection to the periphery as well. Unlike other American cities, Washington could implement as well as legislate improvements. This, too, limited the McMillan Plan's potential application elsewhere. Just as it included no provision for relating private buildings to proposed public improvements, the plan had no place for the individual speculator, who played a decisive role in shaping metropolitan improvements in other American cities.

Figure 3.12

Figure 3.13 Map of the District of Columbia showing the existing park system (in light green) and proposed additions (in dark green). From Senate Report No. 166 by the Senate Park Commission, 1902.

The circumstances that produced a unified plan for the fair in Chicago also produced a unified plan for metropolitan improvement in Washington. Both sympathetically expanded and transformed existing plans for clearly defined sites. Both created public precincts that were self-consciously abstract and monumental, qualities that were enhanced rather than undermined by the traffic moving through them.[25] And both expanded a given program into a model for general improvement. Both plans therefore intimated a further and more-ambitious application. The McMillan Plan was the second step in an evolving approach that expanded on earlier successes. New problems recalled previous ones but added a layer of complexity or removed an earlier constraint. Paradoxically, they required simpler solutions—more-flexible models that could accommodate greater variety. What could this approach achieve in cities that had evolved according to an implicit commercial order rather than from specially designed plans? And who would impose new plans? Washington's successful exercise in metropolitan planning assured that these questions would be explored.

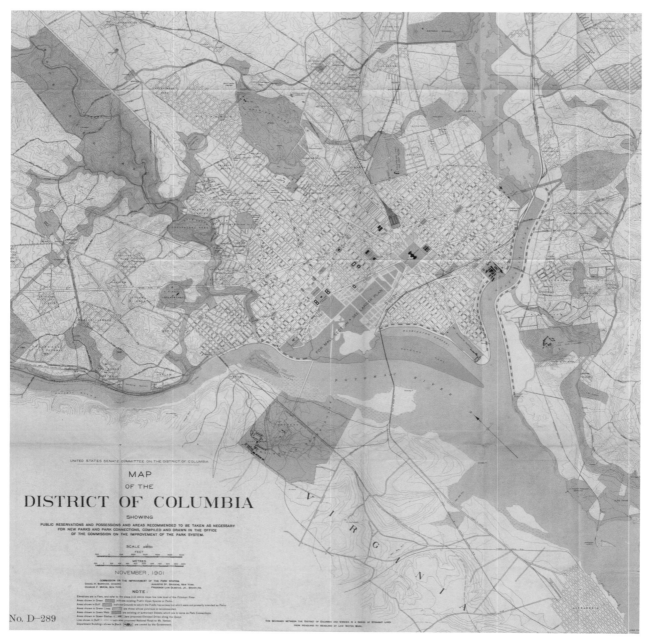

Figure 3.13

CHAPTER 4

PLANNING FROM THE
CENTER IN THE *PLAN OF CHICAGO*

OPPORTUNITIES AND ATTEMPTS AT COMPREHENSIVE NARRATIVE
PLANNING · CIRCUMSTANCES OF A COMPREHENSIVE PLAN AND EXISTING
CONDITIONS IN CHICAGO · THE PRECEDENT OF HAUSSMANN'S PARIS
THE *PLAN OF CHICAGO* DESCRIBED · THE PLAN ASSESSED
THE PLAN'S RECORD OF IMPLEMENTATION

OPPORTUNITIES AND ATTEMPTS AT COMPREHENSIVE NARRATIVE PLANNING

Like the World's Columbian Exposition before it, the McMillan Plan captured the public imagination with a compelling presentation. Its warm reception, and the official endorsement represented by its commission, helped ensure that enthusiasm for coordinated urban planning continued unabated. As in the immediate aftermath of the Chicago fair, the individual components of the McMillan Plan continued to develop along separate courses before an opportunity to address them together on a broader scale presented itself.

Plans for central-city ensembles, boulevard connections, and metropolitan park systems proliferated in the years immediately following the McMillan Plan's publication. In 1903 Burnham's office designed a civic center for Cleveland, Ohio, that included a city hall, a federal office building, a public library, and a train station arranged around a formal landscaped court that recalled the Court of Honor and the Place de la Concorde in Paris (FIGURE 4.2). The Public Buildings Commission of St. Louis proposed a similar plan in 1904. In 1903 the architect Cass Gilbert planned three radiating axes to relate his Minnesota State Capitol building in St. Paul to the

adjacent central city. The city engineer of Hartford suggested in 1904 that new government buildings be coordinated around the existing Bushnell Park and the Connecticut State Capitol. As in Washington, D.C., where what became the Federal Triangle replaced a slum, these central-city improvements proposed to clear and redevelop existing urban blocks and neighborhoods that the plans' commissioners deemed undesirable. Each design identified urban improvement with a larger presence for public buildings, particularly government buildings. The axial planning, formalized landscape elements, and architectural ensembles of the McMillan Plan appeared in commercial cities and state capitals alike.

Peripheral park and boulevard systems belonged to an older tradition of urban improvement with roots in Olmsted's romantic planning, and in this regard, the McMillan Plan had adhered to established practice rather than breaking new ground. Even before 1901, mid-size American cities began to follow the lead established by Buffalo, Chicago, and Boston.[1] In 1896 Kansas City, Missouri, started to implement a system of peripheral residential parkways proposed by the landscape architect George Kessler in 1893, and during the same decade, Memphis, Omaha, Toledo, and Cleveland followed its example.[2] In 1903 Kessler proposed a park and boulevard system for St. Louis modeled on the Kansas City plan. Planners continued to combine landscape and circulation to connect and relate the central city to peripheral parks and suburbs. In Chicago in 1896, Burnham proposed a lakefront park and boulevard between the 1893 exposition site, now reconfigured as a park, and the central city; he presented this plan again in a revised form in 1904. Based on legislation passed by the Philadelphia City Council in 1892, ground was broken in 1907 for a parkway

Figure 4.2

Figure 4.1 View of the Civic Center for the *Plan of Chicago* by Jules Guerin, 1908.
Figure 4.2 Cleveland plan for public buildings by Daniel Burnham, 1903.

41

Figure 4.3 Proposed metropolitan park system for Chicago. From the *Report of the Special Park Commission to the City Council of Chicago on the Subject of a Metropolitan Park System* by Dwight Heald Perkins, 1904.

between the central city and Fairmount Park that would include major public and institutional buildings.[3]

By their transitional nature, boulevard connections continued to encourage related improvements in the central city and on the periphery. Kessler's 1893 boulevard proposal for Kansas City also recommended reestablishing the natural character of the bluff occupied by the central city. The proposed Philadelphia parkway was eventually attached to plans for a river parkway, a system of peripheral boulevards and playgrounds, and a town extension in South Philadelphia. In 1904 the architect Dwight Perkins and the landscape architect Jens Jensen incorporated Burnham's proposed lakefront park and boulevard in a metropolitan parks plan for Chicago that also included the existing North, South, and West park systems (FIGURE 4.3).[4] Their plan treated these as an inner park ring, to be complemented with an outer belt of preserved natural landscapes beyond the periphery, whose contours would be determined not by settlement patterns but by existing landscape

Figure 4.3

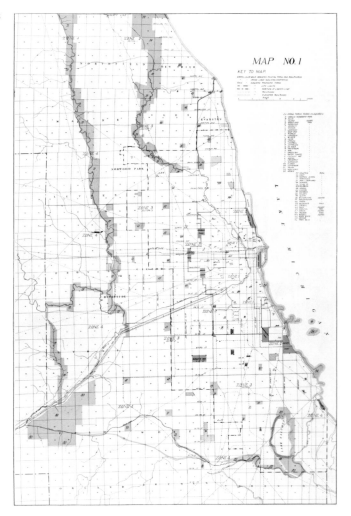

features. The entire Des Plaines River Valley and that of the undeveloped portion of the Chicago River's north branch would be preserved, along with Lake Calumet and ten miles of lakefront. Perkins and Jensen also proposed that the expanding periphery include extensions of the existing park and boulevard system. They divided their plan into zones to facilitate implementation and accommodate distinct planning strategies within a larger framework. This was the most ambitious metropolitan parks plan put forward in the years following the McMillan Plan; in 1909 some of its proposals were incorporated in the *Plan of Chicago*. By 1905 peripheral park systems had been established in Baltimore, Philadelphia, Providence, Minneapolis and St. Paul, Portland, and Seattle.[5]

Whether presented together, as in Kansas City, or assembled from separate proposals, as in Chicago, Cleveland, St. Louis, and Philadelphia, these metropolitan improvement plans lacked the unified brief and the clear path to implementation of the McMillan Plan. The first opportunity to apply the strategies of the McMillan Plan to a more-typical American city fell to Burnham in 1904, when he was commissioned by the Association for the Improvement and Adornment of San Francisco, a civic association of local business leaders, to create a comprehensive plan for the city. The plan's brief stressed a program of public and cultural enrichment that, combined with San Francisco's dramatic site, invited ensemble planning in the central city, natural preservation on the periphery, and landscaped connections that might be combined with port facilities. These elements, all of which were prefigured in the Washington plan, appeared in the plan for San Francisco devised by Burnham and his associate Edward Bennett in 1905 and presented by the association to the city in September of that year.[6] The plan also included a new emphasis on efficient circulation and a prescription for introducing new streets into the existing urban fabric.[7] San Francisco's topography had produced multiple, differently oriented street grids with haphazard collisions; Burnham and Bennett identified these as impediments to smooth circulation. A proposed central circuit of diagonal streets that would negotiate colliding street grids and create a network of through circulation around a series of monuments and boulevards reflected a new rationale for ensemble planning that was based on improved circulation rather than symbolic effect (FIGURE 4.4).[8]

As the basis for a comprehensive plan for a commercial city, however, reprising the primary strategies of the McMillan Plan was inadequate. The San Francisco plan did not squarely acknowledge the centrality of the city's commercial requirements and consequently did not privilege its commercial interests. Though it proposed expanding the financial district and the port and manufacturing facilities that were the engines of San

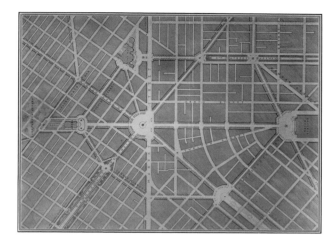

Figure 4.4

Figure 4.5

Francisco's economy, these changes were made pendant to a civic and cultural program and a series of dramatic enhancements to the surrounding hills (FIGURE 4.5). The commissioners of the San Francisco plan, though businessmen themselves, had also overlooked the central role of economic improvements in a commercial city.[9]

Two plans for cities in the Philippines—commissioned by the United States government and undertaken in Burnham's office in 1905, while the San Francisco plan was being drafted—were largely irrelevant to the development of comprehensive American urban planning, and they may even have frustrated the evolution of a more-pragmatic approach to narrative planning. A plan to improve the capital, Manila, and another for a new summer capital at Baguio both employed the kind of sweeping planning gestures that were rendered impractical by the circumstances of most American cities.

Public enrichment in the center and on the periphery was not an adequate framework for comprehensive metropolitan improvement in the typical American city. Chicago provided perhaps the foremost example of a commercial city where urban improvement served economic interests. Early peripheral park planning had shown that the marketplace could distribute

urban amenities as evenly as centralized planning: parks and boulevards circumscribed the city because the North, West, and South sides had all used them to attract potential residents. Unless narrative planning could appeal directly to commercial interests, its potential application was limited in cities where cultural and quality-of-life issues remained secondary to economic ones.

CIRCUMSTANCES OF A COMPREHENSIVE PLAN AND EXISTING CONDITIONS IN CHICAGO

The conditions that produced the *Plan of Chicago* recalled those that generated the San Francisco plan. Burnham was approached by a civic group composed of local business leaders to prepare a comprehensive improvement plan for the city. Circumstances that were peculiar to Chicago produced a plan focused from its inception on economic issues, and therefore better suited to implementation in a commercial city.

This economic focus owed something to a more-established, powerful commissioning body. In contrast to the Association for the Improvement and Adornment of San Francisco, which had coalesced around the idea of a metropolitan plan, the Merchants Club had existed for ten years when it commissioned Burnham in 1906. In 1907 it merged with the older and more-prestigious Commercial Club (of which Burnham was a member), partly to centralize private support for the *Plan of Chicago*. Individually, the members of the enlarged Commercial Club already made many of the decisions that guided Chicago's commercial and cultural development, and with good reason they viewed its larger public interest as contiguous with their own. The *Plan of Chicago* represented their collective attempt to coordinate these interests, which were fundamentally entwined in the program they devised in consultation with Burnham and Bennett.[10] In Chicago commercial interests rather than the government commissioned and would implement a centralized metropolitan plan.

The unprecedented rate of Chicago's recent growth and unbridled optimism about its future produced a need and desire for coordinated planning. Hardly seventy-five years old in 1906, Chicago was already the second-largest city in the United States. On the evidence of its phenomenal growth, its leaders and boosters predicted that it would become the world's largest and most important city, an attitude that Burnham and Bennett summarized in the *Plan of Chicago*:

> Chicago is now facing the momentous fact that, fifty years hence, when the children of to-day are at the height of their power and influence, this city will be larger than London: that is, larger than any existing

city. Not even an approximate estimate can be ventured as to just how many millions the city will then contain.[11]

Chicago's rapid expansion had created an urgent need to coordinate the systems of circulation on which the city's growth depended. Its radial pattern ensured that further growth would increase congestion, both in the commercial center—the common destination of a growing peripheral population—and along the roads and rail lines that connected it to the periphery.[12] Such congestion, compounded by the structural inefficiencies of the local rail network, already threatened Chicago's security as the national rail hub.[13] In 1906 trains approached the central city slowly, through urban surroundings, holding up and being held up by the activity around on-grade crossings. Separate ownership of the rail lines forced passengers and freight to negotiate multiple terminals around the central city and required new rail lines to enter Chicago by torturous paths to avoid their competitors' rights-of-way (SEE FIGURE 1.6). Devising a better method of moving passengers and freight through Chicago was critical to the city's economic efficiency and its future growth.

Earlier proposals for improving the rail network awaited coordination with one another and with a larger metropolitan plan. Frederic Delano, a former manager of the Burlington Railroad and one of the Merchant Club members who originally approached Burnham, had proposed a consolidated rail terminal along Twelfth Street, between State Street and the Chicago River, in 1904.[14] In a 1905 report, the engineer Bion Arnold addressed Chicago's transportation problem as a whole, advocating a comprehensive intracity rapid-transit system with subway and surface rail lines and a system for routing rail traffic through the central city.[15]

The plan's organizers also had reason to believe that separately owned railroad and mass-transit lines could be combined into larger systems. In 1897 the separate spokes of the elevated mass-transit system were connected with a loop that allowed the trains on each line to run continuously (this loop defined and lent its name to the densest part of the urban center, hereafter the Loop). Nine railroads had jointly founded the Union Stock Yards in 1865 and thereby centralized meat-packing in Chicago, demonstrating that shared risk and the promise of higher profits could overcome the inertia of established individual competition. In both cases, individual elements were put in place separately before they were combined into larger systems.

The evolving scale and sophistication of narrative planning had prepared Burnham and Bennett to address the coordination of commercial infrastructure on a large scale. The World's

Columbian Exposition depended on a comprehensive rail system that delivered passengers, freight, and livestock to separate facilities. Both the Washington and San Francisco plans included consolidated railroad terminals, and in the latter proposal, Burnham had placed new emphasis on coordinated infrastructure and circulation as the primary concerns of a metropolitan plan. Making these concerns central to a plan for Chicago would cement the relationship between functional and monumental planning. The benefits of a coordinated railroad network, since they could be measured objectively by time and money saved, could justify a monumental narrative plan for Chicago on functional grounds alone.

Chicago's own crucial role in the history of narrative planning, and its particularly clear and simple urban pattern, appeared to suggest that this city could offer American cities another object lesson in coordinated planning. In 1890 the city's leading business interests had undertaken the World's Columbian Exposition on their own terms, as a commercial venture, and its success on all counts had demonstrated that private profit and cultural and aesthetic achievement were not incompatible. With the gridiron street plan and functional zoning that were typical of American cities, Chicago offered a site for experimental planning with a potentially wider application. Uninflected by geographical incident, the city's radial arrangement could accommodate rational central-city planning and romantic peripheral planning in a clear, legible relationship, and implicitly—through the piecemeal implementation of a new central business district, improved transportation connections, and peripheral parks and boulevards—it already did. Chicago could continue to expand radially without losing its shape or its focus on the central city, which additional radial and circumferential connections would further reinforce. These, too, were already present: the former as a converging array of diagonal streets, early roads from surrounding towns engulfed by the expanding periphery; the latter as a circumferential park system connected by straight boulevard segments. The rational, cellular character of the grid also appeared to support established techniques of ensemble planning. The straight lines and major demarcations of the existing street grid could be enlisted as axial reinforcements where they coincided with the basic divisions of the larger circle, and the grid's standard divisions could be viewed as the common module of such a composition.

The impulse to create a unified metropolitan plan in Chicago was thus a product of converging circumstances. An optimistic and invested client had the power to implement the plan it commissioned. The growth of Chicago's economy and population demanded a more-efficient system for circulating people and freight. Internal developments in coordinated

Figure 4.6   Section and plan of the boulevard des Batignolles and the boulevard d'Italie. From *Les Promenades de Paris* by Adolphe Alphand, 1873.
Figure 4.7   *Paris Street; Rainy Day* by Gustave Caillebotte, 1877.

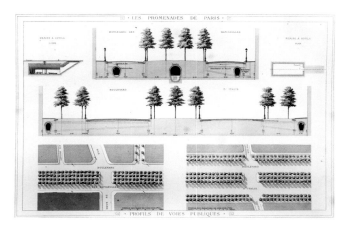

Figure 4.6

Figure 4.7

planning called for a wider application that addressed functional and economic concerns. An amenable urban pattern and local precedents for consolidating park and transportation systems offered sound points of departure for further coordination. All of these circumstances paved the way for a narrative plan that was unified to an unprecedented degree.

THE PRECEDENT OF HAUSSMANN'S PARIS

As in the earlier plans for Chicago and Washington, a French precedent supplied a concrete example and an additional point of departure. Paris, as it was reconfigured from 1852 to 1870 by Emperor Napoleon III and his prefect, Baron Georges-Eugène Haussmann, possessed precisely the functionally and aesthetically unified urban plan that Burnham sought for Chicago. As a national capital with an explicitly public character, Paris might seem a more-relevant precedent for Washington than for Chicago,[16] but its growth and reconfiguration during the nineteenth century, though implemented through official centralized control, were fueled by and designed for primarily commercial interests. The middle class, whose members were the prime producers and consumers of newly mass-produced goods, was the engine of France's nineteenth-century urban industrial economy and the ultimate source of a boom that doubled Paris's population over thirty-three years.[17] Historically at home in the city, which was a zone of free trade, the growing middle class demanded urban housing and shopping opportunities on a new scale, along with the improved circulation, services, and public enrichments that attended urban industrialization everywhere.[18]

Paris's existing urban fabric, based on medieval patterns of land use, was hardly prepared to accommodate these requirements. Despite the gradual replacement of a successive series of fortifications with boulevards,[19] urban space remained at a premium, with members of all classes housed together in vertically stratified, multiuse buildings. Streets were narrow, and by later standards, public space was restricted (FIGURE 4.8). Historically, consumer goods were the province of artisans who specialized in a particular craft, serviced a local population, and lived above their shops. The monuments of a national capital floated as isolated events within this dense and otherwise uniform fabric. The introduction of rail lines—which terminated, as in Chicago, in a ring of train stations around the central city—confirmed the inadequacies of this outmoded pattern of settlement. Having arrived in the capital by newly quick and convenient means, the traveler was prevented from finding his way to its center or across town to another station by twisted and congested streets.

The emperor and Haussmann introduced a structural skeleton into this fabric to improve circulation and house the middle class.[20] They took the old national monuments and new transportation nodes as their starting points and channeled straight streets between them to accommodate through traffic (FIGURE 4.9). They ran tunnels for gas, water, drainage, and sewage beneath these streets to service new multiuse buildings on either side (FIGURE 4.6). Shops on the street with apartments above provided the urban middle class with places to buy, sell, and live. The planners regulated the floor heights and facades of these buildings to give streets a uniform visual order (FIGURE 4.7), enriching them with lights, benches, and trees to create continuous public space. The new buildings supplied these spaces with people but also preserved the character and function of the existing fabric behind them, which continued to offer goods and services not available on the avenues.[21]

45

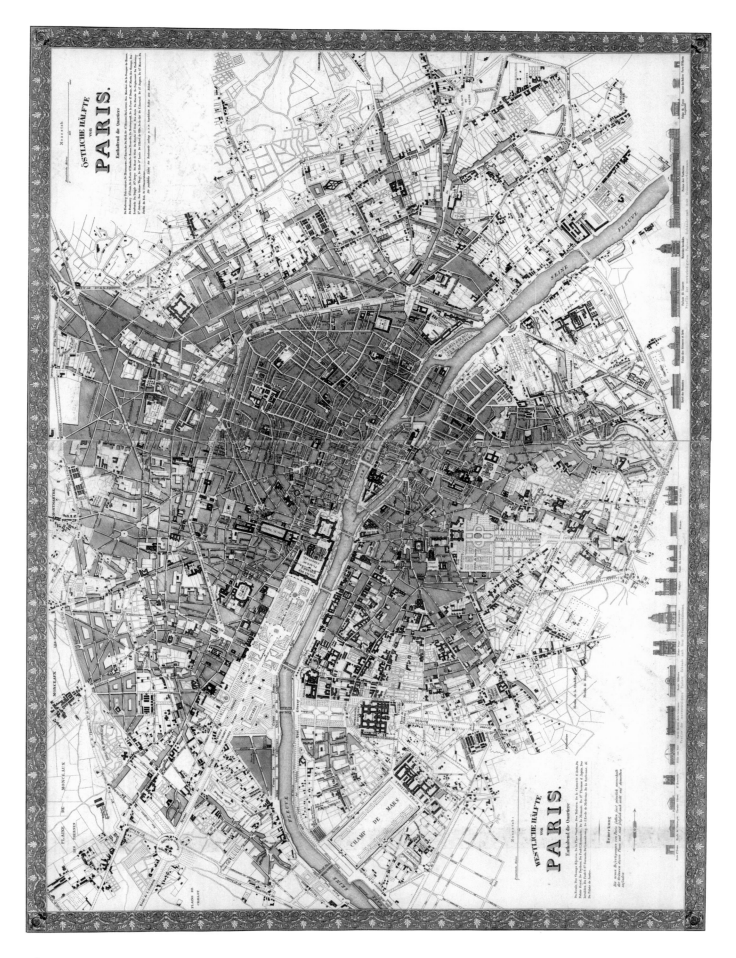

46 Figure 4.8 Map of the western and eastern halves of Paris by Joseph Meyer, 1860. Copied from the 1834 maps published by the Society for the Diffusion of Useful Knowledge, London.

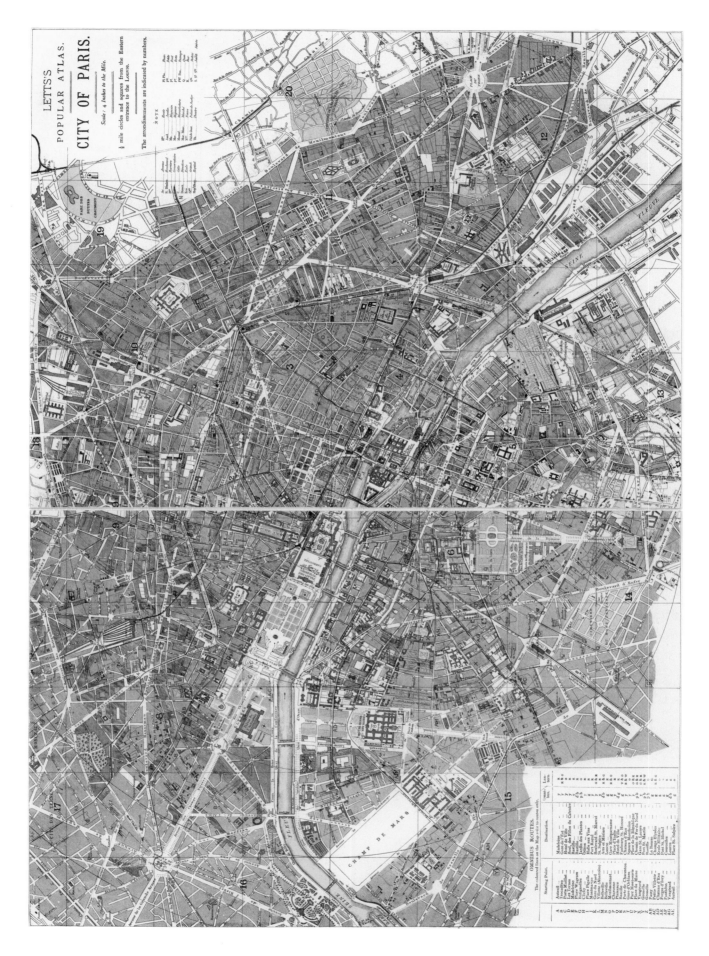

Figure 4.9 City of Paris by Letts, Son and Co., 1883. The omnibus lines are shown in color.

Figure 4.10 *View of the city from Jackson Park to Grant Park, looking towards the west. The proposed shore treatment as a park enclosing a waterway (or a series of lagoons) is shown, together with the enlarged yacht harbor, recreation piers, and a scheme for Grant Park*, by Jules Guerin, 1907. Plate 49 from the *Plan of Chicago*, 1909.

Figure 4.11 *Lake shore from Chicago Avenue on the south to Wilmette on the north*. Plate 50B from the *Plan of Chicago*, 1909.

Figure 4.10

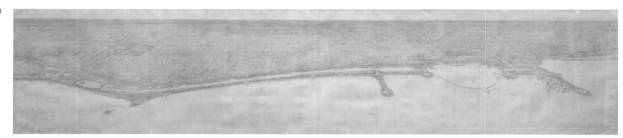

Figure 4.11

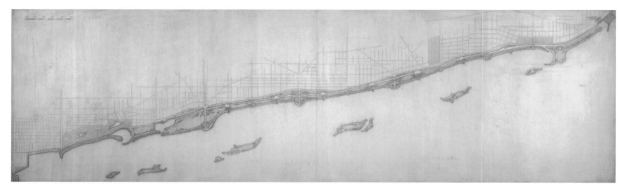

Some aspects of this reconfiguration were irrelevant to circumstances in Chicago. The Paris plan was not a narrative plan in the American sense because it remained focused on a clearly defined urban area where commerce and housing intermingled. Peripheral park improvements did not seek to attract residential settlement but rather to provide a destination for excursions from the city. Connections within the multiuse core therefore took precedence over those with the periphery. It was these latter connections that, in joining urban surroundings to a natural landscape, gave American metropolitan planning its narrative quality. Always able to expand, American cities had no tradition of multiuse buildings and no real need for them.[22] In Chicago land use was intensive enough to support remaking the old fabric only in the central city, and as this space already conformed to the rational divisions of the street grid, it could be (and had been) remade on the same pattern.[23] Burnham and Bennett and other American planners instead looked to the example of the Paris plan for its coordinated methods, unified results, and successful negotiation of new systems of circulation and public space with existing conditions. They also drew encouragement from its method of implementation. Through a complex financial arrangement, the French government relied on private speculators to build new streets, services, and buildings, demonstrating that private commercial interests could theoretically implement a comprehensive metropolitan plan.[24] In Paris, the administration and design of such a plan were nevertheless in the hands of a centralized government authority.

THE *PLAN OF CHICAGO* DESCRIBED

In Chicago, Burnham and Bennett applied the relevant aspects of the Paris plan to the goals of improving circulation along existing lines and establishing a unifying metropolitan narrative that could accommodate infinite peripheral expansion. Improved road and transportation networks connected and serviced the complementary poles of a rational urban core and a romantic natural periphery while reinforcing their existing radial arrangement. This simple system of connections and destinations, equally focused on circulation and public space, incorporated earlier proposals for improvement and relied on the boulevard system, an existing combination of circulation with public space, for additional reinforcement.

Burnham and Bennett emphasized the narrative arrangement of their plan by describing it in a larger historical and geographical context. The *Plan of Chicago* was published by the Commercial Club in 1909 with a run of 1,650 copies. It opened with a historical survey of city planning that ranged from its Mesopotamian origins to the most recent European and American metropolitan improvements, including both Haussmann's reconfiguration of Paris and Burnham's previous coordinated planning efforts in the United States and abroad. The plan presented urban industrialization and coordinated metropolitan planning as simultaneous and related phenomena, the former allowing and demanding the latter on an ever-larger scale. The authors emphasized Chicago's unprecedented rate

Figure 4.12 *Plan of a park proposed at Western Boulevard and Garfield Boulevard, being an extension of Gage Park*. Plate 62 from the *Plan of Chicago*, 1909.

of growth, the exceptional scale of its functional requirements, and its unparalleled capacity for systematic improvement as the latest development in this progressive history.

By elaborating Chicago's spatial, economic, and cultural continuity with its hinterland, Burnham and Bennett identified their plan's narrative quality with existing geographical realities. They emphasized the size, population, and productivity of a "domain . . . larger than Austria-Hungary, or Germany, or France,"[25] over which Chicago held sway:

> When Chicago is adverted to as the Metropolis of the Middle West, the meaning is that throughout this area Chicago newspapers circulate, and Chicago banks hold the banking reserves; that in Chicago are the chief offices of the larger industrial enterprises, and the market for their products.[26]

Burnham and Bennett proposed two regional road networks to reinforce these abstract connections. A roadway around Lake Michigan would bring all the towns on its shores more firmly under Chicago's influence. To the north, west, and south, recognizing that "there exist between this city and outlying towns within a certain radius vital and almost organic relations,"[27] Burnham and Bennett proposed an outer highway system with four concentric circuits (FIGURE 4.22). These distant refrains connected metropolitan Chicago with its hinterland and projected its radial pattern far beyond the city's existing periphery.

The plan's three basic elements—interlocking systems of transportation, streets, and open space—progressively focused Chicago's "vital and almost organic relations" with its hinterland on their imagined source at its center, the plan's fourth and final element. Though successively presented as a sequence of tighter rings, each of these systems of circulation and public space was in reality more difficult to isolate. Park, transportation, and street systems all spanned the distance between the periphery and the central city, which was a connection between the surrounding sections of the city as well as a common destination. The simple arrangement of a small number of elements supplied the Burnham and Bennett plan with conceptual clarity. Their complementary roles and shared components gave it a rich texture and physical unity.

The park system proposed by Burnham and Bennett incorporated earlier peripheral park and boulevard plans into a concentric sequence of progressively larger and more-naturalistic landscapes (FIGURE 4.23). A lakefront park in the central city was designed as a rationally planted formal garden and the central link in a continuous public landscape that revived and extended Burnham's 1896 proposal (FIGURES 4.10 and 4.11). The existing West Park District was an inner park

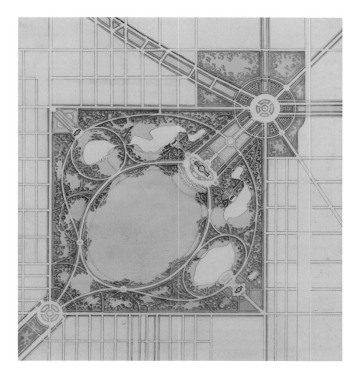

Figure 4.12

ring; the South and North park districts were the lakefront terminations of an outer park ring that included three large parks evenly distributed along a continuously curving peripheral boulevard that belonged to a "grand circuit"[28] of circulation around the city (FIGURES 4.12 and 4.23). Beyond this ring, a belt of forests and river valleys would remain undeveloped and preserve a natural setting for Chicago; this scheme incorporated and extended the proposals of the 1904 metropolitan parks plan. A complementary system of smaller neighborhood parks and playgrounds snipped from the street grid provided recreation facilities for areas remote from the spokes and rings of the park and boulevard system. Burnham and Bennett referred to these as neighborhood centers; they might contain more built than natural space, and they serviced a civic as much as a recreational program.[29]

The transportation system proposed by Burnham and Bennett incorporated the earlier proposals of Arnold and Delano into a network of tangential rail loops that separated freight and passenger traffic bound for Chicago from traffic passing through it. A larger version of the elevated transit loop, implemented on the model of the Union Stock Yards by coordinated private interests, allowed trains to move through and around the central city. This ring was studded with passenger and freight stations at its major points of intersection with elevated and subsurface rapid-transit lines (FIGURE 4.13). Along its western side, it ran tangent to three larger rail loops, which expanded westward, nested one within the other. These serviced existing and expanded industry and allowed freight

Figure 4.13

Figure 4.13 *Diagram of the city, showing complete system of inner circuits.* Plate 75 from the *Plan of Chicago*, 1909.

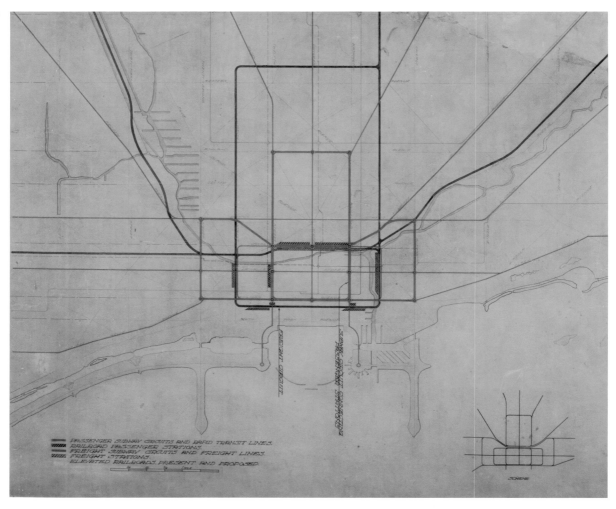

and passenger traffic passing through Chicago to bypass the city altogether (FIGURE 4.24). A consolidated freight-handling center was located southwest of the city between the outermost loops, largely beyond the existing periphery and convenient to national markets. This transportation system freed the central rail ring to process local freight. Stations divided by level into passenger and freight facilities, an existing network of subterranean tunnels, and the regularity of the daily work schedule also allowed the central city to process freight arriving by boat—which was significantly diminished by the rise of the railroad—and pass it to the freight-handling center.[30] A continuous circuit of loops, yards, piers, and stations could reroute trains around impediments and shuttle cars not in use to dormant corners of the system for service and repair.

This transportation network participated both directly and indirectly in other systems of circulation and public space. Consolidated railroad stations contained public halls and faced public plazas (FIGURE 4.14). Raised viaducts incorporated police stations where they arched over city streets. The relocation

of manufacturing and storage facilities from the lakefront freed it for public use. Consolidating central-city rail traffic along the Chicago River and Twelfth Street expanded the central business district and reinforced the radial composition and symmetrical arrangement of the metropolitan plan.[31]

The proposed street plan forged from the existing diagonal streets, which were implicitly ordered by their common destination in the central city, an explicit radial web that channeled circulation through the central city and improved access to the natural periphery (FIGURE 4.25).[32] Burnham and Bennett pointed out that Chicago's pervasive street grid, though it supplied a common module for their larger composition, suggested, in concert with the surrounding landscape, a certain monotony that inhibited its legibility at a larger scale and, more practically, impeded long-distance through circulation because it was unable to accommodate diagonal movement.[33] As in their transportation plan, Burnham and Bennett separated traffic according to its destination, dividing it between avenues carrying through traffic, general streets

Figure 4.14 *Railway station scheme west of the river between Canal and Clinton streets, showing the relation with the civic center*, by Jules Guerin, 1905. Plate 122 from the *Plan of Chicago*, 1909.

Figure 4.14

conveying local traffic—either through the central city or on the periphery—and boulevards with recreational circulation and park space. The existing diagonal streets and the major divisions of the street grid, supplemented by new diagonal routes and extensions, concentrated inbound through traffic on a central-city web (FIGURE 4.26) and outbound circulation on radiating spokes, which crossed and were connected by the concentric park boulevards and the outer concentric highways.

Burnham and Bennett, while pointing out that some incursion into the existing urban fabric was necessary to accommodate through traffic, sought to limit the intrusive effects of such changes and preserve the patterns established by the grid. General streets and boulevards—with the exception of the park boulevard on the grand circuit—conformed to the grid's established divisions and character. Burnham and Bennett protected these transportation routes from new diagonal avenues by lining the latter with commercial buildings. They placed the greatest emphasis on the point where the radial web coincided with the street grid, envisioning Congress Street, the central east-west spoke, as the backbone of Chicago. In addition to being the most heavily trafficked peripheral connector, with lanes for street traffic and lines of mass transit, Congress Street was a boulevard and the primary visual axis between the central-city architectural ensembles, a major peripheral park, and a natural reserve beyond.[34] It was a single, concentrated slice of the metropolitan narrative.

The central city envisioned by Burnham and Bennett was the functional and symbolic focus of these park, transportation, and street systems. Their plan reconciled improved circulation to, through, and around the central city with the axial planning and hierarchical arrangement of an enriched civic center and

the natural landscape of a public lakefront (FIGURES 4.27 and 4.28). A T-shaped intersection of complementary axes brought these three elements into an explicit relationship. At one end, the diagonal street web converged on a forecourt defined by the buildings of the Civic Center, which collected the federal, state, and local government offices into a single ensemble, presided over by a domed administration building on the Congress Street axis that, in form and situation, recalled the Chicago fair's Administration Building on the Court of Honor (FIGURES 4.1, 4.15, 4.28, and 4.29). The Civic Center faced the Field Museum, the center of a perpendicular cultural ensemble in Grant Park, which preserved the identification of nature with culture but acknowledged its place in the central city with a formal garden plan (FIGURE 4.16).[35] Congress Street—divided into lanes for local and through traffic, defined by the unifying facades of office buildings kept to a common height, and enriched with "the highest class of adornment known to civic art"[36]—channeled through traffic toward the lakefront, where the perpendicular line of Michigan Avenue directed it north or south along Grant Park.

This emphasis on movement in the central city reconciled practical and symbolic ends. The T-shaped ensemble concentrated Chicago's major lines of through circulation on two intersecting channels. Additional diagonals connected the Civic Center to Canal Street, Twelfth Street, and the riverfront boulevard that became Wacker Drive. Together with Michigan Avenue, these circulators bounded the central city and drew through traffic from Congress Street, allowing it to fully assume its symbolic role. In this capacity, Congress Street reprised the metropolitan narrative, connecting a clearly defined public space with an open, natural landscape, and

Figure 4.15 *View, looking west, of the proposed civic center plaza and buildings, showing it as the center of the system of arteries of circulation and of the surrounding country*, by Jules Guerin, 1908. Plate 132 from the *Plan of Chicago*, 1909.

Figure 4.15

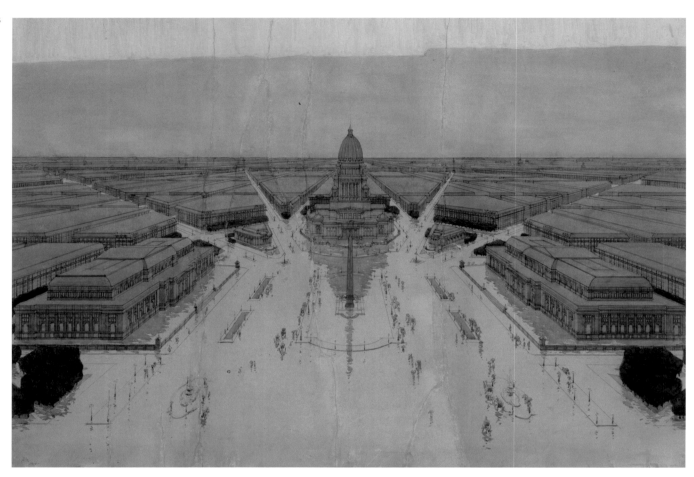

creating a tableau in which government, business, culture, and nature played complementary parts. The bounding circulators defined the enlarged central city as a closed precinct with open connections, the corners of which were accessible by diagonal as well as orthogonal streets. Boundary streets carried passing through traffic and incorporated public plazas and train stations. Michigan Avenue, the preeminent urban boulevard, ran northward from a public plaza at Twelfth Street (FIGURE 4.17) along the eastern edge of the central city and over the Chicago River to its termination at the existing Water Tower. The raised riverfront boulevard that became Wacker Drive,[37] which defined the western and northern edges of the central city, continued beyond it along the north and south branches of the Chicago River as a boulevard built over working quays and warehouses (FIGURE 4.18).[38] The central city's natural edge along Grant Park continued north and south,

incorporating athletic grounds, promontories, and working piers enriched with public space.

The principal element of the central axial ensemble also dominated the larger city (FIGURES 4.19 and 4.21). The dome of the city administration building, as the hub of Chicago's radial order, terminated multiple axes and anchored multiple connections with the natural landscape. As a radially symmetrical object itself, it reflected, in concentrated form, the character of the expanding periphery, from which it would always remain visible. The radial expansion of an open edge around a fixed central point demonstrated the simplicity and completeness that planning from the center had attained.

Figure 4.16 *Proposed Plaza on Michigan Avenue west of the Field Museum of Natural History in Grant Park, looking east from the corner of Jackson Boulevard,* by Jules Guerin. Plate 128 from the *Plan of Chicago,* 1909.

THE PLAN ASSESSED

This simple image of a metropolitan circle also demonstrates the extent to which compositional ideals remained central to narrative planning. Chicago's existing conditions, however, only appeared to harmonize with those ideals. The sympathetic elements—a radial arrangement of functional zones, uniformly well served by systems of circulation and recreation—had evolved organically from commercial pressure on a standard grid and a specific site, not from a specific plan. In formulating an explicit plan from these elements, Burnham and Bennett did not recognize the nature of the process that had put them in place. Their emphasis on the requirements of the city as a whole, their enthusiasm for a simple and potent diagram that would address these together, and their hope for its centralized implementation caused the planners to disregard typical conditions in Chicago.

In this context, the larger systems' relationships to one another took precedence over their engagement with immediate surroundings. Conceptual and compositional clarity, not the requirements of local populations, determined the placement of the largest proposed new parks, which were connected by a boulevard whose constant curve ignored the precedent for introducing boulevards into the grid.[39] The railroad loops west of the central city did not adequately incorporate the emerging industrial belt on the southern periphery, which was equally accessible to water and rail and closer than the western periphery to national markets.[40] Though Burnham and Bennett squarely faced the problem of moving vehicular traffic between core and periphery through the intervening urban fabric, their radial network could not ensure smooth through circulation because it did not conform to Chicago's existing pattern of streets and blocks.[41] Slicing through the street grid not only compromised this existing pattern, in which major half-mile streets protected the interstitial residential streets from through traffic, but it also produced more intersections on the through-traffic streets themselves.[42] Chicago's existing diagonal streets avoided the former problem because the peripheral street grid had been extended outward around them, but the obstacles to circulation created by additional, irregularly spaced intersections must have already been observable on them.[43] Moreover, these streets only vaguely intimated a more-coherent network of circulation. Proposed diagonal streets significantly outnumber existing diagonals in Burnham and Bennett's plan (FIGURE 4.25); only one diagonal street out of six was already in place at the proposed convergence of this network on the Civic Center.[44]

The ensemble plan proposed by Burnham and Bennett for the central city, which they envisioned as a concentrated version of the larger city, exposed the practical limits of their larger strategy of imposing an explicit plan on an implicit order. Both the placement of the T-shaped intersection and the balance of its components owed more to conceptual neatness than to existing conditions or practical realities. The business district, contained within the Loop, lay entirely to the north of Congress Street. A southern extension across Congress Street was theoretically feasible because a height limit of 260 feet for new buildings, imposed by the city in 1902, effectively fixed the volume of office space in the business district.[45] The railroads owned much of the land under the proposed expansion and stood to profit from developing new office space that would be serviced by the consolidated rail station on Twelfth Street (SEE FIGURE 1.6).[46] This expansion was prevented, however, by the combined effects of a desire among property owners in the existing Loop for taller, more profitable buildings, the lax enforcement of the height limit, and the practical impediments to consolidating rail facilities and coordinating real-estate development among separate railroads.

Figure 4.16

Figure 4.17 *Michigan Avenue, looking towards the south. Proposed double roadway running to a plaza at its intersection with Twelfth Street, and a suggestion for buildings to surround the place, including rearrangement of the Twelfth Street railway station, by Chris U. Bagge. Plate 118 from the* Plan of Chicago, *1909.*

Figure 4.18 *View looking north on the south branch of the Chicago River, showing the suggested arrangement of streets and ways for teaming and reception of freight by boat, at different levels. Plate 107 from the* Plan of Chicago, *1909.*

The exceptional height and individuality of tall buildings that were endemic to the character of Chicago's central city prevented it from exhibiting the uniform, undifferentiated quality that Burnham and Bennett envisioned for it (FIGURE 4.19).[47] Property owners wanted to maximize profit and distinguish their product from their competitors', perhaps even more so where the building stock was as standard as in central Chicago.[48] More generally, the idea of a business district that was merely a foil and a setting for civic monuments ignored Chicago's commercial character. Since the evolution of the steel frame and the invention of the elevator, the city's most visible monuments were commercial rather than civic or cultural. For reasons of prestige as well as profit, commercial buildings would not collectively defer to civic monuments. Might not commerce itself, through the exceptional height and individual character of tall office buildings, seek the symbolic power reserved in the past for the church and the state? The development of the skyscraper as a civic marker, already well underway in 1909, intimated that it would.

Neither the Civic Center nor the cultural ensemble envisioned by Burnham and Bennett were likely to be implemented when they were proposed. A new City Hall (also the seat of county government) was already under construction on the site of its predecessor in the existing Loop. The South Park Commissioners were engaged in an ongoing legal battle with the mail-order merchant Aaron Montgomery Ward to keep the lakefront, in the words of the canal commissioners who had mapped this section of Chicago in 1836, "public ground—a common to remain forever open, clear, and free of any building, or other obstruction whatever."[49]

The absence of a preexisting plan for Chicago may also partly explain why the engagement of precedent in the *Plan of*

Chicago is less considered than in its predecessors. Both the World's Columbian Exposition and the Washington parks plan owed some of their complex character and experiential richness to the dialogue between a preexisting plan and a European precedent. Absent another plan to engage, the application of Parisian precedent took on a rote quality in Chicago. The example of Haussmann's Paris, moreover, was not wholly relevant to Chicago in 1906. Prior to its improvement, Paris was a clearly defined city with a dense, undifferentiated fabric that was difficult to navigate and already populated with existing monuments. Both the defining context and the terminal markers of new axes were in place. Chicago, by contrast, was a rationally organized city with an open periphery and a fabric that was highly varied by use and density. Such monuments as it possessed were, like every other building, organized by the street grid. Metropolitan zoning and a convenient periphery prevented its fabric from attaining the density and character to accommodate avenues lined with public space and multiuse buildings. Enriching circulation with landscape elements was both more practical and more appropriate in an environment where the home was identified with natural rather than urban surroundings. With its implications for typical conditions and private space, the question of how streets relate to buildings was one Burnham and Bennett largely passed over.[50] This led them to overlook the speculative implementation that was central to the Haussmann plan and the one feature most relevant to Chicago. Without a typical building program, the *Plan of Chicago* was a plan for circulation, public space, and public monuments, which relied for its implementation solely on an enthusiastic public and a degree of private coordination without precedent in Chicago or anywhere else.

Figure 4.17

Figure 4.18

Figure 4.19

Figure 4.19 *View looking west over the city, showing the proposed civic center, the Grand Axis, Grant Park, and the harbor,* by Jules Guerin, 1907. Plate 87 from the *Plan of Chicago*, 1909.

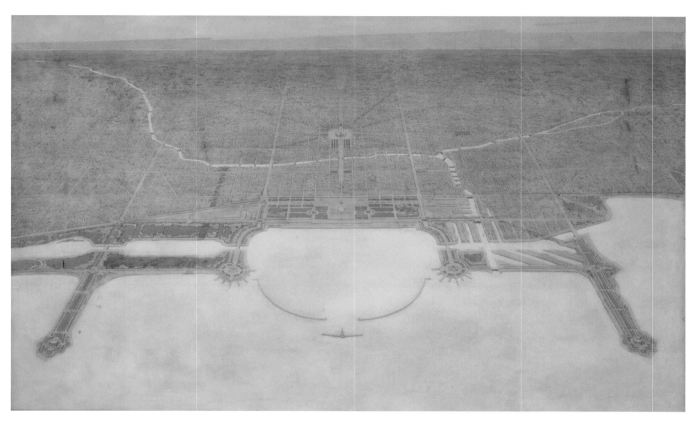

THE PLAN'S RECORD OF IMPLEMENTATION

The willfulness of Burnham and Bennett's plan and its failure to engage traditional means of implementation in Chicago invite speculation that the *Plan of Chicago* was a vision rather than a specific plan for the city. But Burnham's previous experience in Chicago—and in Washington, if not in San Francisco—encouraged him to view a practical plan and a romantic vision as contiguous concepts, and to imagine that a suitably compelling vision could gain the public and official support required to implement its proposals.

Nevertheless, it is as a vision more than a plan that the *Plan of Chicago* has persisted, and this is consistent with the nature of its contribution to American planning. By emphasizing circulation routes—as practical connections, organizers of monumental ensembles, and public landscapes—the plan provided a simple and obvious means for understanding an unprecedented urban phenomenon as a city. By engaging the precedent of Paris, it related the American urban predicament, with its seemingly new and special problems, to a shared past (the appeal of which was demonstrated by the World's Columbian Exposition). By incorporating existing conditions and earlier plans for improvement, it supported and reinforced Chicago's local history and helped foster a view of its improvement as a gradual process with roots in the past. By reinforcing Chicago's radial pattern, it proposed a course of expansion that would maintain the equal importance of the urban center and the natural periphery. That this largely described the city's unplanned expansion is part of the plan's achievement: it supplied that expansion with a narrative. By consistently emphasizing the larger metropolitan picture, even when describing specific proposals, the plan laid a broad framework for implementing these proposals in a general way. It has therefore been easy to ascribe not only the realization of specific proposals but also Chicago's still-persistent radial pattern to the foresight of Burnham and Bennett.

The plan's major concrete legacy is a consistent and pervasive program of public natural space and improved and enriched circulation. An expanded, beautified, and more-efficient central city is part of this program, though it lacks the focal elements envisioned by Burnham and Bennett. Michigan Avenue and Wacker Drive fulfill their intended roles as urban

Figure 4.20 View of the proposed Michigan Avenue Bridge, from the southwest, by Edward Bennett, 1912.

boulevards; both accommodate through traffic on lower levels.[51] The Michigan Avenue Bridge, designed by Bennett, opened in 1920 as a bi-level conduit for through traffic, a spur to real-estate development along North Michigan Avenue and the entire northern lakefront, a public connection to the river, and a civic ornament at the center of an ensemble of adjacent commercial buildings (FIGURE 4.20).[52] All of these routes of circulation were endowed with classical architectural elements that established them as parts of a connective civic system. Existing streets in the central city were widened, and Congress Parkway, introduced into the fabric, was completed in 1956, though as a conduit for through traffic rather than as the multipurpose boulevard Burnham and Bennett planned. Its axial alignment with the center of Grant Park, marked by the Buckingham Fountain, recalls its intended role.[53]

Grant Park remains the focus of an improved public lakefront. It includes multiple routes for through circulation, underground parking facilities, formal gardens, a program of commemorative sculpture, and active recreation facilities. The cultural ensemble Burnham and Bennett intended for Grant Park has been displaced southward, to the Museum Campus. Soldier Field occupies the place designated for athletic fields in the plan. Burnham Harbor and Northerly Island conform in shape and use to the plan's recommendations. To the north, the Municipal Pier, moved from its proposed position at Chicago Avenue to Grand Avenue, was completed in 1916 and combined port facilities with a public promenade. It was renamed Navy Pier in 1927, and it continues to serve in a sympathetic capacity as a family entertainment complex.

The ensemble plans that failed to materialize were not without value in guiding the arrangement of the civic and cultural program that was put in place. Though it remains unoccupied by buildings, Grant Park is a sort of natural forum

Figure 4.20

for an ensemble of cultural institutions around its edges, including the Harris Theater, the Art Institute, and the Symphony Center. The institutions that comprise the Museum Campus—the Field Museum, the Shedd Aquarium, and the Adler Planetarium—constitute a separate but related ensemble that partially shapes and defines the central harbor as Burnham and Bennett intended. The federal, state, and local governments did complete dedicated ensembles, albeit separately and within the Loop, on parcels that they already occupied or on adjacent parcels that they acquired. The plazas of the Federal Center and the Civic Center (renamed the Daley Center in 1976) constitute outdoor rooms shaped by adjacent buildings in the manner, if not the style, of Burnham and Bennett's proposed Civic Center.

A continuous public lakefront and a preserved forest belt are the plan's primary legacy on the periphery. The northern and southern extensions of the lakefront park were implemented as parts of a larger program of improvement that included Lake Shore Drive. The Burnham and Bennett plan also acknowledged and incorporated the metropolitan park system proposed in 1904 by Perkins and Jensen, to whom some of the credit for realizing the Cook County Forest Preserve must go.

The specific character of the landscaped circulation routes that Burnham and Bennett proposed as the basis for their plan was subsequently compromised by the introduction of the automobile. Even though the ultimate implications were not clear, by 1906 a change in Chicago's transportation pattern was underway. In 1895 the *Chicago Times-Herald* sponsored an automobile race along the lakefront from Evanston to Jackson Park, and Michigan Avenue was paved in the early 1900s, attracting automobile traffic and, between Twelfth and Twenty-Sixth streets, sales offices. Most horse and cable-car traffic disappeared by 1910.[54] The *Plan of Chicago* did not investigate the specific requirements of the automobile or speculate about the effects of its widespread use. These effects were ultimately more detrimental to Burnham and Bennett's public vision than the proliferation of tall buildings or the collective failure to coordinate railroad infrastructure. The car celebrated individual privacy and freedom rather than collective public engagement, as Henry Ford foresaw in 1909 when, regarding the Model T, he declared:

> I will build a car for the great multitude. It will be large enough for the family, but small enough for the individual to run and care for . . . it will be so low in price that no man making a good salary will be unable to own one—and enjoy with his family the blessing of hours of pleasure in God's great open spaces.[55]

Figure 4.21 *View of the proposed development in the center of the city, from Twenty-Second Street to Chicago Avenue, looking towards the East over the civic center to Grant Park and Lake Michigan,* by Jules Guerin, 1907. Plate 137 from the *Plan of Chicago*, 1909.

Figure 4.21

Figure 4.22 *General diagram of exterior highways encircling, or radiating from, the city. All the arteries composing the system without the city limits exist, except where shown in dotted lines. City limits shown in red tint; rivers and other waterways in blue.* Plate 40 from the *Plan of Chicago*, 1909.

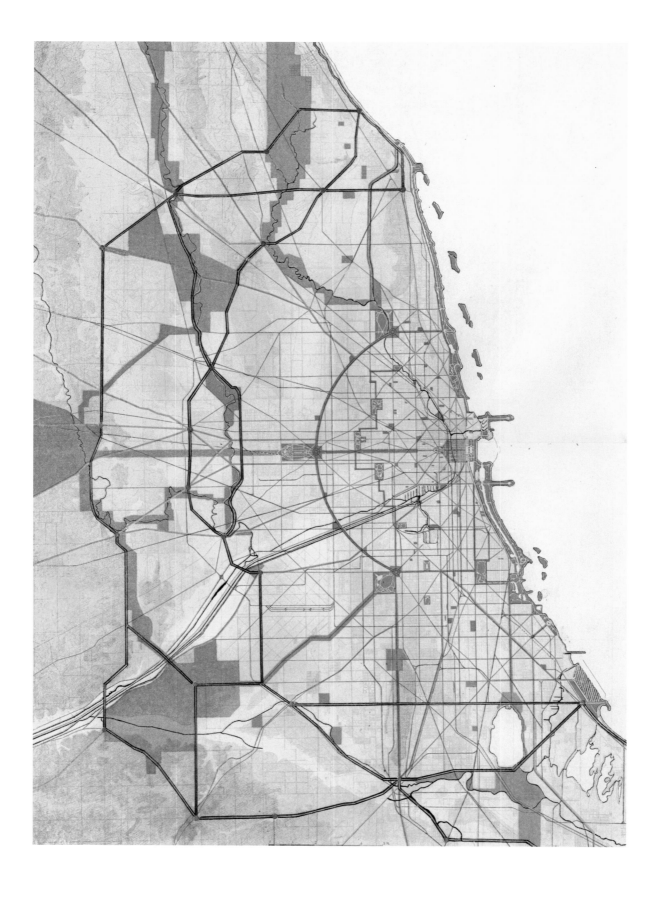

Figure 4.23 *General map showing topography, waterways, and complete system of streets, boulevards, parkways, and parks.* Plate 44 from the *Plan of Chicago*, 1909.

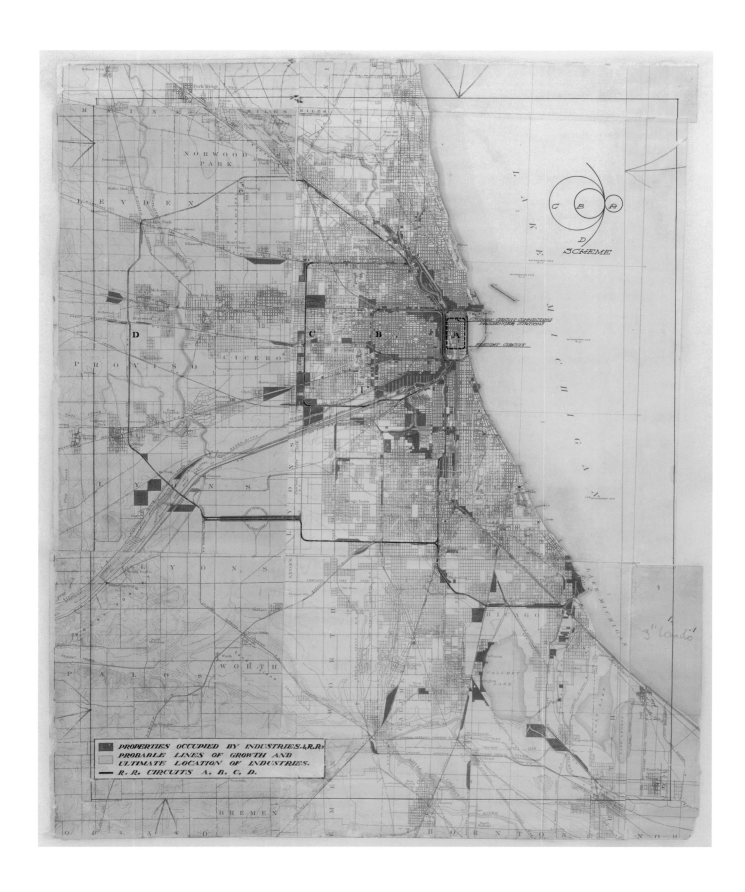

Figure 4.24 *Diagram of the city and surrounding country, showing railroad circuits, B, C, and D, which are, or may become, tangent to the inner circuit A.* Plate 73 from the *Plan of Chicago*, 1909. Circuit E, indicated in the original title, is not listed or shown in the plan.

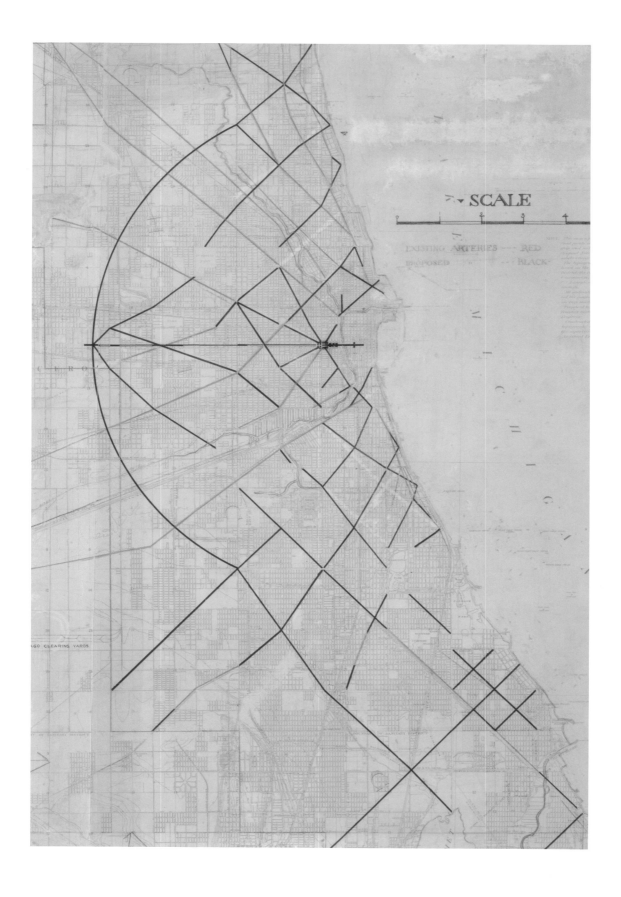

Figure 4.25 *Existing and (in black) proposed diagonal arteries.* Plate 91 from the *Plan of Chicago*, 1909. These are reversed in the original plan.

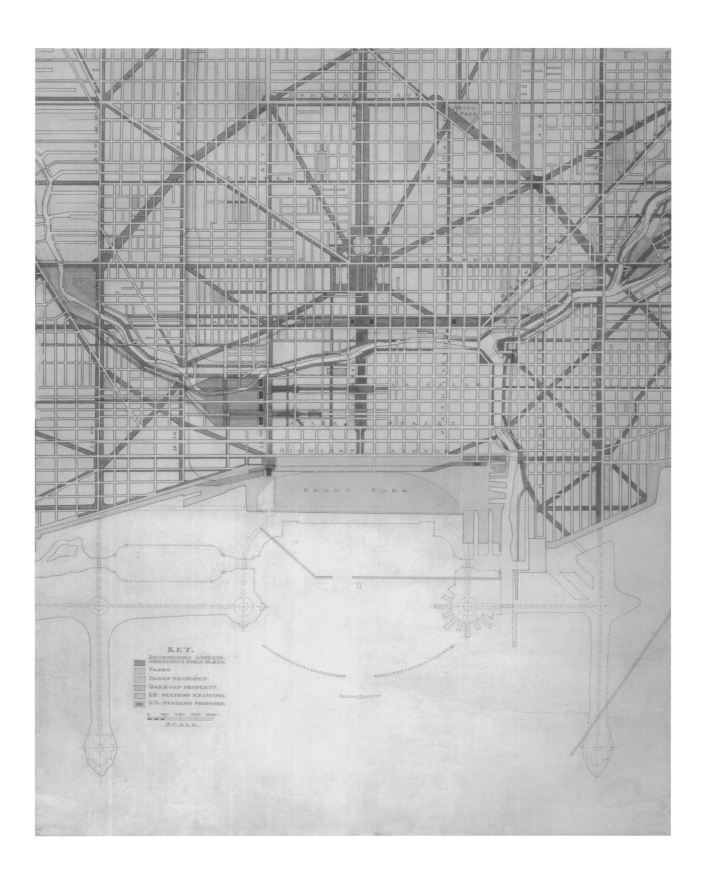

Figure 4.26 *Plan of the center of the city, showing the present street and boulevard system.* Plate 111 from the *Plan of Chicago*, 1909.

Figure 4.27 *Plan of the complete system of street circulation; railway stations; parks, boulevard circuits, and radial arteries; public recreation piers, yacht harbor, and pleasure-boat piers; treatment of Grant Park; the main axis and the Civic Center, presenting the city as a complete organism in which all its functions are related one to another in such a manner that it will become a unit.* Plate 110 from the *Plan of Chicago*, 1909.

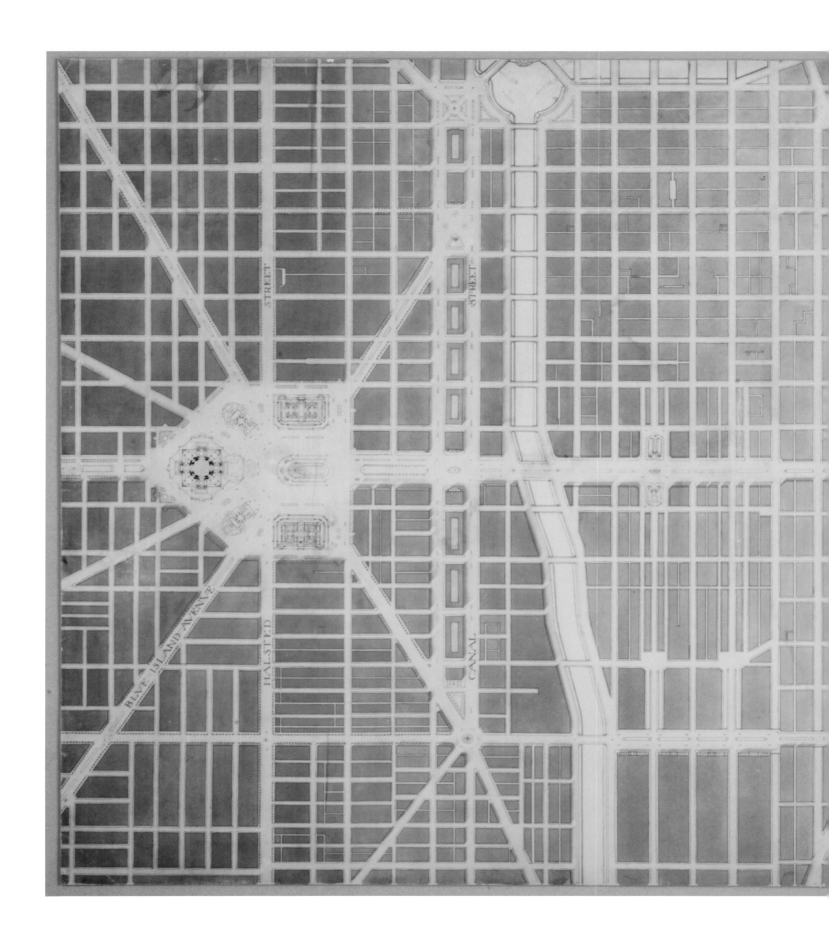

Figure 4.28 *The business center of the city, within the first circuit boulevard, showing the proposed grand east-and-west axis and its relation to Grant Park and the yacht harbor; the railway terminals schemes on the South and West sides; and the Civic Center.* Plate 129 from the *Plan of Chicago,* 1909.

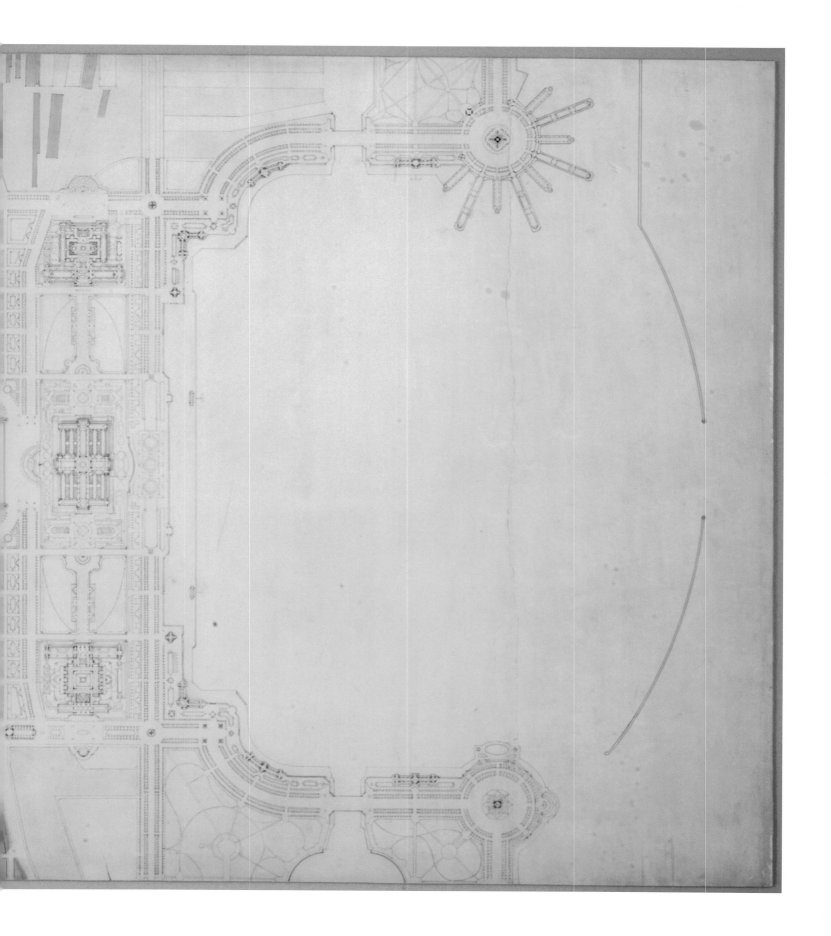

Figure 4.29 *Plan of the proposed group of municipal buildings or Civic Center, at the intersection of Congress and Halsted streets*. Plate 130 from the *Plan of Chicago*, 1909.

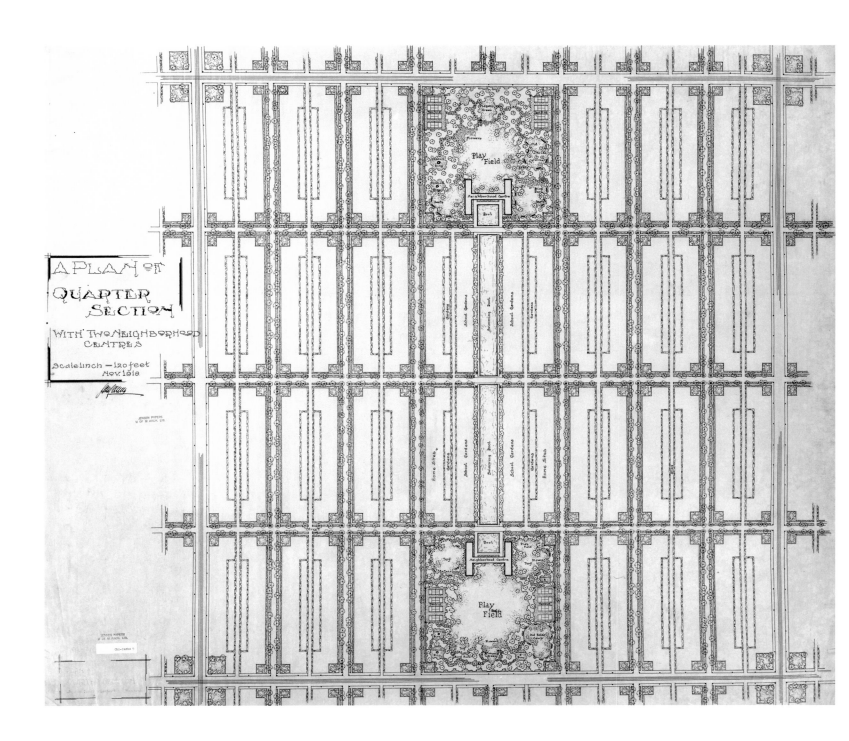

A PLAN OF
QUARTER
SECTION

WITH TWO NEIGHBORHOOD
CENTRES

Scale 1 inch — 120 feet
Nov. 1918

CHAPTER 5

PERIPHERAL PLANNING
BEFORE THE AUTOMOBILE

TYPICAL BUILDING REQUIREMENTS ON THE PERIPHERY

THE QUARTER-SECTION COMPETITION · CONTEMPORARY PARK

PLANNING ON THE PERIPHERY · MODULAR METROPOLITAN PLANS

COMPREHENSIVE PARK PLANNING · CONCLUSION

TYPICAL BUILDING REQUIREMENTS ON THE PERIPHERY

The *Plan of Chicago* did not address Chicago's typical residential, commercial, or industrial buildings or investigate with any thoroughness their relationship to typical streets. What these buildings required individually, and what their individual users required of them, fell outside the scope, or at least the emphasis, of a narrative public plan. Such considerations were of only secondary importance in the central city, where individual building requirements for light and air took second place to the collective need to accommodate as many buildings as possible in a relatively small area. They were more properly addressed on the periphery, where buildings were not forced into close proximity. Thus, in Chicago it was the existing tradition of peripheral planning that took up the issue of typical building requirements.

This tradition also typically addressed the transportation connections on which peripheral settlement depended from the point of view of individual users. The proposals of Olmsted, Jenney, and Beman and Barrett concerned individual access to transportation connections rather than the character or quality of the transportation system as a whole. Peripheral planning was therefore concerned with the local functional relationships between circulation routes, buildings, and open space.

During the early twentieth century, with the metropolitan park and transportation systems in place, further peripheral improvements addressed a smaller scale. They sought an optimum balance between these larger systems and the housing, local commerce, and neighborhood open space they serviced. The potential application to a large and uniform area encouraged peripheral planners to develop ideal neighborhood models that could be adjusted to fit specific conditions.

The character of the peripheral street grid and recent developments in suburban planning encouraged planners to view these neighborhood models as individually autonomous units.[1] The major through streets at half-mile intervals constituted natural boundaries between adjacent quarter sections, whose residents required local shopping and public open space in addition to housing. Planners could imagine quarter-section neighborhood models as small towns in themselves, with the potential for harboring a small town's locally based social relations. A neighborhood model with more local public open space might also mitigate the pervasive and unrelieved sprawl of houses and streets that created constant anxiety about the consumption of the natural periphery.

Actual peripheral development, meanwhile, continued in its established course, with neighborhoods conforming to regular divisions of the surveyor's grid built by speculative developers seeking maximum profit and therefore maximum density (FIGURE 5.2). The gradual division and dissipation of peripheral open space that was a byproduct of this process also continued. Peripheral planning developments that sought an improved neighborhood model amounted to a critique of speculative building practices.

THE QUARTER-SECTION COMPETITION

In 1913 the City Club of Chicago sponsored a competition to find a neighborhood model that combined housing at a relatively low density with public open space, local commerce, and through and local circulation. The organizers sought designs that were suitable for implementation.[2] In their view, this goal complemented the aims of the *Plan of Chicago*, which

---

Figure 5.1 Plan of a quarter section with two neighborhood centers by Jens Jensen, 1918.

69

Figure 5.2 Humboldt Park real-estate advertisement, 1871–74.

Figure 5.2

the competition brief characterized as concerned with "the broad structural features of the city framework" rather than the way in which these features related to typical conditions.[3]

The competition's parameters encouraged entrants to rethink the basic building block of the residential periphery. The site was a typical quarter section, bounded by four half-mile streets, with the interior streets that usually divided quarter sections removed. It was located at the edge of Chicago's city limits, eight miles to the northwest or southwest of the central city as the entrant chose; depending on that choice, transit lines to the central city would run along either the south and east or the north and east sides of the site, with the other two bounding streets able to accommodate future lines (FIGURE 5.3).

These parameters established some basic guidelines for the proposals and even suggested planning strategies. By limiting the site to one quarter section, as opposed to a whole section divided into four parts by two half-mile streets, the organizers ensured that plans would focus on the quarter-section interior rather than on the dividing lines of the grid. By locating the site relatively far from the central city, they guaranteed both a moderately low density, capping the total population of quarter-section proposals at 1,280 families, and a measure of local autonomy for the program's commercial and civic components.[4] By removing the typical street divisions, they encouraged alternative approaches to orthogonal planning while insisting that these acknowledge the grid's larger half-mile divisions.

The American tradition of identifying peripheral housing with nature rather than the city constituted one source for alternative planning approaches; contemporary English town-

planning practice provided another. English industrial town planning had explored the problem of arranging a relatively dense residential program in a peripheral context, as had Beman and Barrett in Pullman at roughly the same time. Bournville, near Birmingham, and Port Sunlight, near Liverpool—begun in 1879 and 1888 for manufacturers of chocolate and soaps, respectively—both used block planning to negotiate between circulation and protected natural space.[5] The individual house in its garden, though it might share a wall with a neighbor, was the basic building block of each plan. Attached houses around the outer edges of large blocks defined adjacent streets and shielded interior public open space containing individual or shared gardens. Public recreation fields occupied open blocks of their own.

The theoretical model of the Garden City, proposed in 1898 by Ebenezer Howard, codified these practical attempts to introduce elements of the natural landscape into an industrial context. Its tenets—land held in trust and population caps that would create leagues of smaller cities—were not directly relevant in Chicago, but the Garden City addressed the same individual requirements, ready transportation connections, and local public open space as American peripheral plans.[6]

The entrants in the City Club's competition applied the principles of English block planning to both the quarter section and its internal divisions. At both scales, they aimed to protect a natural interior from intensive use along the edges. Consequently, most entrants pushed local commerce to the quarter-section boundaries, where it would serve both local residents and passing traffic. This commercial sleeve would

Figure 5.3 Plan of a typical quarter section in the outskirts of Chicago, from the quarter-section competition, 1913.
Figure 5.4 Street subdivisions from the quarter-section proposal of Arthur C. Comey, 1913.
Figure 5.5 Plan of a quarter section by Edgar H. Lawrence, Walter Burley Griffin, advisor, 1913.

also shield residential interiors and public open space. Most entrants controlled access to this protected interior with a hierarchy of streets, in which the smallest circulation routes, intended only for pedestrians, penetrated farthest into quarter-section interiors (FIGURE 5.4). Blocking the center with either landscape elements or a civic ensemble did not necessarily contradict this approach (FIGURES 5.5 and 5.7). One entrant, Arthur C. Comey, combined all these approaches in a diagonal parkway that recalled the street-planning strategies of the *Plan of Chicago* on a smaller scale, using circulation enriched with landscape elements to overcome inefficiencies in the grid (FIGURE 5.6).[7]

Whether these specific strategies adopted or ignored the grid's orthogonal language largely determined their rational or romantic character. Romantic plans emphasized the center as a distinct pastoral order described with serpentine routes of circulation. These might pick up adjacent orthogonal streets but would inevitably lead them across the section to other parallel streets, dissenting from the grid's relentlessness but at the cost of scrambling it (FIGURE 5.7).[8] Geometrical plans, on the other hand, sought to focus the grid with local, radial orientation. These plans pulled adjacent streets inward toward a central circle or octagon, which collected and distributed circulation and set off a central civic ensemble or formalized park space (FIGURE 5.5).

Only those plans that acknowledged the grid's innate resistance to formal manipulation could exploit its inherent ability to accommodate both focal points and through traffic. Frank Lloyd Wright proposed a plan (though not competitively) that was unmatched in the ambition of its program and the extravagance of its expression. The plan had no dominant central space, but rather a switchback park armature that recalled existing park boulevards on a smaller scale; Wright enriched this with a civic and recreational program and threaded it through a residential fabric. Its undulating path impeded through traffic like an open center but also allowed some smaller routes through the quarter-section interior (FIGURE 5.8). Both the plan's ambitious programming and its intricate articulation were out of keeping with the typical nature of the quarter section, the one exceeding its requirements and the other compromising its legibility.

Among the competition entrants, only the Prairie school architect William Drummond combined focal organizing elements with through circulation in a neighborhood model that could be feasibly and gradually implemented as a typical planning unit. His plan was designed around a "nucleus" of educational and recreational buildings that he called a social center. The social center occupied a square block at the center of the quarter section, bounded on all sides by local through streets. Drummond also concentrated local commerce on the

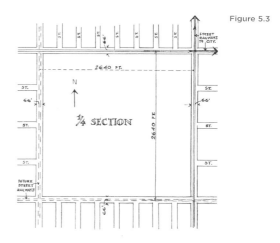

Figure 5.3

Figure 5.4

Figure 5.5

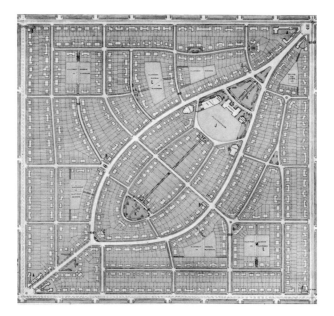

Figure 5.6

Figure 5.7

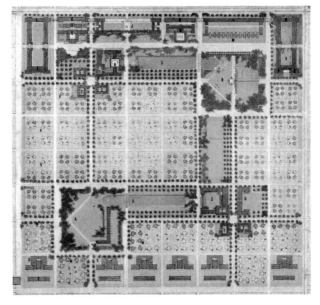

Figure 5.8

Figure 5.6 Second-prize plan for a quarter section by Arthur C. Comey, 1913.
Figure 5.7 First-prize plan for a quarter section by Wilhelm Bernhard, 1913.
Figure 5.8 Plan of a quarter section by Frank Lloyd Wright, 1913.

Figure 5.9 Bird's-eye view of an alternative scheme for a quarter section by William Drummond, 1913 (for the normative scheme, see *Figure 10.1*).

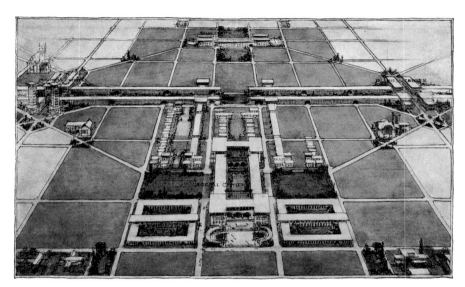

Figure 5.9

corners of the quarter section, creating four secondary foci. Across adjoining sections these would coalesce into nodes of the same size and importance as the quarter-section nuclei; Drummond called these nodes business centers. Social centers and business centers alternated in an even pattern of equal and opposite emphasis (FIGURE 5.9). The architect further endowed the streets and open spaces between these focal points with their own complementary character, with axial parks lined with small apartment buildings leading to the social centers, and urban streets lined with townhouses leading to the business centers (FIGURE 5.10). Higher-density housing thus sheathed the circulation routes that passed around and through the quarter section, freeing the rest of its interior to accommodate single-family homes (FIGURE 5.11). Drummond's proposal created a unified fabric that avoided monotony and tied quarter sections together at their edges and through their centers.[9] However, by concentrating commerce at quarter-section corners rather than along boundaries, and by introducing housing along half-mile streets, Drummond's alternative order ignored a fundamental aspect of the established peripheral pattern.

Many of the other proposals also utilized high-density housing types to maximize public open space. Concentrating population in multifamily apartment buildings and attached housing allowed the private open space that these would have occupied as single-family homes to be consolidated for parks and recreation, which planners often located on the interiors of large blocks (FIGURES 5.5, 5.6, and 5.7). The architect Walter Burley Griffin advised a proposal that successfully reconciled large blocks with duplex houses with the existing street grid (FIGURE 5.5).[10] Wright, on the other hand, maintained small, square residential blocks, with houses gathered into groups of

four placed at the centers of their lots. These houses faced outward across a lawn on three sides, sharing abutting service courts on the fourth (FIGURES 5.8 and 5.12). Wright thereby made private lawns appear as public open space.[11] This recalled Olmsted's treatment of private natural space at Riverside, though whether, in the denser and more-regular conditions of the typical quarter section, the private natural space of a backyard could be turned inside out was debatable.

A lack of effective centralized control among the competition's organizers, and the resistance of entrenched settlement patterns, ensured that these remained theoretical models with little practical influence on peripheral development in Chicago. The City Club, like the Commercial Club, was composed of businessmen of all types with an interest in civic improvement. Proposed improvements thus originated not with the development interests who built the periphery but rather with an outside group. Inventive plans for quarter-section improvement that counseled lower density could not find favor with these interests, who sought maximum profit and therefore maximum density. The periphery's persistent emphasis on individual rather than collective requirements, and the equally persistent allure of private open space that drew residents to the periphery in the first place, would not support the systematic integration of public open space with higher-density housing. The very pervasiveness of the residential peripheral pattern proved that the existing model was at least adequate. The plans for improving this pattern, devised by some of the United States' foremost architects, were therefore without issue in Chicago. Their implied program of social reform, however, rooted in the English Garden City movement, persisted in later modernist plans for the periphery.

Figure 5.10
Left: Street view from the quarter-section proposal of William Drummond, 1913.
Right: Court view from the same proposal.

Figure 5.11 A group of paired single-family dwellings from the quarter-section proposal of William Drummond, 1913.

STREET VIEW

COURT VIEW

Figure 5.10

CONTEMPORARY PARK
PLANNING ON THE PERIPHERY

Parks remained the primary tool of peripheral improvement. Like residential neighborhoods, they introduced elements of the natural landscape into the interstices of the peripheral grid, though as dedicated public space. They were subject to the same requirements of convenient access, and they increasingly became subject to the boundaries of the street grid as well, a process that was already under way during the creation of the metropolitan park system.[12] With this larger park system in place, subsequent parks evolved as smaller divisions of the surveyor's grid, unconnected to one another in any explicit way. The quarter section placed an upper limit on their size, just as it established the basic neighborhood unit. Parks and neighborhoods were therefore interchangeable components of the street grid.

As publicly funded improvements, parks were built where suitable land was available and affordable. Small neighborhood parks and playgrounds, which typically contained more built than natural space, therefore outnumbered the larger parks that promised relief from the peripheral urban pattern and thus constituted the most significant tool for improving that pattern. The demands of convenient access typically located these large parks at the intersections of half-mile streets, where their lack of a protective built edge, such as screened residential neighborhoods, was most apparent. Convenient circulation also demanded that they include interior through streets, either to connect neighborhoods on both sides or to allow access to their recreation facilities. Standard sizes, site conditions, program elements, and circulation requirements pushed peripheral park development, like residential development, toward a standardized model.

Jensen, a landscape architect and the coauthor of the 1904 metropolitan parks plan incorporated in the *Plan of Chicago*, established that model during the first decades of the twentieth century by adapting the existing peripheral approach to parks as characteristic natural landscapes to the more-restricted conditions of a developed periphery. His design for Columbus Park—located on Chicago's far-western periphery, against its border with the suburb of Oak Park—which he undertook as superintendent for the West Park District between 1915 and 1920, emerged as the local prototype for the large peripheral park. Occupying a quarter section between half-mile streets and surrounded on three sides by residential neighborhoods and on the fourth by industry, from which it was separated by a railroad line, this was a typical large peripheral park in terms of its size, situation, and program requirements. Jensen expressed two primary goals for the park's design: "to realize a complete interpretation of the native landscape of Illinois" and to use that landscape to convey to the city dweller "a message of the country outside his city walls."[13] Like the entrants in the quarter-section competition, Jensen emphasized the periphery as a transitional zone between urban and natural landscapes. As the grid extended the character of one, so should peripheral parks extend the other, pulling its distinctive elements—the

Figure 5.11

Figure 5.12 Bird's-eye view of a typical residential block, from the quarter-section proposal of Frank Lloyd Wright, 1913.
Figure 5.13 Proposed group planting for Austin Park site (later Columbus Park) by Jen Jensen, 1916.

Figure 5.12

watercourses that cut through the prairie and the hawthorn and crabapple trees that edged it—into close daily contact with peripheral residents.

Jensen enlisted the existing conditions of the site for Columbus Park to create a characteristic natural landscape; many of its final elements were therefore already in place (FIGURE 5.13). A broad, flat meadow occupying its center and used informally for golf became a protected landscape. Strategically planted stands of native trees prevented park users from seeing the entire space at once and thereby enlarged its apparent size. Nor did retaining this central meadow as a golf course violate its pastoral character, which park visitors around its edges could visually experience even when it was in use. Jensen employed the required routes of through circulation to reinforce the pastoral quality of this central landscape. He joined through streets along the park's northern and southern edges with a ring road, creating a circular boulevard that divided a pastoral landscape from an edge devoted to the more-structured activities of active recreation. Tennis courts, athletic fields, swimming pools, and a formal planted walk occupied the space separating this boulevard and the park's boundary, where, as in the active recreation program proposed by Olmsted for the South Parks, they were convenient to adjacent neighborhoods.

Jensen also enlarged an existing watercourse at the site's northeast corner and excavated a depression running down its eastern side, which marked an ancient section of the shoreline of Lake Michigan, to create a linear lagoon that recalled a prairie river. He mounded the excavated fill along this lagoon's eastern edge to further protect the center and provide park users with an elevated view of its natural landscape. Jensen did the same at the lagoon's northern end, at the imagined source of the "prairie river." He re-created this as a hilltop spring concealed within a grove of trees that also sheltered a performance space called Player's Green, where stage and seating were

separated by the passing brook. Here, in the "wildest" part of the park, was a place for celebrating culture. Jensen placed a field house and social center just to the north of Player's Green, at the intersection of woodland, lagoon, and prairie landscapes, related to each of them by terraces or planted fields.

As conceived by Jensen, Columbus Park demonstrated that the stringent requirements for through circulation and program arrangement in a limited space could enhance rather than compromise the natural character of peripheral parks. As in the quarter-section proposals, the confinement of through circulation routes and intensive uses to site edges allowed natural elements to dominate the center.

Jensen explored how park and residential planning might be further integrated based on this common strategy. He had been one of the judges in the quarter-section competition, and

Figure 5.13

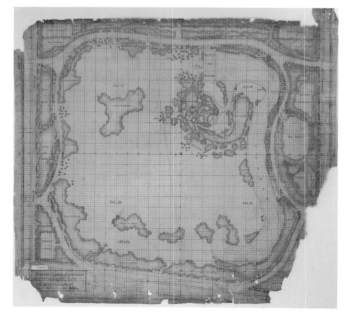

Figure 5.14 Plan of a section of Broadacre City by Frank Lloyd Wright, 1932.

he subsequently published his own noncompetitive entry. Like Drummond, he used the grid's orthogonal, open character to accommodate continuous natural space. This traversed the entire quarter section, bisecting it along a vacated street, which Jensen replaced with a linear park and canal between two square parks. Each of these contained a school that also functioned as a civic and community center (FIGURE 5.1). A protected park corridor might either stand on its own or continue through adjacent sections, creating long natural striations rather than the uniform points of emphasis Drummond had proposed. Where Drummond reinforced quarter-section corners with higher-density development, Jensen opened them up with small parks. Both planners, however, successfully reconciled the continuous through streets and uniform character of the peripheral grid with the continuous natural open space and civic significance appropriate to residential neighborhoods imagined as small towns.

MODULAR METROPOLITAN PLANS

How parks and neighborhood planning models might engage the city at a larger scale was a question that both Jensen and some of the quarter-section competition entrants addressed explicitly, regardless of the likelihood that their proposals would be implemented. These expanded plans negotiated the typical peripheral resident's individual requirements for convenient transportation connections and open space with the collective requirements of regional park and transportation systems, priorities heretofore associated with narrative planning.

Not all of the modular metropolitan plans were designed to be implemented in Chicago. Wright's 1932 Broadacre City was a theoretical, polemical planning model that proposed a universal pattern of settlement based on the one-mile divisions of the surveyor's grid. Though it shared with his earlier quarter-section proposal a modular composition, a hierarchical circulation system that separated through traffic from local traffic, an emphasis on private open space, and a complete program of public and private uses, Broadacre City employed these on a scale and at a density that were not urban. As an endlessly expandable grid, this "city" had no overall shape and thus no center, no need for density, and no metropolitan zoning. In effect, every separate use received its own section, and the elements of Wright's earlier proposal, while integral to an organizing system of circulation, lost their coherent relationship to one another. Wright recognized and celebrated this abandonment of urban settlement patterns when he described Broadacre City as being "everywhere and nowhere."[14] His "urban" proposal was consequently always presented as a typical section (FIGURE 5.14).

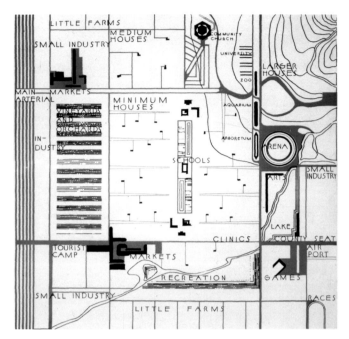

Figure 5.14

Modular metropolitan plans proposed by Drummond and Marion Mahony Griffin (utilizing her husband's quarter-section proposal) did not push the theoretical limits of their earlier proposals but instead engaged with Chicago's problems of metropolitan zoning and circulation. Griffin's 1945 plan, built from an octagonal module, would have introduced a new model that was related to but distinct from the square quarter section and thus necessitated a total metropolitan reconfiguration (FIGURES 5.15 AND 5.5).[15]

Indeed, plans based on multiple geometric units, like their Beaux-Arts predecessors, required cleared or vacant sites under centralized control. The Australian government provided both for Walter Burley Griffin in 1912, when he won an international competition to design the capital of Canberra with a scheme that resembled the later quarter-section proposal incorporating his advice (FIGURE 5.16).[16] The British colonial capital of New Delhi, designed by Sir Edwin Lutyens and Sir Herbert Baker at the same time, also adapted geometric modules to a new site. Newly founded government cities were thus the most likely candidates for geometrically regular modular city planning; it was not a viable planning alternative in an existing commercial city like Chicago.

Among the quarter-section entrants, only Drummond, whose proposal combined minimal intervention and gradual implementation with the formal language of the street grid, successfully extended those qualities to a larger scale. The architect presented his metropolitan plan in 1913, in response to another invitation from the City Club, in this case for improvements to the central-city railroad infrastructure, which

Figure 5.15 Site plan of Chicago, north and south sections, by Marion Mahony Griffin, 1945.
Figure 5.16 Plan of Canberra by Walter Burley Griffin, 1912.
Figure 5.17 Plan of a civic subcenter by William Drummond, 1913.

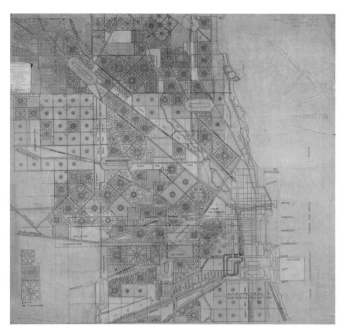

Figure 5.15

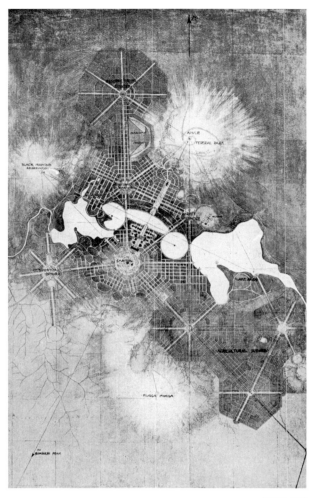

Figure 5.16

Figure 5.17

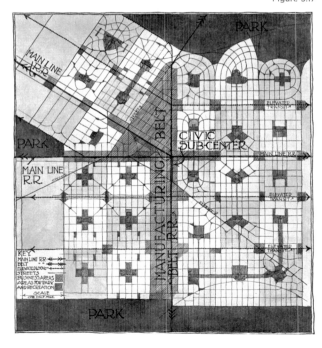

remained in 1913 much as Burnham and Bennett had found it.[17] Drummond's proposal lined radial railroad and rapid-transit lines with improved quarter sections. Where these lines intersected, he created "civic sub-centers," larger versions of the commercial nodes at quarter-section corners that included passenger stations, civic buildings, markets, and freight-storage and handling facilities (FIGURE 5.17). These reinforced intersections were joined by a circumferential manufacturing belt that recalled Burnham and Bennett's transportation plan but adjusted its regular geometries to actual site conditions. The railroad "spokes" that passed through the belt were separated from one another by linear park space, giving every peripheral resident convenient access to the natural landscape (FIGURE 5.18). The hub of this spoke system was a consolidated central-city rail terminal on the west bank of the Chicago River, which incorporated multiple office towers, passenger rail stations, and freight terminals, as well as through rail traffic.[18] Drummond thus adapted the complementary points and connections of his orthogonal quarter-section proposal to the multiple scales and radial arrangement of the larger city.

COMPREHENSIVE PARK PLANNING

Jensen used parks rather than neighborhood models as the building blocks of a larger regional plan. He incorporated within this nominally limited program, however, educational and agricultural components not usually associated with parks. The gradual reintroduction of a natural landscape into the existing peripheral fabric was the goal of his 1918 proposal for

Figure 5.18 Plan for the future development of the city of Chicago by Guenzel and Drummond, Architects, 1913.
Figure 5.19 Plan for a Greater West Park System by Jens Jensen, 1919.

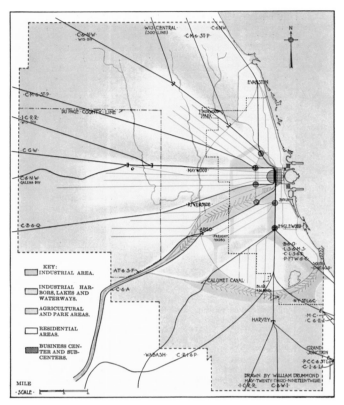

Figure 5.18

a Greater West Park System.[19] Like Drummond's scheme, his design organized a metropolitan park system along existing lines of circulation, allowing available land and existing natural features, rather than the regular geometries that guided Burnham and Bennett, to dictate the placement of new parks (FIGURE 5.19). Parks were augmented by "kitchen gardens" that could grow food for local residents or the larger population, an art school, and neighborhood centers planned around schools. These could either be built new (two examples anchor the ends of Jensen's quarter-section plan) or introduced around existing schools, opening up natural "holes" in the peripheral fabric. Some of these parks and gardens were connected by park boulevards that, unlike their predecessors, accommodated uses beyond housing (FIGURE 5.20); others were scattered through the fabric.

A metropolitan plan committed to a constant natural presence on the periphery appealed to a domestic ideal that was appropriate for the periphery's primary use. Jensen imagined the city as a larger version of the house in its garden, a simple analogy that prized typical conditions over exceptional ones and the everyday over the occasional. He wrote that "the human mind is not influenced by excursions. . . . We are molded into a people by the thing we live with day after day."[20] This was the heart of a planning tradition that served the peripheral

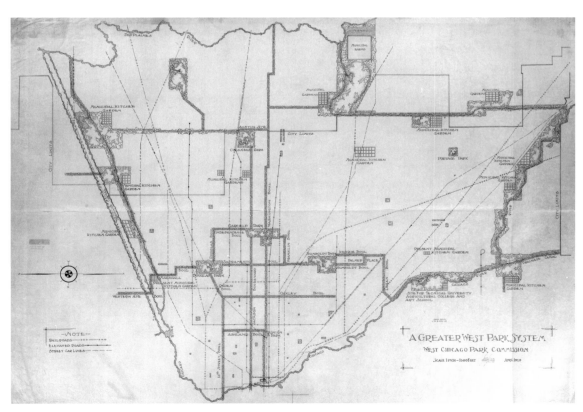

Figure 5.19

Figure 5.20 Plan of Prairie Drive, south of Columbus Park between Austin and 58th avenues, by Jens Jensen, 1919. North is at the right.

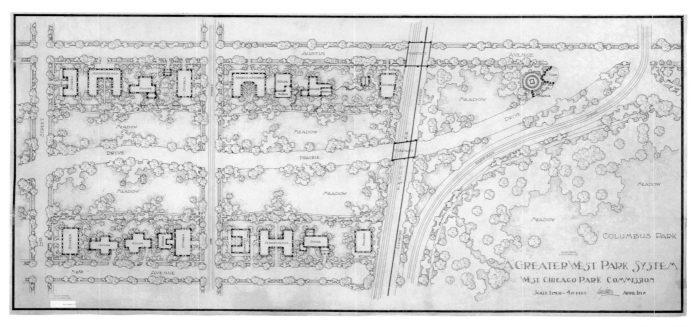

Figure 5.20

resident rather than the metropolitan citizen. In this context, Burnham and Bennett's grand central monuments were common touchstones in name alone, rarely seen and only abstractly shared.

The peripheral planning tradition cannot be separated from the larger social program that it shared with the proposals for an improved neighborhood model. Jensen saw the speculative pursuit of profit as the enemy of the livable city, and he believed that the purpose of town planning was "to guide the city so that it will retain a livable atmosphere."[21] Thus, he identified the expert planner with urban improvement and set him against the speculator in pursuit of profit. He went further, identifying better living conditions with a better democracy and characterizing the American home as "the foundation on which the world's greatest democracy rests."[22]

Despite their focus on typical transportation requirements, Drummond and Jensen, like Burnham and Bennett, failed to engage the automobile or to imagine the possible repercussions of its widespread use.[23] By offering uniform peripheral access, the automobile actively undermined the regular lines of emphasis on which their plans relied. It reduced parks to convenient destinations for individual drivers, thus destroying them as places where citizens might come into regular and incidental contact with one another.

CONCLUSION

Together these peripheral developments described, as had their predecessors, an order distinct from, and only sometimes complementary to, the centralized metropolitan order of the Burnham and Bennett plan. Each addressed the individual

requirements of residents and park users through functional planning, an approach that invariably involved transportation connections as plan organizers and zone separators.

On the residential periphery, this produced an alternative urban pattern, one that combined the suburban romantic planning of Riverside and the English Garden City with the street grid's rational arrangement of through circulation. Quarter-section interiors became, at least in theory, natural hollows, which Jensen's park and urban plans proposed to expand and endow with educational, agricultural, and civic as well as recreational uses.

These park and neighborhood plans catered to the special requirements of the periphery, as did the regional park and transportation plans that took existing conditions rather than geometric ideals as their points of departure. Peripheral residents could not relate to improvements in the city center simply by using the enhanced connections that led there; they required improvements addressed to their lives on the periphery, as they lived them every day. To that end, architects and planners promoted local civic amenities and parks as a response to peripheral monotony. Both Drummond and Jensen argued that the city's expansion must not sacrifice natural open space. Theoretically, the major divisions of the grid could go on forever as high-traffic corridors and high-density armatures, as long as they admitted an accessible natural landscape into their interstices. Ultimately, however, the grid's strength—probably as a measuring tool that aided speculation more than as a metropolitan circulator—overwhelmed systematic attempts to improve local conditions.

CHAPTER 6

PERIPHERAL PLANNING
AFTER THE AUTOMOBILE

EFFECTS OF THE AUTOMOBILE · BAUHAUS PLANNING IN CHICAGO

APPROACHES TO FUNCTIONAL PLANNING · HILBERSEIMER'S

PLANNING MODEL · APPLICATION IN CHICAGO · HILBERSEIMER'S

PLANS ASSESSED · RECORD OF IMPLEMENTATION

EFFECTS OF THE AUTOMOBILE

The automobile reconfigured Chicago's physical pattern as drastically as the railroad before it, though in a different way. Drivers could go where they wanted when they wanted, along any route they wanted to use. As Henry Ford had indicated, the automobile combined individual freedom of movement with access to a natural landscape, thus reconciling the two primary aspects of the periphery's persistent appeal. Therefore, like its predecessor, the automobile developed a new periphery beyond the existing city, according to its own requirements. It liberated suburbs from radial railroad lines, gradually filling in their interstices with low-density housing. Eventually, through a network of limited-access highways, it forged another spokelike pattern of peripheral growth at a larger scale and lower density.

The automobile's effect on the existing urban fabric, which had developed from the requirements of other modes of transportation, was drastic. The old periphery became an intermediate fabric, no longer adjacent to a natural landscape. The automobile had removed the area's comparative advantage over the central city, and its established neighborhoods, with their tightly packed houses, could not compete with the suburban neighborhoods of newer houses arranged on wide intervals in an unspoiled landscape. The fabric's half-mile streets became conduits for a more-aggressive mode of through traffic, and because cars could easily stop anywhere, the regular stops of trolley and streetcar lines ceased to regulate commercial growth on these streets. Half-mile intersections, once attractive to street-side commerce, became impediments to through traffic and a danger to pedestrians. The automobile also introduced new requirements for parking. Parking spaces not only lined residential and commercial streets but also eventually surrounded commercial buildings on half-mile streets, pulling apart the commercial sleeve that sheltered interior blocks.

The automobile's requirements for efficient through circulation and parking were concentrated on the central city, where multiple routes of through circulation converged. Eventually, limited-access expressways channeled through or around the central city satisfied the first requirement, and consolidated parking fulfilled the second; both opened holes in a dense, continuous urban fabric. Parking lots replaced outdated commercial buildings on some central-city blocks.[1] Larger lots proliferated on cheaper land just beyond the central city, isolating it in a sea of parking (FIGURE 6.2).[2] Peripheral values were also projected back onto the central city's building stock, whose uniform high density blocked light and air, at least by the standards of the periphery. To remedy this, and to emphasize buildings as discrete objects set off from their surroundings, architects incorporated public plazas into designs for tall office buildings. Opening the central-city fabric was therefore an

Figure 6.2

Figure 6.1 *A new settlement unit. A—Industry. B—Main highway. C—Local highway. D—Commercial area. E—Residential Area. F—Schools in the park area.* Illustration 80 from *The New City*, 1944.

Figure 6.2 Consolidated automobile parking in Grant Park, 1931.

81

Figure 6.3 *Traffic diagram of London.* Illustration 36 from *The New City*, 1944.
Figure 6.4 General view of a contemporary city of three million inhabitants by Le Corbusier, 1922.

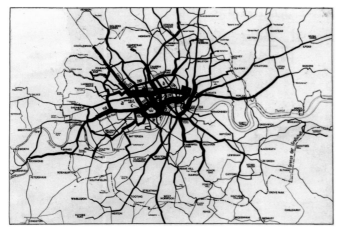

Figure 6.3

Figure 6.4

aesthetic strategy for increasing architectural presence as well as a functional measure for accommodating the circulation and parking requirements of automobiles. Neither the *Plan of Chicago* nor the peripheral park and quarter-section plans that followed it addressed or anticipated these effects.

BAUHAUS PLANNING IN CHICAGO

In 1938 the German architect Ludwig Mies van der Rohe immigrated to Chicago to direct the school of architecture at the Armour Institute of Technology (later the Illinois Institute of Technology). He was joined there that same year by his colleague Ludwig Hilberseimer, who became the director of the school's department of city planning. Both had taught at the Bauhaus, the German design school that sought to integrate emerging technology into the design process, historically the private concern of a craftsman producing a custom work for a patron.[3] Mass production of all sorts of objects—tools, decorations, building parts—had not only rendered obsolete the traditional processes of producing them but had also changed the way they were designed. The process by which an object or building was fabricated, the precisely defined function it would serve, and the inherent properties of the materials from which it was made replaced the particulars of its site or the requirements of its patron as guidelines for its design. The Bauhaus curriculum also espoused social improvement through better design, which would allow for the creation of mass-produced products that were cheap and available to everyone. Users who were equally well serviced by the same products and environments could become social equals and would together devise further social improvements.[4]

Bauhaus design relied on a method that distilled design problems into their essential terms and discarded anything not vital to the new requirements of production or the inherent properties of materials. Thus, Mies van der Rohe's architecture relied for its aesthetic effect on a clear demonstration of the structural logic and standard, factory-assembled character of the steel frame (SEE FIGURE 11.3).[5] These abstract concerns fostered the development of generalized, archetypal models that could be refined and adjusted to specific requirements of function and site.

Hilberseimer applied this approach to urban planning, seeking an ideal planning model based on the purely functional requirements of the city's different uses. This model relied on objectively verifiable observations, such as the amount of sunlight entering a room at a given time on a certain day at a particular latitude, or the spread of factory smoke given prevailing wind patterns. Such observations guided the planning of standardized models for housing, commerce, and industry, as well as their relationships with one another and with circulation routes and open space. Planning consisted primarily of satisfying the individual requirements of each component without impinging on those of the others.

The abstract, generalized nature of this process distinguished the ideal models it produced from those developed earlier for parks and quarter sections in Chicago. The latter were rooted in the requirements of a particular site and program, while the former evolved exclusively from the functional requirements of component parts that could be assembled anywhere.[6] The Chicago planners described their models in terms of location, with metaphors that tied them to a specific place. Jensen, for example, appealed to the familiarity and comfort of a home in a garden when describing the city in its setting. In contrast, Hilberseimer described his planning model in terms of work, appealing to the efficiency and specific purpose of the machine, whose performance was theoretically

Figure 6.5 Plan of a contemporary city of three million inhabitants by Le Corbusier, 1922.

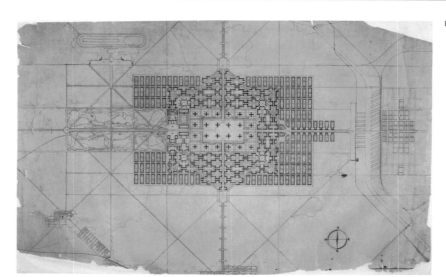

Figure 6.5

unrelated to its location. In this context, the adjustment of ideal models to specific sites was one step in a standardized process of functional optimization. The metaphor of the machine governed Hilberseimer's understanding of the city, his diagnosis of its problems, the formation of the solutions he proposed to improve it, and the ideal for which those solutions strove.

APPROACHES TO FUNCTIONAL PLANNING

A planning approach based on the machine metaphor sought to adjust the existing urban pattern to the requirements of the machines that comprised it—the automobile, the factory, the tall building—rather than vice versa. From this point of view, the existing pattern was itself merely a product of earlier technological advances, which were now obsolete. The relatively recent development of new machines was therefore bound to transform this pattern. In Chicago the introduction of the automobile had already initiated such a process of transformation.

In his book *The New City*, published in 1944, Hilberseimer charted the historical development of urban form in response to social, economic, political, and technological developments, concluding with the rise of industrialization as a distinct historical phenomenon. He elaborated the specific requirements of automobiles, factories, and tall buildings and discussed their incompatibility with traditional urban patterns. He also investigated these patterns at the fundamental level of their overall structure. He argued that the efficiency of the traditional radial city—or, as he termed it, the centric city—was theoretically limited by its inability to accommodate central-city through circulation beyond a certain point. Radial peripheral growth inevitably increased pressure on a center whose limits were fixed by the adjacent surrounding neighborhoods and whose capacity for accommodating through traffic was further limited

by its concentration of buildings and activity. Thus, the center of the centric city would eventually be either paralyzed or erased by the requirements of through circulation (FIGURE 6.3).[7] The scale of peripheral growth enabled first by the railroad and then by the automobile had brought cities closer to this theoretical limit. Hilberseimer identified the metropolitan zoning that had evolved in centric cities as the source of additional through traffic, as people traveled across the city between home and work. This constant local through circulation could not be distinguished from that moving between more-distant points.

The New City featured a discussion of proposals by other architects and planners that addressed the possible solutions to the structural problems of the centric city and the various strategies by which the city might accommodate the automobile. It included, among others, earlier projects by Howard and the Spanish engineer Don Arturo Soria y Mata and more-recent projects by Wright and the French architect Le Corbusier. Howard and Wright addressed the problems of the centric city on the periphery; Le Corbusier reconstituted the traditional centric city; and Soria y Mata proposed a settlement pattern that did not distinguish between core and periphery.

Howard's English Garden City and Wright's Broadacre City relocated work to the periphery, where Howard constituted smaller centric settlements around local industry and Wright proposed an endless, low-density street grid without zoning.[8] Neither precluded the gradual consumption of the natural landscape, and the latter, while it did not increase regional through traffic, did not necessarily reduce it.

Le Corbusier's 1922 plan for a hypothetical "Contemporary City" approached the problem of increased through traffic from the center, adapting the dense settlement pattern and distinct edges of the traditional European city to the scale and

Figure 6.6 Perspective view of a contemporary city of three million inhabitants by Le Corbusier, 1922.
Figure 6.7 Perspective view of Broadacre City by Frank Lloyd Wright, 1932.

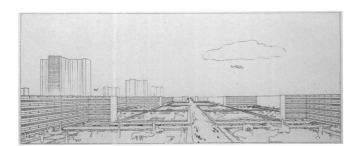

Figure 6.6

Figure 6.7

requirements of automobile through circulation (FIGURE 6.4). A geometrically regular city plan organized by two perpendicular axes focused on a central intermodal transportation hub, with a rooftop airport raised over an interchange through which automobiles, trains, and subways passed.

Le Corbusier reconciled this radical strategy with conventional notions of urban form by employing the geometric regularity and hierarchical arrangement that were recognized elements of the primary European urban-planning tradition. He maintained the placement and form but altered the function of the public spaces and building types with which this tradition typically worked. Thus, the singularity, central placement, and regular geometry generally reserved for public spaces and religious and government buildings here endowed a transportation hub. Concentric divisions separated dedicated business and residential zones rather than the space within the city from the space outside its walls (FIGURE 6.5).[9]

This geometric regularity concealed a radically different urban experience from that of the traditional European city. The automobile demanded a large scale that opened up the urban fabric and prized apart its traditional components of buildings, streets, and public space. Le Corbusier discarded the reciprocal relationship between streets and adjacent buildings, in which exterior walls defined the street as a public space and internal plans were shaped by it in return. For Le Corbusier, these components were tools dedicated to specific tasks. Streets were therefore intended exclusively for automobiles, pedestrian paths were used only for foot traffic, and buildings were shaped primarily by their occupants' individual requirements for maximum exposure to natural light. Into the interstices of this pulled-apart urban fabric Le Corbusier introduced elements of a natural landscape, which complemented the idea of the city as machine (FIGURE 6.6). The results were hardly urban in

a traditional sense. By reconfiguring the city from the center, Le Corbusier arrived at a model that resembled in its scale, separated program, and natural character the peripheral planning model later proposed by Wright (FIGURE 6.7). The Contemporary City, however, retained the metropolitan through traffic of a zoned city.

Only the *ciudad lineal,* or linear city, proposed by Soria y Mata accommodated urban expansion without sacrificing either efficient circulation or access to the natural landscape.[10] In 1883 the engineer proposed an alternative pattern for suburban development on the outskirts of Madrid, built around a circulation route between existing centric cities. This would contain a railroad line, a tramway, trunk lines for plumbing and sewage systems, and a linear park; it would be lined with public and commercial buildings and perpendicular residential streets (FIGURE 6.8). These would accommodate single-family homes with convenient access to circulation, services, and public space in one direction and open countryside in the other. Thus, a simple perpendicular arrangement allowed for intensive use and low-density settlement in close proximity. Expansion would occur at one end of the linear city through the addition of new perpendicular streets and could proceed without compromising efficient circulation in the existing city.[11]

Hilberseimer culled from the precedents of Howard, Wright, Le Corbusier, and Soria y Mata the basic features of a planning model based on the requirements of the industrial city. On one hand, this model needed to incorporate the large scale that serviced the automobile's requirements for uninterrupted through circulation. The plans of Wright and Le Corbusier demonstrated that such a scale could accommodate buildings configured to the individual requirements of their occupants, with generous exposure to the natural landscape. On the other hand, this planning model should exhibit the

Figure 6.8
Top: Topographic plan of Madrid in 1875, superimposed with the plan of the Linear City as realized (top center). Drawn by Manuel Sanmartín Fernandez.
Bottom: Plan detail of a section of the Linear City, showing the perpendicular arrangement of residential streets on either side of a central boulevard.

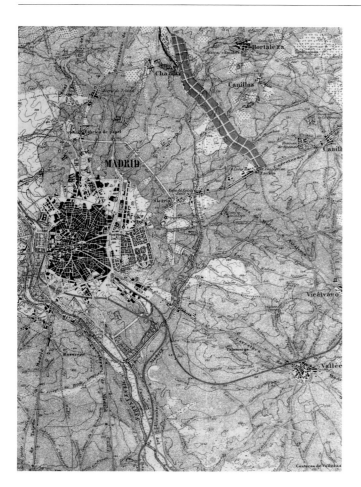

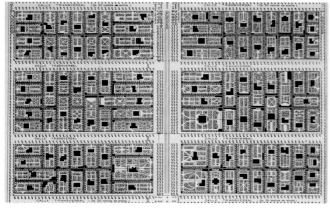

Figure 6.8

small scale and local zoning that allowed Howard's garden cities to limit metropolitan through circulation. Like Soria y Mata's linear city, it should be capable of expanding without compromising the efficiency of the existing city or its access to the natural landscape.

HILBERSEIMER'S PLANNING MODEL

Hilberseimer based a planning model that reconciled multiple scales on the requirements of its smallest components. Thus, the building occupant's individual requirement for direct exposure to sunlight, which Hilberseimer called insolation, determined the smallest unit of plans with a regional scope.[12] As insolation could be reliably predicted for different times of year at any given latitude, it could be graphically projected onto the surfaces of rooms with different orientations (FIGURE 6.9). From the results of this analysis, Hilberseimer designed a typical house plan, factoring in the privacy requirements of individual rooms and their accepted patterns of use. Living rooms and bedrooms faced south (in the northern hemisphere) to receive direct sunlight at the appropriate times of day, the former in the evening and the latter in the morning. Placing these in perpendicular wings separated public and private space and created a protected courtyard outside. Service rooms and circulation space around the outside edges of this L-shaped plan received less direct sunlight and screened the primary living rooms from the street (FIGURE 6.10). Houses could be turned forty-five degrees on their lots where streets were planned on a cardinal grid. Thus, Hilberseimer used a simple, quantifiable criterion to evolve a housing prototype that retained an essentially domestic character.

The shadows cast by individual houses limited the buildings' proximity to one another and thus the overall density of residential neighborhoods. However, Hilberseimer's L-shaped prototype could be tightly packed because its courtyard absorbed the shadows cast by adjacent houses. Maximum insolation also guided the arrangement of larger structures; taller buildings required a greater amount of space between them, which limited the clustering of tall buildings and intensive uses.

Separate requirements for automobiles and pedestrians governed how houses were arranged on streets. Landscaped pedestrian pathways alternated with closed-end residential streets that only local residents had a reason to use. Hilberseimer placed houses on the borders between these two circulation routes; these opened from one side onto the street and from the other onto the pedestrian path. The closed-end residential streets connected at one end to a larger perpendicular through street that was also closed at one end. It was connected

Figure 6.9 *Diagrams showing how different orientations affect the penetration of sunlight into a room at 10 A.M. on December 21.* From top to bottom, rooms are oriented to the east, southeast, and south. Included in illustrations 54–56 from *The New City*, 1944.

Figure 6.10 *L-shaped houses at a density of 120 people on one acre.* Illustration 67 from *The New City*, 1944.

Figure 6.9

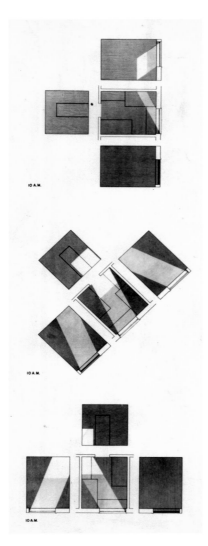

Figure 6.10

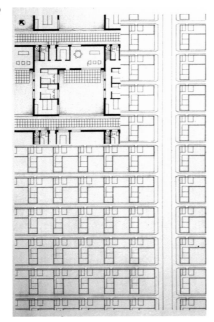

at the other to a perpendicular expressway (FIGURE 6.1). Thus, perpendicular relationships divided changes in use and scale, separating houses from residential streets, residential streets from local through streets, and through streets from major through circulation along the expressway.

A typical closed-end neighborhood was one of many, arranged along the expressway like leaves on a branch (FIGURE 6.11; SEE FIGURE 11.1). These neighborhoods, which Hilberseimer called settlement units, were enlarged and elaborated versions of the perpendicular residential streets of Soria y Mata's linear city. They were also small, closed-end linear cities themselves. In their small size, discrete character, and relative isolation, individual settlement units recalled English garden cities. Like those, the settlement units were functionally autonomous "country towns" that accommodated local industry, commerce, and cultural and educational buildings. Hilberseimer placed factories across the expressway from settlement units, as far from houses as possible; he situated commercial buildings along the local through street—between the expressway and the residential streets—and schools (which doubled as cultural centers) in the open landscape between adjacent settlement units. He limited the size of each settlement unit so that there was a comfortable walking distance between these elements. A continuous natural landscape, itself a network of paths interlocked with the street system, was the primary pedestrian route between home, work, and school. Children could walk to school without crossing a street. By giving settlement units their own complete functional program, separated by the linear-city system into local zones, Hilberseimer removed metropolitan through traffic from the expressway, which was reserved for long-distance travel. The architect thus proposed a modular linear city as the urban pattern appropriate to the Industrial Age. This planning model lacked a central point of convergence and therefore a hierarchical spatial arrangement. As it satisfied the requirements of every individual function, it did not privilege any one over the others. Finally, its full embrace of the machine metaphor paradoxically permitted a full engagement with a natural landscape, which, unlike that of Broadacre City or the Contemporary City, was not divided by streets into clearly bounded parcels. The modular linear city was therefore not experienced as a machine but rather as a continuous landscape.

APPLICATION IN CHICAGO

In 1944, the year *The New City* was published, Chicago remained a large, prototypical industrial city of about four million people, with the radial pattern and metropolitan zoning typical of a centric city.[13] A significant section of *The New City* was

Figure 6.11 *Commercial area with residential sections on both sides.* Illustration 91 from *The New City*, 1944.
Figure 6.12 Marquette Park and two proposals, showing existing conditions and implementation in two stages, by Ludwig Hilberseimer, 1950.

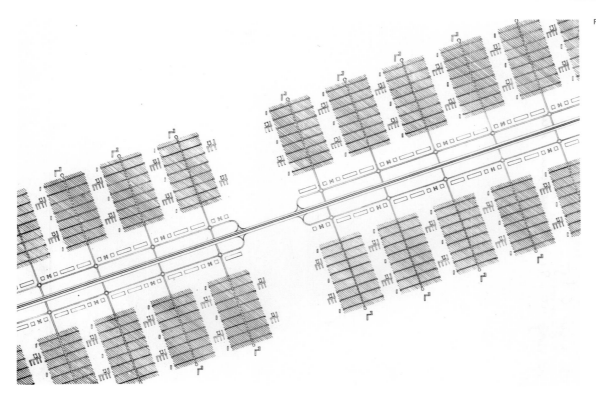

Figure 6.11

consequently devoted to the city's hypothetical reconfiguration as a modular linear city. Over the next twenty years, Chicago provided Hilberseimer with the context and opportunity for refining this idea. A series of academic projects and professionally commissioned plans increasingly conformed to the city's existing radial organization and the established character of its street grid.

Like Hilberseimer's settlement units, this existing street grid relied on orthogonal arrangement and a separation of through traffic on major streets from local traffic on minor ones. While Chicago's grid was open-ended and expandable with regard to streets, it divided land into clearly defined blocks that precluded the continuous natural landscape that Hilberseimer imagined as a pedestrian realm. The planner relied on the established Bauhaus technique of erasing inessential elements to adapt his ideal model to the existing fabric. By closing through streets and eliminating the redundant intersections that posed a danger to both cars and pedestrians, he could reintroduce a continuous pedestrian landscape into the existing fabric, initially as linear extensions to existing parks (FIGURE 6.12). Half-mile streets would remain as local through streets; existing residential streets would become cul-de-sacs; and the buildings along each would remain intact. Gradual implementation was inherent in a process that improved the fabric through subtraction. Complete settlement units, composed of houses oriented for maximum

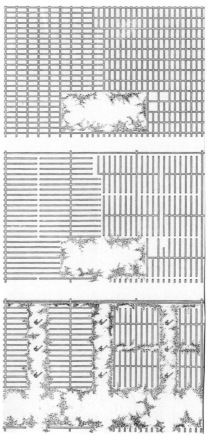

Figure 6.12

Figure 6.13
Left: *City of Chicago. Diagram of present state and condition.* Illustration 103 from *The New City*, 1944.
Right: *City of Chicago. A diagram of its proposed replanning, 1940.* Illustration 104 from *The New City*, 1944.

Figure 6.14 *Aerial view of the replanned city of Chicago.* Illustration 105 from *The New City*, 1944.

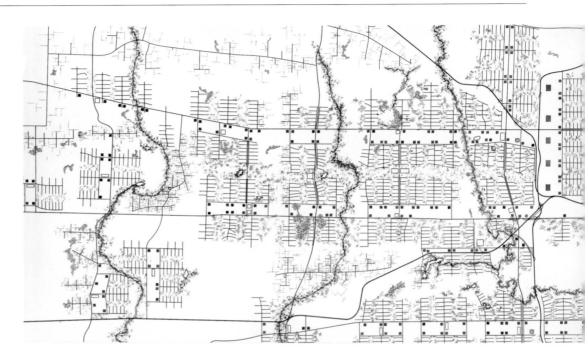

Figure 6.13

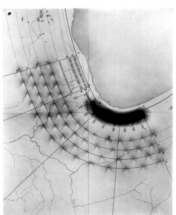

Figure 6.14

insolation, would evolve over time as obsolete housing was gradually replaced.

These latent settlement units were the basic modules for a series of theoretical regional plans and more-localized professional commissions undertaken by Hilberseimer between 1944 and 1963. The latter included two plans for cooperative housing—Evergreen I and II, designed in 1945 and 1947, respectively—one for the area around Marquette Park in 1950 (FIGURE 6.12); and two for urban renewal on the South Side, one between 39th and 47th streets in 1950, and another in Hyde Park in 1956.

The regional plans gradually acknowledged and accepted Chicago's entrenched metropolitan zoning, regional through circulation, and specific geographic character. The early plan featured in *The New City* divided a modular linear plan into two major zones with settlement units dedicated to commerce and industry, reflecting existing concentrations of those uses in the Loop and along the southern lakefront (FIGURES 6.13 and 6.14). Housing in the southern zone of heavy industry was located beyond the range of polluted air, connected to work by local highways and railroads; in the commercial zone, it followed the normative pattern of the ideal model (FIGURE 6.11; SEE FIGURE 11.1).[14] A 1963 plan shows a finer grain, avoiding a complete reconstitution of major zones of commerce and industry and accepting the existing half-mile and diagonal streets and radial expressways as organizers of localized zones of commerce and smokeless industry. This plan also preserved, though at a very large scale, Chicago's existing grid (FIGURE 6.15). It further recognized the existing industrial zone along

Figure 6.15 Detail of a plan for the area between Lake Michigan and the Fox River by Ludwig Hilberseimer, 1963.

Figure 6.15

the Sanitary and Ship Canal, the exclusively commercial character of the Loop, and the desire for high-rise housing along the lakefront.[15]

During the same period, the plans for specific neighborhoods also increasingly engaged the existing character of Chicago's street grid. From the cooperative housing proposals to the redevelopment plans for the South Side and Hyde Park, the last of which was undertaken in collaboration with Mies van der Rohe, these plans gradually accepted the established terms of Chicago urbanism. The Hyde Park proposal included recognizably urban building types—rowhouses, courtyard buildings, and slab towers—oriented to the street grid and arranged according to existing patterns of use, with commercial buildings on major streets protecting the residential buildings behind them (FIGURES 6.16 and 6.17).

HILBERSEIMER'S PLANS ASSESSED

Peripheral requirements remained at the heart of Hilberseimer's proposed urban transformation. The mobility of the automobile, the restful character of the closed-end residential street, and the solitude of the natural landscape appealed to the individual requirements of peripheral residents rather than to the collective needs of the city as a whole. The collective identity supported by the limited size and common work and recreation facilities of the settlement unit was that of a village rather than a city. Beyond circulation routes, there was little to bind these self-sufficient modules together, either physically or conceptually. Consequently, there was no place in

Hilberseimer's plans for the kind of urban public space that defined the *Plan of Chicago*.

The emphasis on convenient circulation and exposure to a natural landscape was a common feature of the mid-twentieth-century efforts to create an urban pattern for the automobile. Le Corbusier, Wright, and Hilberseimer all produced urban plans without an urban character, none of which addressed the collective commercial pressures that had created dense urban conditions in the first place. Urban plans that do not acknowledge the spatial limitations that these forces produce cannot properly be applied to an entire city any more than a plan devised from the center can address the specific problems of the periphery.

The nonurban character of these plans owed something to the machine metaphor, which recognized only those uses that it could specifically define and improve in isolation. It was the interdependence of multiple uses, however, where some possible benefits were yielded for the enjoyment of others, that produced an urban character. An urban street is regularly divided into blocks that limit the speed of through traffic and lined with buildings whose rooms receive unequal exposure to sunlight. It defines a clear path, onto which slow-moving vehicular and pedestrian traffic enters and leaves, and along which automobiles and pedestrians periodically stop to park or enter shops, offices, or houses. It is therefore a destination as well as a passage, and in this role its urban quality lies. A method that separates and isolates elements cannot recognize this kind of complex character; indeed, it dismantles it. Thus, when circulation, building use, and open space are separated, places

Figure 6.16 Hyde Park redevelopment plan by Ludwig Hilberseimer and Ludwig Mies van der Rohe, 1956, showing three stages of development from top to bottom. Lake Shore Drive runs along the bottom of each image and Kimbark Avenue along the top; 55th Street becomes the spine of the redeveloped neighborhood.

Figure 6.16

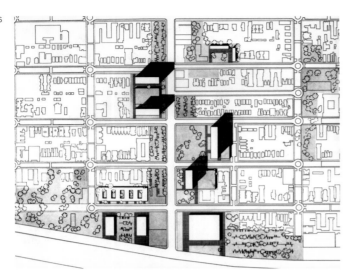

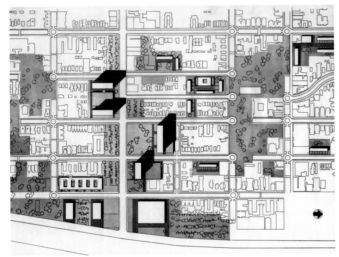

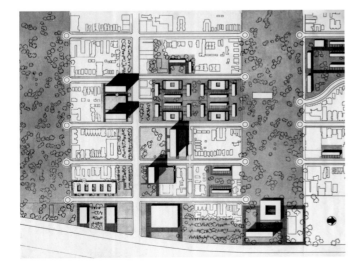

where multiple uses converge are suppressed. This suppression has wider implications, for a convergence of multiple uses is one basic definition of a city.

RECORD OF IMPLEMENTATION

Neither Hilberseimer's regional plans nor those for individual neighborhoods were implemented in Chicago. The 1956 plan for Hyde Park, however, might have been. This was Hilberseimer's second collaboration with Mies van der Rohe and the developer Herbert Greenwald, with whom he had planned Lafayette Park in Detroit the previous year. Hilberseimer's plan for Lafayette Park (originally called Gratiot Park) was largely implemented, and it remains his primary built work. Like that project, the Hyde Park redevelopment plan reconciled the planning ideals of the settlement unit with a speculative method of implementation.

The theoretical premises of Hilberseimer's planning, however, directly contradicted typical speculative practice. Speculators were more interested in reaping the profits provided by high-density settlement than in providing prospective residents with equal access to light and air. A distinction must thus be drawn between these theoretical premises and their application, and between Hilberseimer's regional planning, largely undertaken in an academic setting, and his neighborhood plans, which were professional commissions. In these the planner fully tested the flexibility of his models when confronted with existing site conditions and program requirements for high-density settlement.

The formulation of a distinct peripheral pattern of settlement is Hilberseimer's primary planning legacy. On the periphery, shared experience is less important than a working relationship between circulation, housing, and the natural landscape. In separating and isolating the individual requirements of these components, he found a conceptually succinct and mutually beneficial relationship between them. His planning model provided for urban extension that would preserve the natural landscape. Its combination of multiple uses at a small scale theoretically solved the persistent problem of regional through traffic by eliminating metropolitan zoning. It thus pointed the way to possible peripheral autonomy. The current incarnation of the urban periphery is a compromised version of this ideal model.

Figure 6.17 Hyde Park area plan, showing the location of proposed redevelopment and existing patterns of land use, by Ludwig Hilberseimer and Ludwig Mies van der Rohe, 1956.

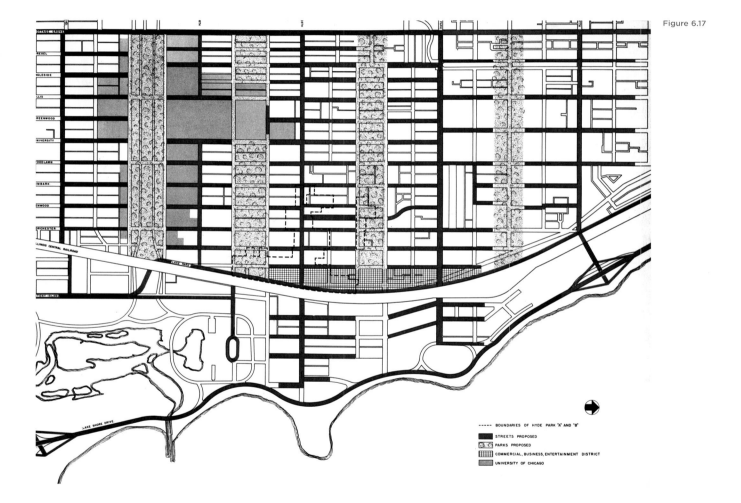

Figure 6.17

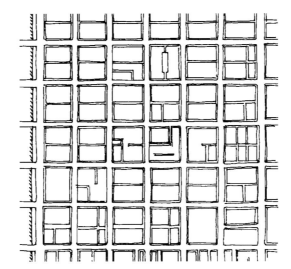

Plan for a quarter section from the *Plan of Chicago*, 1909.   Central City

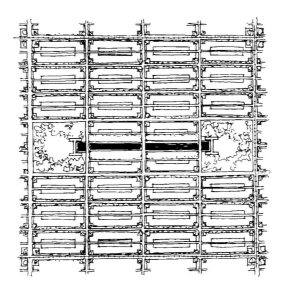

Plan for a quarter section by Jens Jensen, 1918.   Intermediate Fabric

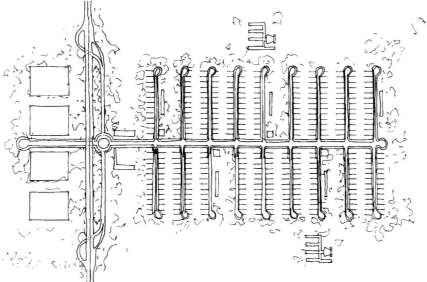

Plan for a quarter section by Ludwig Hilberseimer, 1944.   Periphery

CHAPTER 7

RELATING THE CHICAGO PLANS

TWO PLANNING TRADITIONS DESCRIBED · OBSTACLES TO
RELATING THESE TRADITIONS · COMPLEMENTARY RELATIONS AND
SHARED ELEMENTS · THE PRECEDENT FOR A NEW PLAN AND THE
PERSISTENT PROBLEM OF SPECULATIVE DEVELOPMENT

TWO PLANNING TRADITIONS DESCRIBED

The plans discussed here can be grouped under two broad headings—peripheral planning and planning from the center. The early plans for residential suburbs, regional parks, and factory towns, and the later prototype-based plans intended to improve typical settlement patterns, both before and after the arrival of the automobile, belong to the latter tradition. This tradition has its roots in Chicago's phenomenal expansion during the second half of the nineteenth century, when residential sprawl raised fears about the destruction of the city's natural landscape. Its components are the transportation connections, low-density housing, and natural landscape elements that comprise the periphery. Peripheral planning relies heavily on convenient transportation connections and assumes that long distances are easily traversed and further expansion is always possible. Indeed, it presupposes that land is available and, per capita, inexpensive. The scale of the periphery is larger than that of the central city, with more distance between buildings and streets and a greater variety of street types separating through traffic from local traffic. The requirements of the periphery are those of individual users—convenient connections to the city and the natural landscape and optimal access to natural light and air. Since at any given time in its history the majority of Chicago's population has lived on the periphery, these are also the typical requirements of most of the city's residents. Peripheral planning has therefore increasingly focused on prototypical planning models that can be applied to many specific sites.

In contrast, the World's Columbian Exposition, the McMillan Plan for Washington, D.C., and the *Plan of Chicago* belong to a tradition of planning from the center that addresses collective rather than individual needs. In Chicago the roots of this tradition lie in the last decades of the nineteenth century, when, at the end of the city's period of fastest growth, it had attained the second place among American cities in terms of population and importance and had reason to hope for the first. Planning from the center is consequently concerned with the city as a singular entity with which even the region outside its political jurisdiction identifies. This emphasis on totality, focused on the central city as the point where multiple systems and uses converge, is the primary distinction between planning from the center and peripheral planning. Planning from the center assumes that the other parts of the city are dependent on this point of convergence; it is central-city planning whose scope also includes the central city's connections to its dependent territory. This approach further presupposes that available space, at least in the center, is limited and must be used as efficiently as possible. It therefore seeks to combine rather than separate uses, as is common practice on the periphery. The efficient through circulation and intensive land use demanded in the central city are products of convergence; plans for improving the city concentrate on this special character and are therefore not applicable elsewhere. Their implications, however, affect all areas of the periphery.

OBSTACLES TO RELATING THESE TRADITIONS

An undue emphasis on the transformative effects of new technology and an assumption that the modes of architectural expression associated with individual plans are incompatible with one another have obscured the complementary nature of these two planning traditions. Constant change, however, has clarified rather than altered Chicago's persistent physical

---

Figure 7.1 Comparative plans for improving typical quarter sections of the central city, intermediate fabric, and periphery.

Figure 7.2 Arbor seat and lamp, Lincoln Park Lily Pool, by Alfred Caldwell, 1936.

Figure 7.2

character. The technological innovations that drive peripheral expansion and central-city concentration also service a more-basic impulse to separate commercial, residential, and industrial uses according to their functional requirements. In Chicago this is demonstrated by the fact that the periphery has continued to expand and the center has become increasingly dense as new modes of transportation and building reconfigure these areas.

Evolving architectural styles are largely irrelevant to the primary concerns of Chicago's two major planning traditions. Buildings, like circulation routes and public open space, are only one element of planning, and changes in the way a small number of buildings are designed cannot seriously affect the development of planning traditions that are concerned with the larger questions of how buildings with different uses relate to one another and to systems of circulation and open space.

Architecture can, however, convey larger planning priorities at the small scale of individual buildings and neighborhoods. Burnham and Bennett's use of classical architectural elements appealed to civic dignity and thus emphasized the public nature of their plan, just as Hilberseimer's use of steel-frame houses with large, glazed openings emphasized continuity between building interiors and the natural landscape, and thus the individual access to light and air that were central to his plans. The different priorities of these larger plans account for many of the differences in their choice of architectural idiom.

Figure 7.3 View of Thomas Paul Hardy House in Racine, Wisconsin, by Frank Lloyd Wright, delineated by Marion Mahony Griffin, 1905.

For much of the twentieth century in Chicago, Beaux-Arts, Prairie school, and modern architecture were grounded in a common pragmatic approach based on frame construction and the practical demands of economic and functional efficiency, which was evident in the gridded organization of their plans and elevations. Though Beaux-Arts architects in France employed grid-based planning for reasons that were largely independent of structure, most Beaux-Arts buildings constructed in the United States (including those of the World's Columbian Exposition) used frame construction. A common strategy of hierarchical planning and organization of building masses into a base, middle, and top produced buildings with some shared, basic characteristics, which allowed them to coexist reasonably well on a street or in a group. On this fundamental level, Sullivan's commercial buildings and those produced by D. H. Burnham and Compnay as well as other contemporary architectural practices were quite similar. Shared characteristics balanced the differences in material, vocabulary, spatial effect, and ideology that are often used in critical discourse to contrast these approaches. Burnham's office produced the Monadnock Block in Chicago, an early high-rise building bereft of ornamental embellishment; the Reliance Building in Chicago with its stylistically indeterminate and mostly glazed skin; and Union Station in Washington, D.C., a heavily enriched exercise in Beaux-Arts design. Corporate firms such as Graham, Anderson, Probst, and White (the primary successor to D. H. Burnham and Company) and Holabird and Root designed commercial and institutional buildings in a similar range of styles. The Monadnock Block and other later commercial buildings by architects of the Chicago School demonstrated, in their expressive heterogeneity and ever-increasing height and floor area, that the imperatives of the commercial marketplace were in opposition to any plan that imposed a constraining architectural program.

The career of Chicago landscape architect Alfred Caldwell demonstrates that an arcadian conception of the natural landscape, and more broadly a design approach based on the order found in nature, accorded equally well with the aims of Beaux-Arts, Prairie school, and modern architecture. Over the course of his career, Caldwell, best known through his affiliation with the Prairie school, worked with Wright, Jensen, Hilberseimer, and Mies van der Rohe. Between 1927 and 1932, he served as Jensen's protégé and a superintendent in his office. From 1936 to 1939, he worked for the Chicago Park District, in which capacity he designed the lakefront public park extensions that were implemented as part of the Burnham and Bennett plan[1] and redesigned an existing lily pool in Lincoln Park. This latter design exhibited the complex, synthetic character that is typical of his work, combining elements of the Prairie landscape

Figure 7.3

Figure 7.4
Top: Plaza level plan of Lake Point Tower, Chicago, by Alfred Caldwell and Schipporeit-Heinrich Associates, 1964.
Bottom: Section, Lake Point Tower, Chicago, by Schipporeit-Heinrich Associates, 1964.

Figure 7.4

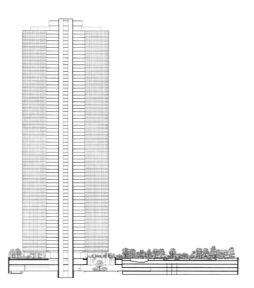

with garden architecture that evokes the work of Jensen and Wright. These characteristics are all evident in his drawing for a proposed poolside arbor seat and lamp, as is the Japanese influence that this drawing shares with those of Wright and Mahony Griffin (FIGURES 7.2 and 7.3). In his capacity as an instructor at the Illinois Institute of Technology (IIT) between 1945 and 1960, Caldwell came into close professional contact with both Hilberseimer and Mies van der Rohe, with whom he collaborated on the design of the campus and a later plan for Lafayette Park in Detroit.[2] Caldwell delineated Hilberseimer's early regional plans for Chicago (SEE FIGURES 6.14 and 11.1). His 1968 landscaping plan for Lake Point Tower in Chicago, designed by the architects and former IIT students George Schipporeit and John Heinrich, further demonstrates to what degree an arcadian vision of the natural landscape was central to modern ideals (FIGURE 7.4).

Thus, in Chicago at least, the boundaries between different architectural styles have remained relatively fluid.[3] All are subject to a pervasive rational character, and in a planning context, they are simply vessels for communicating the characteristic priorities of the two planning traditions.

COMPLEMENTARY RELATIONS AND SHARED ELEMENTS

In Chicago technological innovations and changing architectural fashions support an enduring and independent physical character, in which a compact center serves the requirements of the larger city and a diffuse periphery caters to the individual requirements of its residents. Peripheral planning and planning from the center each address one aspect of this character. They have evolved from persistent and complementary attitudes to available space and an ongoing dialogue between the individual and collective requirements of urban life. Certain attitudes prevail and certain requirements are privileged in particular parts of the city. The plans that belong to these traditions are therefore plans for parts of the city, or partial plans for the whole city. Their strategies are not valid where their assumptions do not hold. The central city, for example, cannot be reconfigured along peripheral requirements for maximum individual access to light and air, as Hilberseimer proposed. The periphery possesses distinct requirements and an autonomous impulse not recognized by the *Plan of Chicago*; these are best serviced by plans that endorse a distinct peripheral pattern of settlement.

The plans of Burnham and Bennett, Drummond, Jensen, and Hilberseimer address the specific requirements of Chicago's primary physical zones: the central city, the pre-automobile periphery (which has now become its intermediate residential fabric), and the current periphery, configured for the automobile.

The layered circulation system enriched with open space and civic ornaments proposed by Burnham and Bennett reconciled the central city's role as a through-traffic circulator with its status as a privileged public precinct. The quarter-section prototypes of Jensen and Drummond protected peripheral housing and public open space from necessary routes of through circulation while providing points of focus for individual neighborhoods within an undifferentiated street grid. Hilberseimer's modular linear city reconciled the large scale of the automobile with the small scale of communal neighborhoods, and individual access to an uninterrupted natural landscape with the prospect of infinite peripheral expansion. These plans are the precedents for further improvement of the central city, the intermediate fabric, and the periphery.

These four models share more than a complementary correspondence to constituent parts of the city. The *Plan of Chicago* and the Drummond, Jensen, and Hilberseimer plans all utilized the same regional systems of circulation and open space, with common strategies for relating circulation routes to buildings and elements of the natural landscape. They separated through traffic on wide streets from local traffic on narrow streets, establishing a hierarchy that also guided the arrangement of different building uses. In each one, through-traffic streets and intersections were lined with commercial buildings that served and negotiated between passing traffic and adjacent neighborhoods; individual houses, uniformly set back behind a regulated strip of green space, occupied the quieter, narrower streets. Boulevards and neighborhood parks and playgrounds periodically introduced public landscaped open space into residential neighborhoods. Hilberseimer imagined all streets as part of an uninterrupted natural continuum.

The planners all treated the natural landscape in a way that recalled its original state. Occasionally, they assigned landscape elements a civic role and treated them with architectural regularity. Burnham and Bennett proposed a formal garden where the public lakefront overlapped with the central city, and Drummond and Jensen organized their quarter-section prototypes around axial lawns and canals. These plans imagined natural elements as extensions of a larger public landscape, and they made parks and public open spaces the primary sites for cultural and institutional buildings.

The site-specific plans of Burnham and Bennett and the prototype plans of Drummond, Jensen, and Hilberseimer all acknowledged Chicago's existing street grid. All four plans therefore incorporated quarter-section divisions and thus shared a common planning module based on the surveyor's grid (FIGURE 7.1).

THE PRECEDENT FOR A NEW PLAN AND THE PERSISTENT PROBLEM OF SPECULATIVE DEVELOPMENT

Together these plans, with their common elements, strategies, and measurements, constitute the precedent for a metropolitan plan with a complex character that reflects Chicago's own. Such a plan should address the central city, the intermediate fabric, and the periphery, both independently and in relation to one another. In the unique circumstances of the central city, this plan should utilize the site-based planning of the Burnham and Bennett plan, and in the pervasive and typical conditions of the intermediate fabric and the periphery, it should employ the prototype-based planning of Jensen, Drummond, and Hilberseimer.

A new metropolitan plan should also address a common problem of previous plans from both traditions. Though these plans proposed a gradual implementation, they all failed to attract the speculative investment that is the principal driving force behind Chicago's physical development. In Chicago the interests of the speculative builder have consistently determined the relationships between circulation, building program, and public space, and this is why, to varying degrees, Burnham and Bennett, Jensen, and Hilberseimer all imagined him as the enemy of good planning. In the center, the speculator's urge to distinguish his product from his competitors' compromised the uniformity of the fabric that Burnham and Bennett's monuments required as a foil and setting. On the periphery, the developer, who sought the most intensive use for (and therefore the most profit from) a given parcel of land, opposed the efforts to limit density on which many peripheral plans were based.

The common failure of these plans to adequately engage the participation of private capital explains, to some extent, their overall poor record of implementation. The planners' hostility to speculators extended beyond their profit motivation and into the realm of appearances, which the planners believed should advance their own vision. The individual freedom of expression usually afforded to the developer directly challenged the unified physical character of the architects' plans. This impasse exposes the limited effect of any explicit plan on a city in which market forces establish a strong implicit order. Planning that seeks implementation should address this implicit order directly, without trying to enlist it in an explicit plan, and encourage speculative builders to put its proposals in place.

Central City

Intermediate
Fabric

 N

Periphery

CHAPTER 8

MAKING AN IMPLICIT PLAN

EXISTING CONDITIONS IN CHICAGO: POPULATION, ECONOMY,
AND PROSPECTS · POINTS OF DEPARTURE: RECENT PRECEDENTS FOR
COORDINATED PLANNING AND THE PHYSICAL ELEMENTS AND IDEAL
MODELS OF A METROPOLITAN PLAN · AN IMPLICIT PLAN PROPOSED: ITS
CONSTANT ELEMENTS, CHANGING CHARACTER, AND IMPLEMENTATION

EXISTING CONDITIONS IN CHICAGO: POPULATION, ECONOMY, AND PROSPECTS

A metropolitan plan for future growth should encompass distinct strategies that consider the specific requirements of the central city, the intermediate fabric, and the outer periphery. A plan for the central city needs to accommodate the exceptional conditions of a specific site; the more typical conditions of the intermediate fabric and the periphery can be addressed through generalized prototypes. The larger plan should integrate these specific proposals with one another by relating them to a common, overarching system of circulation and open space. It should be capable of gradual implementation by profit-motivated private entities and interested public stakeholders, whose attention and endorsement it must first attract. The last comprehensive metropolitan plan for Chicago based on physical improvement was proposed by Hilberseimer in 1963 (SEE FIGURE 6.15).[1] As the changes Chicago has undergone since this time have been extensive and specific, the city's current conditions and prospects for future growth require discussion before another metropolitan plan is advanced.[2]

Chicago is the third-largest city in the United States and the center of the third-largest metropolitan area.[3] Between 1990 and 2000, the city of Chicago (as distinct from the Chicago metropolitan area) posted its first population gains in five decades, over which time continuous peripheral expansion ensured the slow and steady growth of the metropolitan area.[4] The increase in the urban population, however, was modest compared to suburban growth, and this proportional relationship will likely continue as the population of the metropolitan area slowly and steadily increases over the next twenty years.[5] These population projections suggest that new settlement will conform to Chicago's established physical pattern, adding density to urban areas and more space to the periphery.

Chicago remains a commercial capital dependent on transportation connections; this has produced one of the country's most diverse urban economies.[6] Transportation and trade are the city's leading employers, followed by commerce, which is dominated by a professional service sector and filled out by financial and hospitality services.[7] An institutional component comprised of government, education, and health care is almost as large. Manufacturing, once the economic cornerstone of the city, continues to face a gradual decline caused by the departure of heavy industry, although it remains a prominent fixture of the local economy.[8] The decline of manufacturing has been partially offset by the growth of less-intensive transportation-related industry, such as warehousing.

Chicago has remained the national transportation hub, even as the appearance of new transportation modes has altered the character of the national transportation network. This network now relies on a combination of air, rail, water, and highway connections. These modes are concentrated in Chicago to a unique degree, owing to its geographic location and established transportation network. The city remains the major North American railroad hub, with fifty percent of all freight traveling by rail passing through it.[9] Its airports rank second in terms of passenger traffic and fifth in cargo handling (O'Hare International Airport is the second-busiest airport overall), and only New York City enjoys immediate access to more interstates.[10] Chicago's metropolitan area ranks fifth in terms of the total tonnage passing through its combined ports.[11] These transportation connections remain the ultimate source of potential new growth in the metropolitan area.

Chicago's geographic location and the stability of its population growth and economy suggest that, in terms of

---

Figure 8.1 Comparison of proposed improvements to the central city, intermediate fabric, and periphery along the Eisenhower Expressway.

99

population and economic importance, it has settled into a role as the nation's third city, after New York and Los Angeles.[12] Chicago is the center of a continental transportation network whose terminal points, and thus connections with overseas markets, are the largest cities on either coast. This apparently stable arrangement suggests that Chicago can retain its position by consolidating interior commerce and improving distant transportation connections.[13]

Large-scale regional developments and local transportation inefficiencies threaten the viability of this strategic model. The Midwest, Chicago's traditional hinterland, appears to be in decline. Growth in the commercial service sector has not offset the departure of heavy industry in other parts of the Midwest in the same way that it has in Chicago, and the midwestern states surrounding the Great Lakes—Illinois, Indiana, Michigan, Ohio, and Wisconsin—regularly post the smallest rates of economic growth among eight national regions. Illinois's consistent gains are offset by the equally consistent contraction of Michigan's economy, which has been crippled by the departure of the heavy industry devoted to automobile production.[14] It is not clear whether the decline of midwestern economic power will encourage further commercial consolidation in Chicago, undermine the strategic value of the city's transportation connections, or do both.

Meanwhile, the southern and western regions of the country have continued to gain population and wealth at an accelerating rate over the last five decades.[15] Transportation hubs that are closer to these areas of recent growth have thrived at Chicago's expense. Memphis and Louisville have emerged as major points of transfer for airborne freight.[16] In recent years, population and economic growth in the South have allowed Atlanta, previously the regional transportation hub, to challenge Chicago's national role. Its airport is now busier than Chicago's, and as in Chicago, converging transportation systems have enticed companies with links to transportation to establish headquarters there.[17]

The internal inefficiencies of Chicago's local transportation network also undermine its effectiveness as a hub. To some extent, these inefficiencies are characteristic of any place where converging transportation routes foster urban growth, because in such conditions through traffic and local traffic compete for use of the same circulation routes. Chicago was once a bottleneck for freight moving by rail and water; now airport and expressway congestion make the metropolitan area a bottleneck for freight moving by air and truck.[18] This problem is not unique to Chicago, but because the city is larger than its competitors, its effects are more pronounced.

The extent and structure of Chicago's peripheral pattern of settlement therefore further threatens the efficiency of its transportation system. The expressways are equally central to the national freight-distribution network and the regional transportation network that services distinct commercial, residential, and industrial zones. Peripheral expansion has impinged on the warehousing that is Chicago's primary source of new industrial growth and another key component of the national freight network. The warehouse districts around the airports, now immured in low-density residential surroundings, provide limited opportunities for expansion.

The current transportation situation—in which various types of traffic compete for limited space on circulation routes, and uncoordinated growth fails to service different uses equally—recalls Chicago's urban predicament in the late nineteenth and early twentieth centuries. The automobile and airplane have together forged a transportation network that is theoretically faster and more flexible than its predecessor, though it is similarly plagued by congestion and inefficiency. The unforeseen consequences of unconstrained peripheral growth enabled by the automobile and expressway have again compromised the quiet repose and access to a natural landscape that are the primary attractions of peripheral settlement.

The automobile and the expressway are also responsible for those features that distinguish the Chicago of the early twenty-first century from its early-twentieth-century predecessor. By removing through traffic from surface streets, expressways have separated it from local traffic and established a regional hierarchy of circulation. Sunk below or elevated above the surrounding area, they avoid the at-grade crossings that obstructed rail traffic in an earlier era. Expressways have also established a large-scale peripheral settlement pattern and thereby enabled the development of a more-extensive metropolitan area. The former, marked by mile rather than half-mile divisions, has filled in the open space between the pre-automobile periphery and the early railroad suburbs and expanded beyond them.

Expressways appear as invasive elements within the existing urban fabric. In the intermediate fabric, they separate once-contiguous neighborhoods and upset the existing balance of streets, buildings, and open space. They also erect limiting boundaries around the central city that recall nineteenth-century rail yards. Such superimposed circulation routes and an intermediate fabric based on "obsolete" transportation modes were not features of early-twentieth-century Chicago.

The concentration of social and economic ills within some parts of this intermediate fabric is one indirect consequence of automobile-based suburbanization. This zone was formerly the home of the urban middle class; it was often repopulated by poorer residents when the middle class relocated to the suburban periphery. The loss of tax revenue, another consequence of middle-class abandonment, has limited the local government's efforts to remediate the effects of physical fragmentation and a decaying housing stock. The suburban periphery, meanwhile, has preserved its political autonomy, preventing Chicago from annexing peripheral development as it did in the nineteenth century, and thus from recovering lost tax revenue.

The breakdown of a persistent pattern of metropolitan zoning is another unprecedented development that can be traced in part to automobile-based peripheral expansion. Though Chicago remains loosely divided into commercial, residential, and industrial zones, these appear to be vestiges rather than extensions of established patterns. Heavy industry has either consolidated on the southern periphery or departed from the region altogether.[19] New lighter industry does not impinge on other uses but continues to require easy access to transportation routes. This development has coincided with a more-flexible relationship between commerce and housing, both in the city and on the periphery. During the second half of the twentieth century, automobile-based suburbanization brought shopping and offices to the residential periphery, while a series of multiuse tall buildings made the central city a place to live as well as work. Indeed, tall buildings erected in the central city over the past two decades are as likely to contain apartments as offices. With a stable population of workers and residents and a steady influx of visitors, the central city reassumed its role as a shopping destination. Throughout this process, however, the physical characteristics of the central city and the periphery have remained largely intact: one is concentrated, while the other is diffuse. As both provide opportunities for working and living, physical character rather than functional designation has emerged as the primary distinction between them.

Chicago's future economic prospects and its persistent and unprecedented planning challenges have a common root in its transportation system. More specifically, the expressway system that carries both metropolitan through traffic and regional freight is a common source for uncoordinated peripheral growth and physical fragmentation and isolation in the central city and intermediate fabric. It has also been instrumental in the breakdown of existing patterns of zoning. The improvement of the expressway system, and the intermodal network of which it is a part, is therefore the foundation of a metropolitan plan that addresses the related issues of transportation, urban planning, and zoning. As Burnham and Bennett pointed out, circulation routes are both the major connections between core and periphery and the primary means of relating them to a larger whole.[20] The primary shared element of the central city, intermediate fabric, and periphery is therefore the common thread of a metropolitan plan comprised of distinct improvements to these areas.

POINTS OF DEPARTURE:
RECENT PRECEDENTS FOR COORDINATED
PLANNING AND THE PHYSICAL
ELEMENTS AND IDEAL MODELS OF A
METROPOLITAN PLAN

A climate favorable to coordinated planning has emerged in Chicago over the past three decades, as planners and private industry have begun to improve regional systems of infrastructure, including but not limited to transportation. Area municipalities are coordinating efforts to manage regional requirements for drainage, water supply, and open space, recalling similar initiatives undertaken in Chicago during the late nineteenth century. Suburban development of land that once absorbed water runoff has forced the creation of a regional strategy for drainage management. Beginning in 1975, Chicago and fifty-one municipalities in Cook County implemented, with federal support, the Tunnel and Reservoir Plan, which consolidates and diverts water runoff through a subterranean system that holds and treats water before releasing it into surface reservoirs. A central section—from the northern suburb of Wilmette, on Lake Michigan; to southwestern Hodgkins, on the Sanitary and Ship Canal—came into service in 1985; the entire system, with 109 miles of tunnels, is scheduled to be completed after 2015. In a 2005 report, the Chicago Metropolitan Agency for Planning projected water demand in the next fifty years across eleven Illinois counties around Chicago and laid the foundation for a regional program of water use and conservation.[21] The same agency's comprehensive regional plan calls for a unified policy to acquire and preserve open space. Though the current efforts of the Illinois Department of Natural Resources on this front have been hindered by budget cuts, smaller public agencies like the Cook County Forest Preserve continue to augment their holdings through public referenda.

Both policy makers and local governments have begun to consider the protection of natural resources as one aspect of a more-ambitious agenda for regional development. The latter have realized that protected open space attracts commercial and residential development. Peripheral suburbs, for example, tout their proximity to the Cook County Forest Preserve as a lure to investors. Recognizing Lake Michigan's value as a water resource, as well as its historic ability to attract concentrated development, policy makers have called for the establishment of clean water-related industries along the lakefront, as well as intensive private development that combines buildings, infrastructure, and open space.[22] In diverting wastewater from the Chicago River, the deep tunnel system has made the river attractive as another possible

Figure 8.2   Satellite view of Chicago, showing the subdivision of land into grids of varying size. The inscribed circle has a radius of approximately eighteen miles, with its center at the Buckingham Fountain in Grant Park. Within this circle, which is more or less coterminous with the extent of the intermediate fabric, the grid is divided into quarter sections measuring a half mile on each side. Beyond it, the periphery is divided into sections that are one mile on each side. Chicago's original system of land division remains in place (see Figures 1.2–1.5). The small circle and rectangle within the larger circle and the dark rectangle beyond this circle show the relative size and location of the sections of the central city, intermediate fabric, and periphery proposed for improvement.

Figure 8.2

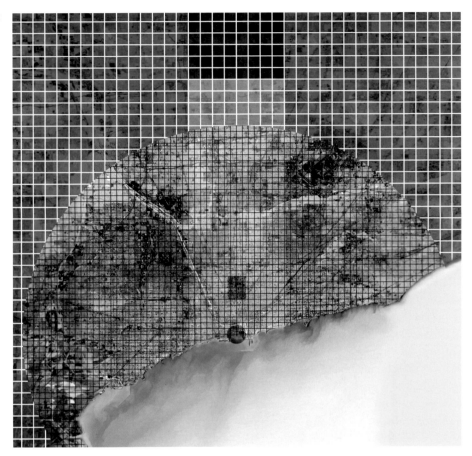

site for such improvements, a development intimated in the *Plan of Chicago*.[23]

Chicago is better prepared than other cities to increase the efficiency of its transportation network. Its expressways already operate as circulation bundles that incorporate lines for rapid transit and regional rail as well as routes for automobiles, and efforts to further coordinate these modes at a regional scale are already underway.[24] The Association of American Railroads, the State of Illinois, and the City of Chicago announced the Chicago Regional Environmental and Transportation Efficiency Project in 2003 to eliminate grade crossings and reduce trucking between separate rail lines. The project received federal funding in 2007. Additional components of a regional freight-transportation network with an increased capacity have been put in place by private industry. In 2009 the Canadian National Railroad acquired the Elgin, Joliet and Eastern Railway, which forms a loop around Chicago from Waukegan to Gary, bypassing the city with a rail-based alternative to interstate trucking. In 2003 the Union

Pacific Railroad opened an intermodal terminal in Rochelle that handles rail and trucking freight, and the Burlington Northern Santa Fe Railway opened a similar facility in Elwood in 2002.[25] Private industry has thus realized a central goal of Burnham and Bennett's transportation plan: the separation of local traffic from regional freight on the far periphery. These intermodal terminals remain, however, individual elements that can be incorporated into a more-efficient regional freight system.

The change in zoning patterns that is already under way will promote more-efficient transportation connections by curbing regional through traffic. This does not mean that Chicago will attain the exclusively local zoning that characterizes Hilberseimer's ideal planning model. The prevalence of particular uses in certain areas of the metropolitan region will persist to some degree, but the volume of constant traffic between these areas will abate as the periphery develops a higher level of autonomy and the central city achieves a more-diversified program.

Figure 8.3

Figure 8.3 Satellite view of Chicago, showing the schematic relationship of the areas proposed for improvement and their relationship to the Axis of Chicago, planned by Burnham and Bennett (straight line), and the Eisenhower Expressway (irregular line).

 N

Because distinct parts of the city have maintained their specific physical character despite changes in zoning patterns, the earlier plans proposed for their improvement remain compelling and relevant. Burnham and Bennett's plan for the central city, Jensen's and Drummond's quarter-section plans, and Hilberseimer's settlement unit can therefore be imagined as potential arrangements of multiuse building program in distinct physical zones (SEE FIGURE 7.1). Since all of these plans conform to Chicago's existing street grid, they can all be accommodated within its radial pattern of increasingly large square divisions (FIGURE 8.2). Together with the expressway system, specific plans derived from these precedents, considered in light of current existing conditions, can serve as the primary elements of a new metropolitan plan.

The expressway system in its entirety, however, need not constitute the site for this metropolitan plan. Four major expressways—the Kennedy to the northwest, the Eisenhower to the west, the Adlai E. Stevenson to the southwest, and the Dan Ryan to the south—divide Chicago's radial pattern into five

pie-shaped pieces. Each of these conduits is a standard and typical component of the larger expressway system, passing through the central city, intermediate fabric, and periphery alike. The Eisenhower Expressway, and its westward extension, Interstate 88, can be singled out as a particularly representative example.[26] As the metropolitan area's primary east-west conduit, the Eisenhower Expressway divides Chicago into two parts that are roughly equal in terms of area but unequal in population and wealth. The evidence of damage to the intermediate fabric along this dividing line, wrought by the expressway's introduction, is particularly acute but also uneven. In some places, the expressway appears as an impenetrable boundary between rich and poor neighborhoods. Where it engages the Loop as Congress Parkway, it also penetrates the central-city fabric, and further east, as a network of surface streets that carry through traffic to Lake Shore Drive, it is intermingled with the public open spaces of Grant Park. Along this course, it follows, more or less, the line identified by Burnham and Bennett as the "Axis of Chicago," as well as one of the lines of Chicago's ubiquitous orthogonal street grid. It is therefore analogous, in placement and function, to a typical half-mile street, a circumstance that makes the prospect of its reconciliation with typical planning models based on the grid less difficult. This process will establish the normative example on which the reconciliations along the diagonal expressways can be based.

The particular portions of the central city, intermediate fabric, and outer periphery through which the Eisenhower Expressway passes, and which will be reconsidered in light of earlier planning precedents, are the final components of the metropolitan plan. The relevant sections of the fabric and periphery exhibit a standard and typical character, and plans for their improvement can—like Jensen's, Drummond's, and Hilberseimer's—utilize normative planning models. The expressway's interaction with the central city is unique, however, and this relationship must be considered as a specific design problem for a particular site. The strategies for improving the Eisenhower Expressway, the central-city fabric on either side of it as it extends from the lakefront to the Chicago River, and paired, standard sections of both the intermediate fabric and the outer periphery are therefore the basis for a new metropolitan plan (FIGURE 8.3). Earlier plans offer physical precedents for improvement that are suited to specific site characteristics and environmental objectives, while new patterns of use establish a guide for endowing these varied arrangements of streets, buildings, and open space with multiple uses.

AN IMPLICIT PLAN PROPOSED:
ITS CONSTANT ELEMENTS, CHANGING CHARACTER, AND IMPLEMENTATION

The integration of one spoke of the metropolitan transportation system with its surroundings, which range from urban conditions to a natural landscape, is the foundation of a metropolitan plan organized around improved transportation connections (FIGURE 8.1). A plan that addresses these connections through their relationships to buildings and public open space will improve transportation efficiency by attracting new settlement to those conduits where a variety of transit options are available. The immediate presence of a range of transportation modes will encourage some residents of adjacent neighborhoods to use mass transit, thereby reducing automobile through traffic between different zones. A metropolitan plan that relates the city's major circulators to their surroundings will help preserve open space on the periphery and remediate the damage caused by the unsympathetic superimposition of these transportation connections on the existing fabric.

Some elements of a plan that traces a continuous transit conduit through varied urban conditions will be present in each of the plan's improved parts. These common elements can be identified, and some aspects of their arrangement examined, to establish points of departure for adapting them to particular sites or conditions. Ideally, an integrated circulation spine will include parking, allowing drivers to switch from cars to trains during their commutes. It should engage some kind of public space—which might range from a plaza, park, or shopping arcade to community buildings—to encourage new building program or a ruptured neighborhood fabric to gather around a focal point. When integrated with local circulation and embellished with standard elements—street signs, standing lamps, trees, and street furniture—these public spaces can also relay the message that different parts of a neighborhood or city belong to a larger whole.

Some basic relationships between these common parts can also be established. Where parking is convenient to the railroad and mass-transit lines that follow the expressway, it can serve to shield neighborhoods from traffic. Parking can also be more easily reclaimed for future expansion of circulation right-of-way than other building types or land uses. Housing should, when possible, be protected from unrelated uses, and houses should always face other houses or landscaped park space. Housing and commerce can occupy the same buildings, as long as shops and businesses occur on lower floors—adjacent to streets and public space—and housing is located on upper floors, affording residents an appropriate degree of privacy. A similar strategy, when applied to tall buildings, allows them to be better integrated with surroundings of varying character.[27]

The individual qualities of the central city, intermediate fabric, and periphery can inform how a plan's constant elements change to suit specific conditions. Each of these conditions relates to a larger urban pattern that increases in scale, decreases in density, and incorporates more natural open space as it extends toward the periphery. In the central city, which is dominated by buildings and circulation routes, landscaped open space is exceptional; on the periphery, however, this situation is reversed, and in the intermediate fabric, these elements exist in relative parity. In the central city, therefore, an integrated circulation spine should provide open space; on the periphery, it should organize higher-density building program; and in the intermediate fabric, it should reestablish the equilibrium disrupted by the expressway.

The earlier proposals of Burnham and Bennett, Jensen, Drummond, and Hilberseimer have already facilitated these specific goals to some degree. Burnham and Bennett's plan for Congress Street and Grant Park introduced public open space along a major central-city circulator. The quarter-section proposals of Jensen and Drummond maintained a balance between open space, circulation, and building program, and Hilberseimer's settlement unit concentrated building program along circulation routes. These models can be adjusted to incorporate the expressway in its various configurations. Burnham and Bennett's plan offers a guide for improving through-traffic connections and public open space in the central city (SEE FIGURE 4.28). Jensen's and Drummond's schemes suggest approaches for introducing public open space along the expressway that can knit the fabric back together (SEE FIGURE 5.1). Hilberseimer's settlement unit provides a model for peripheral expansion that will retain a continuous open landscape (SEE FIGURE 6.1).

Persuading people to settle along improved expressways presents a major obstacle to implementing this plan. The challenge specifically lies in attracting private development to these areas, as history shows that in Chicago improvements put in place by private investment are more likely to be successfully implemented than those sponsored by public initiatives. Reframing the perception of a transit corridor as providing convenient, affordable, and environmentally responsible transportation options, and altering its physical character to suggest an amenity rather than an eyesore, are therefore essential components of this strategy.

Public investment that paves the way for private developers offers the surest means of attracting their investment. We should envision the expressways as public platforms for private building. Only the public sector can improve circulation routes or requisition adjacent land. It owns the primary available sites for new construction along and over expressways, and only public investment will help the private sector recognize the potential value of such sites.

The public sector should therefore put in place any new or expanded routes of circulation. It should build the service program (parking and utilities) that will constitute the first step in insulating the interstate and enhancing its utility. The public sector should also implement all public elements — including public buildings, pedestrian pathways and arcades, outdoor public space, and park space — or require that others implement them according to established guidelines. A visually unified public realm will supply a datum for private buildings that can support a variety of architectural expressions. Speculators must be able to distinguish their product from their competitors'. In doing so, they have in the past, when successful, advanced Chicago's architectural development and enhanced the vitality of its streetscape. Distinct public and private components can establish a foundation for continuous and gradual development. This slow accretion, more than any other quality, will yield the carefully balanced relationship

between elements that comprises a place with distinct and memorable qualities.

It is no coincidence that a single strategy of programmed circulation both follows logically from a series of precedents and solves contemporary urban problems. In Chicago these planning problems are persistent. The city's goal — to be the country's and the continent's central transportation hub — remains the same as ever, as does its speculative method for putting buildings and plans in place. A successful metropolitan plan should unite this goal and method.

CHAPTER 9

PLANNING THE CENTRAL CITY

THE CHARACTER OF THE CENTRAL CITY AND ITS CURRENT STATE
THE GOALS AND POINTS OF DEPARTURE FOR IMPROVING THE CENTRAL
CITY · CONGRESS PARKWAY: CONDUIT, ALLÉE, AXIS · GRANT PARK:
GARDEN, LANDSCAPE, ORNAMENT · THE CENTER RECONSIDERED

———

THE CHARACTER OF THE CENTRAL CITY AND ITS CURRENT STATE

Throughout Chicago's history, the central city has been the focus of the region's commercial, civic, and cultural activities and the hub of its circulation system. This confluence of multiple uses and circulation routes has produced a physical character that derives from an economical and intensive use of space, which is evident in the characteristics of individual streets, buildings, and public spaces and in their relationships with one another. Streets with multiple levels—Wacker Drive and Michigan Avenue—separate through traffic from local traffic and incorporate access to structured parking. The lower levels of State and Dearborn streets are occupied by subway lines; tunnel networks for pedestrians and freight also pass beneath much of the central city. Chicago's tall buildings—which are intensive and economical by virtue of their repetitive, superimposed program—are overwhelmingly concentrated here; they occasionally utilize the air rights over railroad lines and incorporate transit stations on their lower levels. Grant Park serves a symbolic purpose as Chicago's principal public space, but it also incorporates active recreational facilities, an art museum, indoor and outdoor performing-arts venues, a transit station, structured parking, and along the railroad tracks that separate it from Michigan Avenue, a dedicated bus route that connects the central city with the McCormick Place convention center to the south.

This degree of concentration of multiple uses and circulation routes is confined to a relatively small area that is further divided into zones of increasing density separated by transit corridors and infrastructure (FIGURE 9.2). The Loop, the most concentrated part of the central city, is bounded by elevated transit lines and, beyond them, three conduits for through traffic—Wacker Drive to the north and west, Congress

Parkway to the south, and Michigan Avenue to the east. The larger central city is bounded by the expressway system to the west, Roosevelt Road to the south, and Lake Shore Drive to the east.[1] The central city thus exhibits, in a concentrated form, the organization into concentric zones of decreasing density that characterizes Chicago's larger urban pattern.

The street and block pattern within these zones is highly uniform, with most blocks accommodating concentrated land use and most streets carrying through traffic.[2] The basic planning module in the central city is the individual block; this area is too small to accommodate the differentiation between through and local streets evident in the fabric and on the periphery. The entire Loop is hardly larger than a typical quarter section, and Madison Street, the only east-west half-mile street that passes through it, carries the same type and volume of traffic and is lined with the same types of buildings as the other streets in the Loop. A hierarchical arrangement of circulation is somewhat evident in the greater importance assigned to certain north-south streets, multilevel roadways at the Loop's northern and western boundaries, and a secondary system of half-block alleys that accommodate service activities including deliveries and trash removal.

Over time, the central city's various uses have become more segregated and their special precincts more extensive. Until the second half of the twentieth century, Chicago's major concentrations of business, government, retail, and culture were contained almost entirely within the Loop. Finance and exchange were concentrated along its western edge, on LaSalle Street. Department stores, theaters, and hotels clustered along State Street, on the Loop's eastern edge, and just beyond, private clubs and cultural institutions lined Michigan Avenue, facing

Figure 9.1 Plan of Congress Street and Grant Park by Burnham and Bennett, 1909 (detail of *Figure 4.28*).

107

Figure 9.2 Satellite view of central Chicago, 2007.

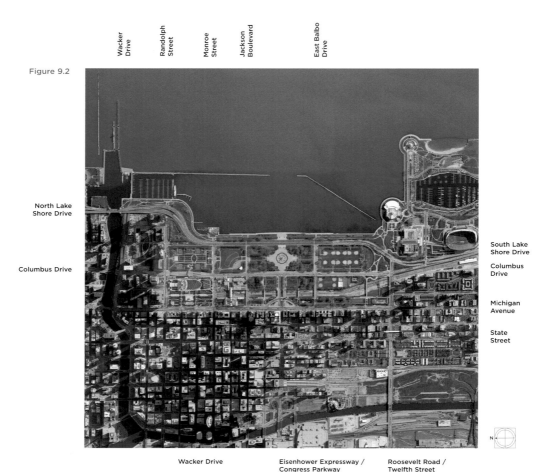

Grant Park. Commercial buildings and offices for the local, state, and federal governments occupied the streets in between. During the last decades of the twentieth century, most of these components expanded beyond the Loop into adjacent areas. Commerce and finance moved westward, first to South Wacker Drive and then across the Chicago River; more recently they have developed northward as well, across the river's main branch. Local, state, and federal governments have expanded from their original sites and now occupy dedicated precincts at the northern and southern ends of the Loop. North Michigan Avenue, not State Street, contains Chicago's highest concentration of central-area retail establishments and major hotels. State Street has become largely a discount retail center, where some flagship department stores have been converted to other uses while a few retain their original function.

During this same period, the central city has also acquired a more-diverse program with a greater range of activities. The gradual removal of industry during the first half of the twentieth century, the abandonment of soft coal as a heating fuel, and more-efficient automobile engines have made the central city cleaner and quieter, attracting residents to what were once exclusively commercial and industrial precincts. Residential neighborhoods, now populated largely by high-rise apartment buildings, have developed north of the Chicago River on both sides of Michigan Avenue, and on its southern bank between Michigan Avenue and the lake. South Michigan Avenue and the Loop have also attracted high-rise apartment development, some of which occupies renovated commercial buildings. The most recent high-rise residential development occurred in the area south of Grant Park, augmenting earlier efforts to rehabilitate the urban fabric to the west with low-rise townhouse blocks around park squares, which now extend as far south as Chinatown.

Existing concentrations of cultural amenities and transportation connections, as well as the availability of suitable building stock, attracted colleges and universities to the central city during the second half of the twentieth century. Chicago's most prominent cultural institutions remain concentrated along Michigan Avenue, south of the Chicago River, in an area whose role as a cultural locus was underscored by the opening of Millennium Park north of the Art Institute in 2004. The central city's public transportation connections are attractive to

Figure 9.3 Plan of the 34th floor of the Sears Tower, Chicago, by Skidmore, Owings, and Merrill, 1974.
Figure 9.4 Site plan of the Federal Center, Chicago, by Ludwig Mies van der Rohe, 1959–64.

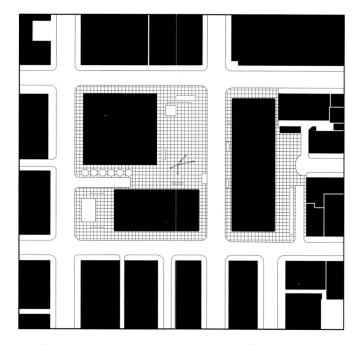

Figure 9.4

students who typically commute to campus from other parts of the city. The vacated office buildings and department stores in the southern portion of the Loop have also proven attractive to educational institutions. The relocation of the main branch of the Chicago Public Library from Michigan Avenue to State Street and Congress Parkway in 1991 gave this emerging educational precinct a public anchor.

A growing number of visitors are drawn to the central city by its concentration of shops and the near-constant improvement, expansion, and renovation of its parks and cultural institutions. These attractions are largely located in the area's eastern half, from North Michigan Avenue to the Museum Campus. In accordance with Burnham and Bennett's intentions, the establishment of North Michigan Avenue and the improvement of the central lakefront have established these as tourist destinations.

The central city's expansion and diversification of program have relied on the maintenance of existing transportation connections and the introduction of new ones. Suburban rail service remained essential and intact during the postwar decades, even as automobiles replaced railroads as the primary means of commuting between the home and workplace. Lines of rapid transit were extended, often along the medians of new expressways. Like the rail network before it, the expressway system connects all segments of the periphery with the central city, but automobiles, unlike trains, also traverse the central area on dedicated routes of through circulation, including Congress Parkway, Lower Wacker Drive, the Ohio Street feeder, and Columbus Drive. Chicago created a municipal parking authority in the early 1950s that built, and in some cases maintained, consolidated parking structures throughout the central city, thereby strengthening its viability as a commuter destination in the automobile era.

Changes in the design and use of tall buildings have enabled the central city to accommodate greater overall density, even as it has expanded outward. The square block with an open central courtyard or light well was the model for the first steel-frame tall buildings in the Loop because it provided

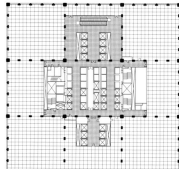

Figure 9.3

ventilation and natural light to every office. Over time, advances in building technology and changes in zoning regulations produced taller office buildings with more usable office space. The introduction of mechanical ventilation systems and efficient artificial lighting in the mid-twentieth century allowed workspaces to be located farther from windows, thereby eliminating the need for the shallow floor plates that determined the size and configuration of earlier buildings. Office floors became vast open lofts, which appealed to modern corporate tenants seeking flexible, consolidated spaces to house workplace populations of dramatically increasing size and diversifying function (FIGURE 9.3; compare to FIGURE 1.7).

Zoning regulations allied with trends in the design of tall buildings to change the way these structures related to the street. Prior to World War II, technological and legal limits on building height encouraged property owners to build to lot lines. Even when, after 1920, the setback tower rising from a full-site block became the model for tall buildings in the central city, zoning regulations demanded that the structures occupy most of their lot areas. These guidelines ensured that even as Chicago's buildings became taller, the central city retained its regular urban character. In 1955 Chicago eliminated explicit height and setback guidelines in favor of a limit on overall square footage.[3] These more-flexible regulations coincided with an emerging preference within the architectural profession for buildings that were discrete, detached objects; architects further emphasized this quality by using glazed curtain walls that contrasted with the opaque masonry facades of neighboring structures. They designed sheer, glass-sheathed towers set back from the street behind plazas to provide oases of light and air to pedestrians. These first appeared as outdoor rooms carved from a uniform, existing fabric (FIGURE 9.4), but the proliferation of towers with plazas eventually undermined the fabric's regularity. The square footage displaced into taller towers became apparent in a bulkier skyline with a larger scale.[4] Over the course of the twentieth century, the central city thus acquired both a greater overall density and a less-uniform urban character.

Chicago's established tradition of large-scale mixed-use buildings has allowed the central city to accommodate uses other than commerce and has limited some of the debilitating effects of the automobile on the urban fabric. By their nature, multiuse buildings operate both during and outside regular business hours, and they provide living spaces in commercial districts, encouraging a lifestyle that does not require commuting between home and work. In Chicago the multiuse building tradition dates to the late-nineteenth-century development of the central city, during which developers combined cultural amenities such as theaters with office and hotel components in integrated projects that they hoped would provide a dependable return on investment. The Auditorium Building, the largest and most ambitious of these early examples, included all three components. As early as 1926, some tall office buildings accommodated parking for automobiles. The Jewelers Building incorporated a 600-car parking garage that rose from the basement to the twenty-third floor and was served by an elevator around which was wrapped a layer of offices, allowing tenants to park directly outside their offices.[5] In the second half of the twentieth century, a series of tall buildings incorporating apartments offered prospective residents an urban lifestyle that might or might not include the automobile. Marina City remains the most ambitious example of this building type in terms of program; when it was completed in 1964, it included two sixty-story apartment towers, each with twenty floors of parking; a marina on the Chicago River; a shopping center; a skating rink; office space; two theaters; and a television studio. The 100-story John Hancock Center, completed in 1969, adapted a multiuse program to the circumstances of postwar tall building construction, accommodating apartments, offices, shops, and parking in a structurally innovative, tapering, trussed-tube frame that gave apartments on its upper floors desirably shallow floor plans. The many multiuse buildings completed since the Hancock Center include Water Tower Place, Olympia Centre, 900 North Michigan, Park Tower, and Trump International Hotel and Tower, all of which are located along or close to North Michigan Avenue, Chicago's preeminent multiuse street.

Available and improved peripheral transportation connections and a concentration of larger buildings with more-varied program have thus allowed the central city to maintain its status as Chicago's commercial hub while expanding into other roles. Chicago's central city captured much of the office space that in other cities developed on the periphery during the last decades of the twentieth century. In 1979 seventy-four percent of all office space in the United States could be found in central cities; in 1999 this share had dropped to fifty-eight percent.[6] In 2000 only Chicago and New York retained over fifty percent of metropolitan office space within their central cities.[7]

THE GOALS AND POINTS OF DEPARTURE FOR IMPROVING THE CENTRAL CITY

Both national and local studies indicate that central cities will, in general, continue to lose office space to suburban peripheries.[8] The Chicago Central Area Plan, published in 2003, projected that downtown Chicago would continue to develop as a multiuse district in which housing played an increasingly central role. It suggested that other uses would grow at an average rate of forty percent between 2000 and 2020, while the central city's residential population would grow by at least sixty-five percent, from 83,500 to 138,000, or one sixth of the projected number of people working in the central city at the time.[9] The plan anticipated slightly lower rates of growth for retail and convention facilities, followed by demand for new hotel and institutional facilities and new office space. It expected the central city to capture between forty and fifty percent of new office construction in the metropolitan area, a high figure compared to that anticipated for other central cities. Based on the more-conservative estimate, it will add 32 million square feet of office space to the 107 million that existed in 2000. The circulation routes on which these uses depend will experience a commensurate increase in traffic.

A central city that is more diversified than other American central cities must therefore accommodate increasingly diverse growth. It must adapt familiar strategies for supporting intensive land use to the full range of urban activities, which, until relatively recently, occupied their own distinct zones within the larger city. Each of these activities has its own special requirements. Office workers who live elsewhere require convenient transportation to and from their homes. City dwellers require public space that is suitable for daily recreational use. Residents throughout the metropolitan area require public space and cultural amenities that remind them that they are citizens of Chicago.

Through an organic process of expansion and diversification, the central city has already begun to address the separate demands of a diversified urban program. It has attracted residents from the periphery and beyond to its multiuse tall buildings since the beginning of the age of automobile-powered peripheral sprawl. High-rise residential development has concentrated largely along the lakefront, convenient to parks and recreational amenities and offering full engagement with the region's defining geographic feature. Grant Park has acquired a more-diverse program that augments its gardens and public gathering places. The business district has expanded westward across the Chicago River, partly because both the rail and road networks used by commuters intersect the central city there. Outmoded commercial buildings have found new institutional uses, convenient to cultural amenities.

These local changes to the central city are part of a more-extensive transformation that has proceeded largely without an explicit plan. This ongoing evolution is the framework for any proposed improvements to the central city, a fact that the four central-city plans proposed since World War II have all recognized. The 1958 *Development Plan for the Central Area of Chicago*, the 1973 *Chicago 21* plan, the 1983 *Chicago Central Area Plan*, and the 2003 plan of the same name share an incremental approach that is actively supported by the central city's established and intensively developed urban pattern, in which circulation routes, buildings, and public space are intricately related. These plans also share an emphasis on transportation improvements, housing, and enhanced public space as a means of reviving and augmenting the central city's functional and symbolic primacy.

Professional consensus and unplanned development have clearly established the larger goals for central-city improvement, which another comprehensive plan would only reinforce. A targeted improvement that accepts and attempts to advance these larger goals is therefore the aim of the central-city plan proposed here. Its scope is limited to issues of circulation and public space, the improvement of which has traditionally catalyzed central-city development. As major routes of through circulation define the boundaries around and within the central city, such a targeted improvement will also address the requirements and character of its expansion.

The central lakefront, between Lake Michigan and the Chicago River, includes a symbolically significant intersection of circulation and public space, the improvement of which could spur a southern expansion of the core central city. This is the major zone of interchange between the through-traffic circulation routes that bound the central city on the east and west. Grant Park is both metropolitan Chicago's symbolic public space and the central city's local park. As the southern boundary of the central-city core, Congress Parkway effectively blocks its extension southward, where the narrow blocks and existing building stock – convenient to Grant Park, the

lakefront, and the Chicago River – can support a mixture of uses with a residential focus.

Burnham and Bennett established a reciprocal relationship among these elements when they proposed to open a major thoroughfare along the centerline of Chicago's primary public spaces (FIGURE 9.1). They planned Congress Street, between the Chicago River and Michigan Avenue, as the final leg of a metropolitan spine of circulation that entered the central city from the west. Grant Park was the central segment of a continuous public park system extending north and south along the lakefront. Their T-shaped intersection organized the city's central ensemble of civic, cultural, and commercial buildings, which proliferated on the blocks south of Congress Street, around a consolidated rail terminal. Circulation and public open space thus lay at the heart of a multiuse plan for the central city.

The gradual and incomplete realization of Congress Parkway and Grant Park has sometimes strengthened, but more often compromised, their reciprocal relationship. Surface streets passing through the park currently constitute the final connection between the expressway system and Lake Shore Drive, disrupting both the constant flow of through traffic and the continuity of public open space, and thus preventing the full functional realization of either.

The requirements of through traffic and public space are two distinct issues. Congress Parkway and Grant Park are therefore considered here as separate but related planning problems. Improving them together will encourage the southern expansion of the Loop and the development of the South Loop riverfront, which plans for the central city have repeatedly proposed but whose realization has remained persistently elusive.

CONGRESS PARKWAY: CONDUIT, ALLÉE, AXIS

Burnham and Bennett conceived the central-city section of Congress Street as the organizing axis of a symmetrically disposed business center and the principal link between the origin of Chicago's radial order and the lakefront, which were represented by a domed Civic Center and a cultural ensemble in a formal garden, respectively. Unlike the proposed extension of Michigan Avenue, however, which was designed as a stately commercial thoroughfare with separated traffic and an architectural program that suggested the boulevards of Paris or Vienna, Congress Street had a relatively unspecified use and character. It was vaguely defined as containing "opportunities for the highest class of adornment known to civic art" and the "theaters, public and semi-public buildings, retail shops, and all the other structures which are to be found on frequented streets . . . of the first importance."[10] A subsequent proposal put

Figure 9.5 Figure-ground diagram showing the existing arrangement of streets, blocks, and buildings along Congress Parkway, from Grant Park to the Circle Interchange.

Figure 9.5

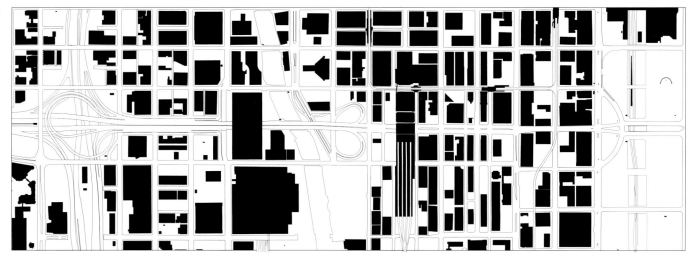

forward by Bennett, Parsons and Frost in 1929 showed an avenue lined by regular walls of substantially scaled buildings that incorporated arcaded sidewalks. This proposal assumed the demolition of significant landmark buildings, including the Auditorium Building and the Second Leiter Building, which lay in the street's proposed path.

The realization of Congress Parkway preserved the location but dispensed with the civic character of these proposals. The street opened in 1956 as a conduit for automobile through traffic and the last leg of the Eisenhower Expressway, connecting the central city with Chicago's western periphery. As Burnham and Bennett proposed, it was introduced into the existing fabric at the midpoint of the long, narrow blocks between Van Buren and Harrison streets, roughly along the line of Tyler Street, which had been partially vacated. In the early 1930s, Bennett, in his capacity as consulting architect for the Chicago Plan Commission, the semiofficial body charged with implementing the *Plan of Chicago*, publicly lobbied against a proposed relocation of the planned westward conduit to Monroe Street, where an east-west thoroughfare and bridge already existed near the densest part of the commercial district. Despite waning interest in the principles on which the original plan was founded, he succeeded. The demolition of buildings on the Congress Street axis, and a tunnel through the lower floors of the United States Post Office that straddled it, finally established the plan's axis along what was to remain a jagged and provisional corridor from Grant Park to the Chicago River (FIGURE 9.5).[11]

The uneven edges of its path emphasize Congress Parkway's intrusive presence in the central city. As it now stands, the street is occupied by as many as nine lanes, which distribute traffic moving to and from the Eisenhower Expressway northward to the Loop and eastward to Michigan Avenue and Lake Shore Drive. The traffic requirements of the parkway's final section, between Michigan and Wabash avenues, necessitated partial ground-floor excavation of the buildings on either side for arcaded sidewalks; this sacrificed Louis Sullivan's famous hotel bar in the Auditorium Building on the north side of the street. Thus, at the critical junction of Congress Parkway and Michigan Avenue, traffic lanes run from building face to building face. Though pedestrian crossings at any point along Congress Parkway are potentially hazardous, pedestrian traffic has increased as a result of the expansion of area educational institutions.

A later addition further compromised Congress Parkway's potential role as a visually significant axis. The construction of a trading floor for the Midwest Stock Exchange in 1985 (later the Chicago Stock Exchange) as a bridge over Congress Parkway at LaSalle Street abbreviated an axis already terminated by the post office. The latter building currently stands empty, awaiting a new use or demolition. Together these obstructions obscure the relationship of the city's principal east-west connector and its primary public space.

The intrusive character of Congress Parkway, changing uses in the surrounding area, and the emergence of the South Loop as a primarily residential extension of the central city to the north suggest a reconsideration of the role of Congress Parkway as an expressway feeder for the business district on one side. An improved Congress Parkway should reconcile the requirements of automobile through traffic with those of a pedestrian-friendly mixed-use urban neighborhood and promote the integration of the Loop and South Loop. In this capacity, it should be compatible with subsequent improvements to the

Figure 9.6 Diagram showing proposed automobile circulation in the central city and Grant Park. Access to the lakefront from the Eisenhower Expressway circumnavigates the Loop via an extended Wacker Drive. Along with a below-grade express route beneath Congress Parkway east of LaSalle Street and a depressed portion of Lake Shore Drive at the proposed central-lakefront terrace, this arrangement allows surface through traffic to be largely removed from Grant Park.

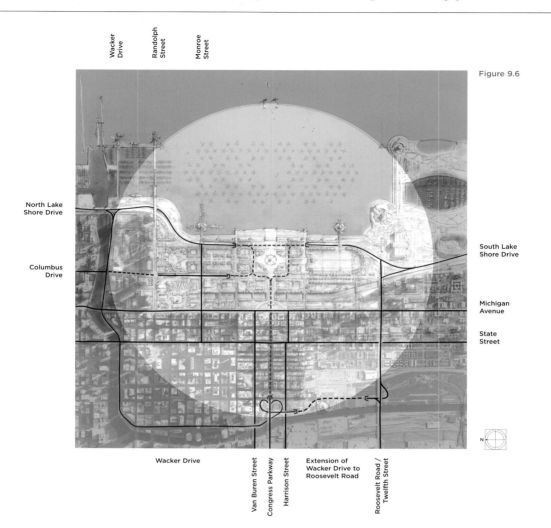

south branch of the Chicago River, which, like Wacker Drive, could combine circulation and open-space improvements to attract development. Finally, an improved Congress Parkway should strengthen its organizational role with regard to the other components of the central city and the larger metropolitan area.

The integration of Congress Parkway with the surrounding city depends largely on its improvement as a through-traffic conduit. A more-efficient circulation route between the Circle Interchange and the lakefront will eliminate obstacles to a southern expansion of the central city, and a proposed redistribution of regional through traffic will rely on both new and established routes (FIGURE 9.6). Existing ramps just east of the river provide access to Loop streets via Upper Wacker Drive, and to Michigan Avenue and Lake Shore Drive via Lower Wacker Drive. The extension of Wacker Drive from Harrison Street southward to Roosevelt Road will also allow through traffic destined for South Lake Shore Drive and the Museum Campus to circumnavigate the Loop. The traffic that currently uses Congress Parkway and the southern segment of

Columbus Drive for this purpose will thereby be diverted, and Columbus Drive south of Jackson Drive, which is already closed during much of the summer for festival events, could be permanently vacated. A southern extension of Wacker Drive should be envisioned, like the existing street, as a comprehensive improvement that combines streets, buildings, and open space with public access to the river. A Wacker Drive extension that organizes a wall of tall buildings could define the eastern edge of a riverfront park south of Congress Parkway and thereby establish a legible boundary for the South Loop.

A more-direct route for through traffic moving between the Circle Interchange and Lake Shore Drive is also possible. A below-grade conduit running beneath Congress Parkway will avoid the regular intersections that are the primary impediments to through traffic. As shown here, the Eisenhower Expressway passes beneath it at a point just east of the river, where the Stock Exchange building that spans the expressway (currently not in use as a trading floor) is removed, and the tower on the north side of Congress Parkway made one of a

Figure 9.7 Plan of the proposed improvement of Congress Parkway by Aric Lasher, 2009.

Figure 9.8 View looking east of proposed improvement of Congress Parkway by Aric Lasher, 2009.

pair that marks a gateway to the central city. From this point east to Michigan Avenue, Congress Parkway continues as a surface street, providing local access to and from the streets of the Loop. The covered expressway, meanwhile, connects to a northbound segment of Columbus Drive and the northbound and southbound lanes of Lake Shore Drive beneath Grant Park. These two improvements could be undertaken as alternatives or in sequence. Together they will establish a system of through circulation between the Circle Interchange, the central city, and Lake Shore Drive that is independent of the surface streets serving local traffic. By providing two routes for through traffic, and thus a choice for drivers moving between these destinations, this system will supply the degree of functional redundancy that an efficient hub requires.

By separating the blocks south of Congress Parkway from the Chicago River, and thereby making them less attractive to development, existing rail lines south of Congress Parkway constitute, after the street itself, the most serious barrier to the southern expansion of the central city and the development of its adjacent riverfront. Currently, these elevated lines, which run along LaSalle Street, terminate at the southern edge of Congress Parkway, where they connect to the Loop via the second floor of the bridged trading-floor annex. Rerouting these lines at a point farther south to terminate at Union Station, or relocating them below grade, will afford the blocks east of LaSalle Street convenient access to the riverfront. Burnham and Bennett proposed the removal of above-grade rail lines at Congress Street to facilitate central-city expansion. The same measure could, a century later, promote similar results.

The improvement of Congress Parkway as an urban boulevard—a surface street enriched with landscape elements that serves local through circulation—could further encourage southern expansion by helping mend the existing breach between the Loop and South Loop. A landscaped parkway could serve both the slower-moving traffic bound for the blocks on either side of it and the pedestrians moving between them, thus reconciling the parkway's east-west through-traffic pattern with the prevailing north-south grain of streets and blocks and pedestrian movement (FIGURE 9.7). The relocation of through circulation will allow the number of traffic lanes to be reduced to two in each direction, with a planted median between them that becomes a turn lane at intersections. This will provide an uninterrupted canopy and thus reinforce the parkway's character as a street to move across rather than along.

Formal landscaping will also establish the street's intended role as a significant compositional element in a central-city ensemble of parks and buildings. Congress Parkway is shown here as an axial extension of the garden landscape of Grant Park into the central city's man-made surroundings. Like Grant Park, it employs natural elements arranged with an architectural regularity that reflects the formal organization of central-city streets and blocks, and as an open, landscaped path between the dense urban fabric on either side, it suggests the inversion of Chicago's one-time motto as "Urbs in horto."[12] In the other direction, along the prevailing north-south grain of central-city streets, the regularly planted trees suggest the former continuity of long, narrow blocks, albeit with natural elements rather than building program.

New construction or additional landscaping could achieve the uniform edges that are appropriate to a symbolically significant circulation route but that the circumstances of the parkway's construction have denied. A regular street wall could be created through "shirtfront" additions to existing historic buildings or new construction of freestanding buildings with small floor plates. Should the commercial viability of new construction on small parcels prove inadequate, irregular block ends could be planted with trees to reinforce the parkway as a greenbelt. Over time, buildings of negligible historical or architectural significance along the street could eventually be redeveloped to specifically address the parkway and thus repair the provisional nature of its edges.

The elaboration of this formal boulevard as a sequential arrangement that relates natural elements to adjacent buildings will further reinforce the parkway as a significant civic axis. Both its sides and center are planted with regular rows of trees between the "gateway" buildings and the Harold Washington Library Center. Here these regular rows are interrupted by a paved plaza with lampposts and other markers, which distinguish the presence of a major public building in a manner that recalls the nearby plazas of the Federal and Daley centers. From the Library Plaza to Grant Park, the parkway's final segment combines planted edges with an open center, maintaining continuous landscaping while acknowledging the street's narrowed intersection with Michigan Avenue. Beyond the rows of trees, sidewalks are reestablished outside the building envelopes of the Auditorium Building and Congress Hotel. Traffic lanes, diverted at Michigan Avenue, no longer extend eastward into the park, though existing ramps are preserved for local park traffic. At the eastern end of Congress Parkway, a pedestrian plaza, monumental staircase, and civic marker identify Grant Park as the origin of the civic axis. The removal of the central portion of the post office will create an outer gateway to the central city that allows this axis to visibly extend westward across the region.

Congress Parkway is not the closed axis that Burnham and Bennett imagined but rather an open-ended path between the lakefront and the western periphery that adopts the formal

Figure 9.9 Diagram showing the arrangement of streets, buildings, and gardens in Burnham and Bennett's proposal for Grant Park, 1909.

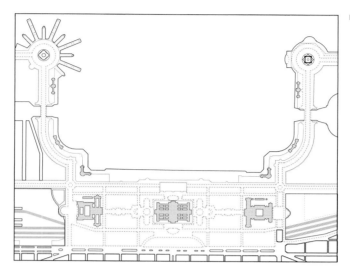

Figure 9.9

language of the central city where it passes through it. The creation of a more-efficient system of through circulation, a provision for the Loop's southward expansion as a multiuse district with a residential focus, and the improved access to parks and the river that it would provide are the more-practical contributions that a redesigned Congress Parkway could make to the central city (FIGURE 9.8).

GRANT PARK:
GARDEN, LANDSCAPE, ORNAMENT

As the focus and point of origin of Burnham and Bennett's regional plan, the proposed city center was a concentrated version of the larger scheme. Like the larger plan, the proposal for the center was defined by separate zones organized within a radial grid of streets that negotiated an urban center and a natural periphery. The character and organization of the larger plan—composed of functionally distinct elements in a formal, hierarchical arrangement—were present in the design of the central city as a refined and orderly sequence of architectural events.

Grant Park played a central role in this sequence as the natural complement to the urban ensemble of the Civic Center. It employed the same axial and hierarchical methods of arrangement but applied these strategies to natural as well as built elements, relating a museum ensemble to its natural setting through formal architectural means (FIGURE 9.1). Its realization over time has complied with the plan's objectives to varying degrees. Changing needs and circumstances have altered its proposed program and organization, but the strength of its original character has persisted in the face of compromising digressions. Comparing the park's current

state with Burnham and Bennett's original intentions provides direction for reconciling real and ideal aspects of its role and function.

In recognition of its exceptional location next to the central city and its complementary relationship to the Civic Center ensemble, Grant Park was envisioned as a garden in the classical European sense, a structured negotiation between architecture and landscape that provides a setting for the former and a transition to the latter. Burnham and Bennett's plan therefore described an architectural order of streets and blocks with the natural materials of garden parterres and allées of trees (FIGURE 9.9). This formal character privileged a larger civic role and a quality of restful repose over the active recreation of organized group activities, facilities for which were consigned to a site south of Grant Park. Burnham and Bennett's design did, however, incorporate working piers and a harbor because these augmented the urban presence of the park, establishing it at a larger scale as a terrace that embraced and framed the lake. Grant Park was therefore a shared civic ornament that worked at multiple scales and addressed multiple functions and contexts.

At the time of Grant Park's creation, the automobile was not yet a ubiquitous presence, and Burnham and Bennett avoided integrating circulation routes for through traffic into this environment. They anticipated neither the central role of the automobile in a new regional transportation pattern, nor the emergence of their proposed lakefront boulevards as major conduits for automobile traffic, circumstances that established the central-city lakefront as a major point of convergence for through traffic moving north, south, and west. Burnham and Bennett did provide a network of through streets within the park, but these were essentially enlarged garden paths, adequate only to support the requirements of existing methods

Figure 9.10 Project for lakefront development in the city of Chicago by Eliel Saarinen, 1923.

Figure 9.10

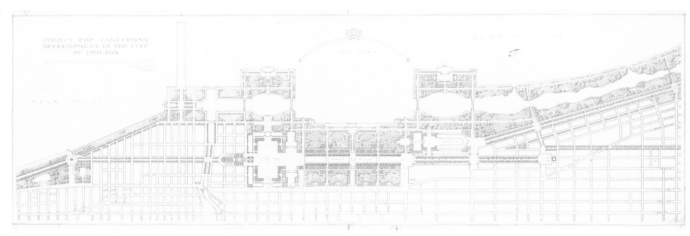

of transport and the adoption of the automobile as a vehicle for leisure use.

A 1923 proposal for Grant Park by the Finnish architect Eliel Saarinen reconciled the functional requirements of high-volume automobile circulation and rail transportation with the formal and aesthetic character proposed by Burnham and Bennett (FIGURE 9.10). A canalized, axial roadway in the location of what is now Columbus Drive was a conduit that provided access to multilevel parking garages on either side, on top of which Grant Park continued uninterrupted as a series of garden parterres linked by bridges over the sunken boulevard (FIGURE 9.11). This drive was anchored at its north and south ends by towers whose design recalled Saarinen's influential second-place entry for the Tribune Tower competition (FIGURE 9.12). The northern tower dominated a plaza that incorporated an expanded Art Institute, a municipal concert hall, and a consolidated railroad station. Saarinen's plan also covered the railroad tracks that at the time separated Grant Park from the central city. East of the park's formal, axial gardens, a landscaped lakefront that incorporated locks for the Chicago River and a recreational harbor fulfilled the scope and intent of Burnham and Bennett's plan for Grant Park. By integrating transportation facilities with commercial buildings, cultural institutions, and landscape elements around a through-circulation route conceived as an organizing axis, Saarinen introduced multiple uses into a park that lay at the intersection of these elements. His idealized architectural treatment of new transportation requirements, however, did not anticipate the noxious realities of high-speed automobile circulation confined in grade-separated, channeled roadways. Nevertheless, his plan represents the first serious attempt to enlist the automobile in the kind of totalizing civic ensemble envisioned in the *Plan of Chicago*.

Grant Park has evolved as both a formal garden with a civic role and a major point of convergence in the automobile-based transportation network. In 1911 the Illinois Supreme Court ruled in favor of a suit brought by Aaron Montgomery Ward to prevent the construction of the Field Museum in Grant Park. Though the building was relocated to the southern edge of the park, as the first element in the institutional ensemble that became the Museum Campus, Grant Park's proposed character as a formal garden was retained. Bennett's revised plan for the park, adopted in 1924, placed a monumental fountain in the central position originally intended for the Field Museum; the fountain was bracketed on either side by formal garden parterres and axial lawns and connected to Michigan Avenue to the west and Lake Michigan to the east by stepped terraces (FIGURE 9.13). The central component of the plan, the Buckingham Fountain and the adjacent garden parterres, was completed in 1927. This sympathetic substitution preserved the most memorable and defining formal and organizational aspect of the original design: the demarcation of the crossing of urban and park axes. The resulting symmetry and legibility are evident at multiple scales, as they can be readily appreciated from the tall buildings of the central city as well as from passing aircraft. The role of Congress Parkway as the central spine of the metropolitan plan has been diminished over the past century, but within the park it is still clearly established.

Other vestiges of the original garden plan occur as isolated incidents. St. Gaudens's statue of Abraham Lincoln occupies one of the islands defined by the park's network of surface streets, and a row of garden parterres along Michigan Avenue reinforces the park's formal relationship to the street. The stairways and terraces of these gardens, the footbridges over the railroad tracks that connect Grant Park and Michigan Avenue, and the pylons,

Figure 9.11 Project for lakefront development in the city of Chicago, plan of the automobile terminal, by Eliel Saarinen, 1923.
Figure 9.12 Project for lakefront development in the city of Chicago, view north along the proposed central boulevard, by Eliel Saarinen, 1923.
Figure 9.13 View of the proposed plan for Grant Park by Bennett, Parsons, Frost, and Thomas, 1922.

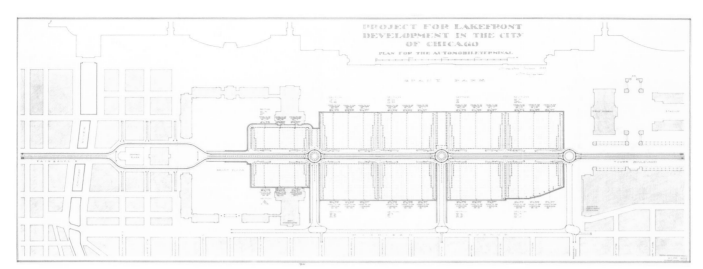

Figure 9.11

balustrades, and pedestals throughout the park employ the unified, neoclassical design vocabulary that sought to identify Grant Park as a shared civic space with a singular, integrated character.

Later additions have altered this established civic character without compromising it. During the 1960s and 1970s, the construction of underground parking facilities provided a platform for additional park space, just as Saarinen had proposed. The Daley Bicentennial Plaza, completed in 1976 on the south side of Randolph Street, added a field house and an ice-skating rink at the park's northern edge. The reconfiguration of Lake Shore Drive in 1985 and 1996 added park space to the northeast and improved pedestrian access to a newly integrated Museum Campus at the park's southeast corner. Millennium Park replaced the rail yards that separated the park's northwest corner from Michigan Avenue and provided additional parking, improved commuter rail access, cultural amenities, and active recreation facilities. This park-within-a-park created a separate but sympathetic focus that appropriately concentrated intensive park activity along the urban edge of Michigan Avenue while acknowledging the presence of an expanding Art Institute. Millennium Park manifests an extension of the rectilinear street grid into the park with terraces and footpaths that conform to the neoclassical expression of the terraces to the south. Moreover, the awkward intrusion of Columbus Drive has been addressed with a broad, meandering footbridge that ambles between gardens on either side of the road. Other smaller improvements have been implemented elsewhere, as over time an implicit physical order has been established in Grant Park, whereby facilities for active recreation around the park's edges are accessible to urban surroundings, and its center is occupied by a formal garden landscape that offers quiet repose in a privileged precinct with a public character.

Figure 9.12

Figure 9.13

Figure 9.14 Diagram showing the existing arrangement of streets, buildings, and open space in Grant Park.
Figure 9.15 Diagram showing the proposed arrangement of streets, buildings, and open space in Grant Park.

Figure 9.16 Diagram showing the proposed arrangement of elements in the park. Park access streets are shown in red. A - Buckingham Fountain. B - Lincoln Exedra. C - South Pavilion. D - Festivals Plaza. E - South Lakefront Pavilion. F - Millennium Park. G - Chicago Yacht Club. H - North Meadow. Red lines indicate park access routes for vehicles.

Figure 9.14

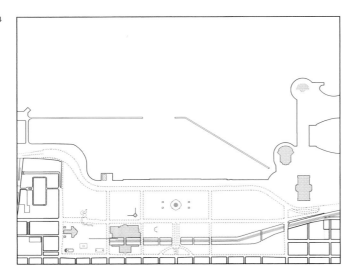

Figure 9.15

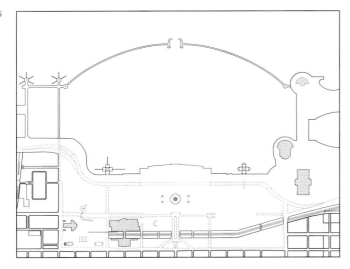

Figure 9.16

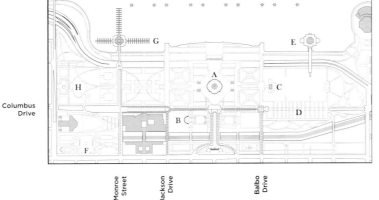

Columbus
Drive

Monroe
Street

Jackson
Drive

Balbo
Drive

The evolution of a network of surface streets that primarily serve through traffic has introduced significant distortions and jarring adjacencies into this implicit order. Currently, the streets that traverse Grant Park are the final link for regional traffic moving between the Circle Interchange and Lake Shore Drive. They also carry local park traffic, which utilizes their edges for additional parking. This extension of the urban grid into public open space necessarily divides it into discrete "islands" (FIGURE 9.14). Lake Shore Drive is both the widest surface street in the park and the feature that, in isolating it from the lakefront, most drastically compromises the quality of its public character.

The uncoordinated nature of Grant Park's concurrent development as a major civic space and a through-traffic circulator has compromised both uses, a condition brought into sharper focus as the park accommodates an increasing number of visitors and local residents. The success of Millennium Park and the additional attention it has focused on Grant Park, the emerging residential character of the Loop's eastern edge, and the extensive redevelopment of the near South Side all further suggest the timeliness of a reconsideration that coordinates Grant Park's varied roles.

The current variety of its components and uses suggests that Grant Park has evolved from a garden into a landscape that incorporates both formal and informal garden elements and recreational amenities. This complex character suggests rules of engagement for a coordinated approach to the requirements of circulation, active recreation, and public open space. Reinforcing the rational, hierarchical arrangement that is concentrated at the park's central section will strengthen its overall identity as a discrete, formal ensemble that contrasts and complements the less-explicit order of the central city. On the other hand, the more-casual arrangement of elements around the park's edges, and the varied character of its boundaries with the surrounding city, provide an opportunity to attract more regular use through an enriched program of activities. New additions should therefore reinforce one of these qualities or the other. Singular elements should be placed along one of the park's two primary axes, while paired elements should emphasize these through symmetrical arrangement; elements without civic significance should be located on the park's periphery, beyond this central sequence. The pattern of traffic moving to and through the park should further reinforce this basic arrangement. A plan thus based in the park's existing conditions can preserve and strengthen the singular character of the most complete, intact, and readily appreciated formal component of Burnham and Bennett's plan.

Overleaf:
Figure 9.17 Plan of the proposed improvement of Grant Park by Aric Lasher, 2009.

As this character is most seriously challenged by the extension of surface streets carrying through traffic into the park, an improved circulation plan is the first step in the coordinated approach proposed here. Much of the through traffic that currently crosses the park is removed by extending Wacker Drive south to Roosevelt Road and relocating the connection between Lake Shore Drive, Columbus Drive, and the Circle Interchange below grade (FIGURES 9.6 and 9.15). A covered conduit between Congress Parkway and Lake Shore Drive provides access to expanded underground parking facilities and through them vehicular access to the park. Balbo and Jackson drives are reconfigured as pedestrian paths and park access routes (FIGURE 9.16). Monroe Street remains as a direct connection between the Loop and Lake Shore Drive. Depressing and covering Columbus Drive south of Monroe Street allows the wide, paved expanse of its current roadway to be similarly reclaimed for pedestrian use and local vehicle access. The central section, reconfigured as a paved and landscaped promenade, provides grade-level parking or accommodates booths and tents during festival events. South of Balbo Drive, it continues as a paved plaza for festivals, sheltered by a canopy of shade trees, that incorporates permanent utility hookups for vendors. An internal network of service streets provides limited local access, allowing the existing street grid to remain in place with an altered character and use. Pedestrian bridges over Lake Shore Drive at Randolph, Monroe, and 9th streets extend this grid to the lakefront. These adopt the traditional method for separating pedestrian and vehicular traffic in and around Grant Park, of which the footbridges over the railroad tracks east of Michigan Avenue at Van Buren and 11th streets and Jackson Drive, and the pedestrian bridges designed by Frank Gehry and Renzo Piano for Millennium Park and the Art Institute, all provide examples.

The park's existing circulation grid is also enlisted in a larger compositional strategy. Its streets currently define discrete districts or quadrants within the park, including the existing Lincoln memorial exedra and gardens and the Buckingham Fountain parterre. These smaller precincts may be developed with an individual character, as in Millennium Park, where a basic organization of terraces and walkways that conform to the Beaux-Arts principles of the original design for Grant Park established a framework for such formally autonomous elements as the Crown Fountain and the Lurie Garden. Here this strategy is applied to some of the sections beyond the central portions of the park, where picturesque planting arrangements and active recreation facilities supplant ornamental gardens.

The Buckingham Fountain and its axial extensions give legible order and hierarchy to a grid that organizes autonomous parts (FIGURES 9.16 and 9.17). These extensions, however, need not duplicate the architectural regularity of the central precinct. The northern axis, for example, acquires a larger scale and a less-formal character as one moves farther from this precinct. It passes between outdoor "rooms" of various sizes regularly defined by rows of trees, which recall the smaller parterres around the central fountain, and into a larger, naturalistically landscaped slope at the southern edge of Randolph Street. There a meadowlike lawn and a pair of markers terminate the fountain axis and informally mirror the semicircular figure found at the opposite end of the park. The southern axis terminates in an open gathering place that maintains aspects of the existing conditions at the park's southern portion, with a depressed grade level and a semicircular termination encircled by trees. This space is left intentionally open to accommodate a flexible range of uses, which might include public concerts, exhibitions, political rallies, or sporting events. A pavilion placed on axis with the fountain, at the southern edge of the central precinct, marks the northern entrance to this area of the park and contains concessions, ticketing, and restroom facilities. Its western edge is defined by the paved plaza for festivals, which overlooks it.

Buckingham Fountain is also the focal point of an axis that extends east and west beyond the limits of the park. To its west, a band of lawn and a monumental stairway mark the foot of Congress Parkway and the regional axis that continues indefinitely westward. To the east, the central parterre extends over a partially depressed segment of Lake Shore Drive, beyond which it descends to the harbor's edge in a series of stepped terraces, thus providing uninterrupted access from park to lakefront. A projecting lakefront promenade marks the Congress Parkway axis within an enlarged harbor. To its north, the Chicago Yacht Club has been rebuilt as an islandlike building surrounded on all sides by water, and in a corresponding position to the south, another pavilion contains restaurant, concession, and entertainment facilities. These dramatic destinations engage the equally dramatic, though currently underexploited, harbor and reinforce Burnham and Bennett's symmetrical order on a smaller scale. On the harbor's eastern edge, a water gate with paired beacons further extends the axis of Congress Parkway eastward, framing a central view of an unobstructed horizon, lending focus to the iconic but presently undifferentiated expanse of Lake Michigan, and identifying the park terrace and its vista as the central focus of the lakefront. An enclosed harbor area at the north edge of the basin is configured to serve those who desire surface access to moorings, while the enlarged central harbor has moorings served by

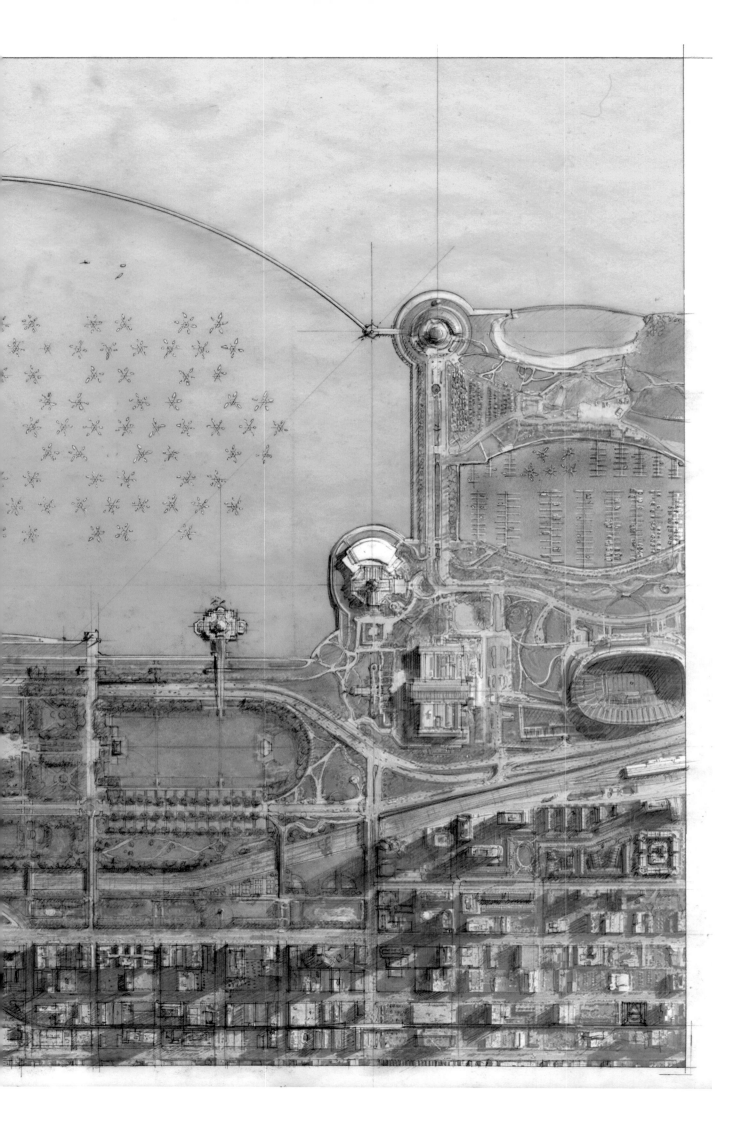

Figure 9.18 Perspective view of the proposed improvement of Grant Park by Aric Lasher, 2009.

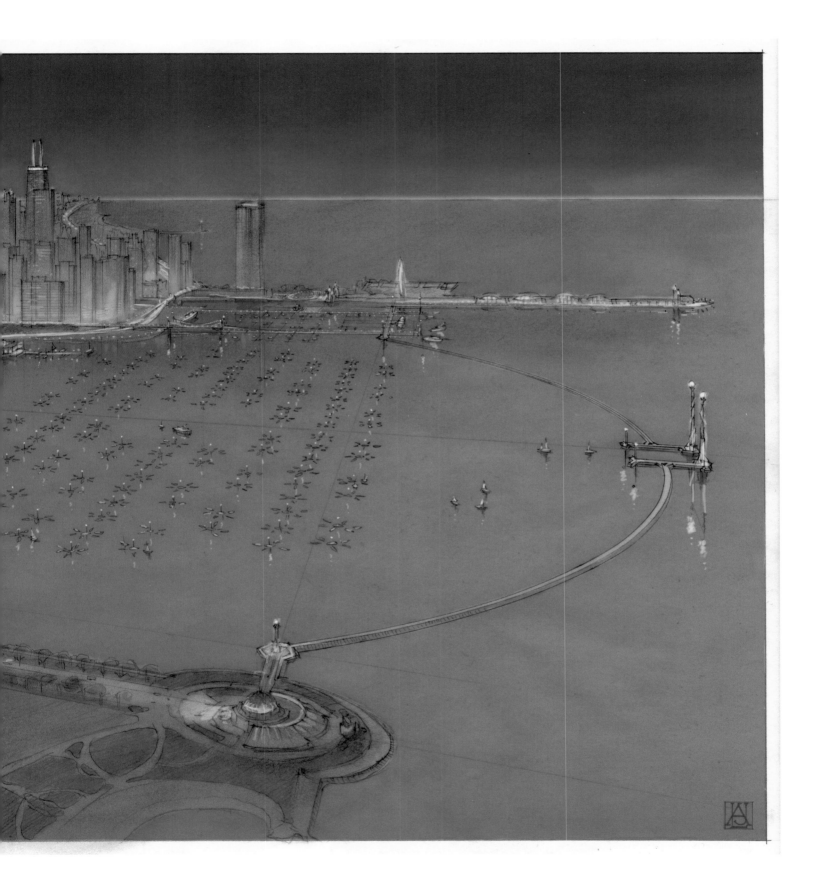

water shuttle. The pedestrian causeway at Randolph Street leads to a landing for tourist lake boats, providing access to this amenity for park visitors. The axially positioned water gate thus becomes a memorable point of departure and arrival, the doorstep of Chicago (FIGURE 9.18).

The breakwater to which this gate belongs extends and reinforces the geometric order of Grant Park. Burnham and Bennett endowed a proposed breakwater in the same approximate position with a similarly formal character and reinforcing role. They envisioned the central lakefront as a recognizable counterpoint to an extensive shoreline of naturalistic landscape parks. At the city's center, the irregular contours of the planted barrier islands and jetties of the north and south shores, as proposed in the plan, gave way to a formal arrangement of low-profile breakwaters that would afford pedestrians at the central lakefront an unobstructed view of the blue horizon. The breakwater shown here employs a deeper arc because it describes a circle whose center is the basin of the Buckingham Fountain. The edge of this circle also touches, to the north and west, the banks of the Chicago River's main and southern branches and thus circumscribes the central city in its entirety: the Loop, South Loop, Grant Park, and the central harbor (FIGURE 9.19). As such, the new breakwater, whose geometry is clearly visible from above, proclaims and reinforces the park's focal position in an integrated ensemble that encompasses all components of the central city.

Any reconsideration of Grant Park should reinforce its latent formal organization while acknowledging its varied landscape of uses and environments. The reconciliation of the park's role as civic ornament, playground, formal setting for cultural institutions, and traffic conduit could successfully reframe and strengthen its role as a linchpin in the urban ensemble that has evolved from the *Plan of Chicago*.

THE CENTER RECONSIDERED

Burnham and Bennett's plan conceived a central city whose character was established by the episodic interruption of an expansive and undifferentiated fabric by exceptional architectural events. The resulting privileged precincts conferred civic prestige to the central city through their position, scale, and formal characteristics. The *Plan of Chicago* attempted to create a city center that had a character commensurate with Chicago's emerging status as one of the largest and most important cities in the world, a task undertaken with the understanding that little of the extant city would figure in the new scheme. We are now confronted by a mature organism that has evolved and incorporated the distortions and enhancements of subsequent circumstances, and any improvements must consequently be considered as refinements or revisions to this manifestation. As it has evolved, Chicago's center is identified as much by an irregular but impressive crescendo of tall buildings as by the disciplined modeling of its central lakefront into a clearly defined, large-scale mandala. The more-compact arrangement of the current central city embraces only one of the two foci proposed by Burnham and Bennett, but the visual potency of its profile has endowed an implicitly ordered composition with the status of an icon. The efflorescence of market-driven development and the partially implemented majesty of a coordinated civic lakefront benefit from their adjacency. The breadth and order of Grant Park becomes more appropriate when it abuts a city of modern scale, and the informal cluster of the Loop gains prestige and focus when it fully engages the park. By rectifying the functional and logistical shortcomings of program, circulation, and organization, both city center and civic lakefront can be improved in such a manner as to clarify their individual characteristics and strengthen their relationship as parts of an indivisible whole. As impressive and iconic as Burnham's coordinated ensemble was, the current incarnation of the central city, with its accommodation of circumstance and its incorporation of individual creativity, represents a fuller and more-robust expression of Chicago's authentic character.

Figure 9.19 Satellite view showing proposed improvement of the central city. A circle with a radius of .88 miles, with its origin at Buckingham Fountain, circumscribes the center.

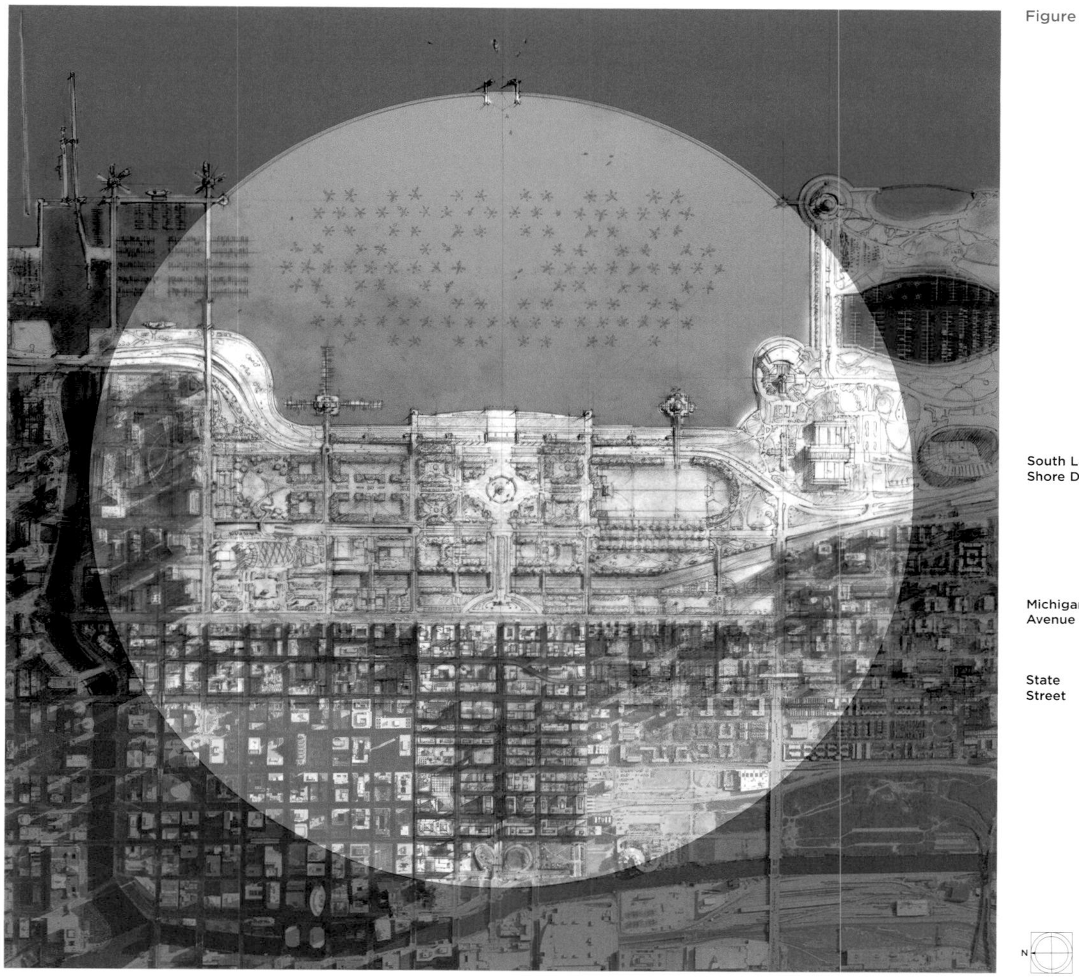

Figure 9.19

Wacker Drive

Randolph Street

Monroe Street

North Lake Shore Drive

Columbus Drive

South Lake Shore Drive

Michigan Avenue

State Street

Wacker Drive

Eisenhower Expressway / Congress Parkway

Roosevelt Road / Twelfth Street

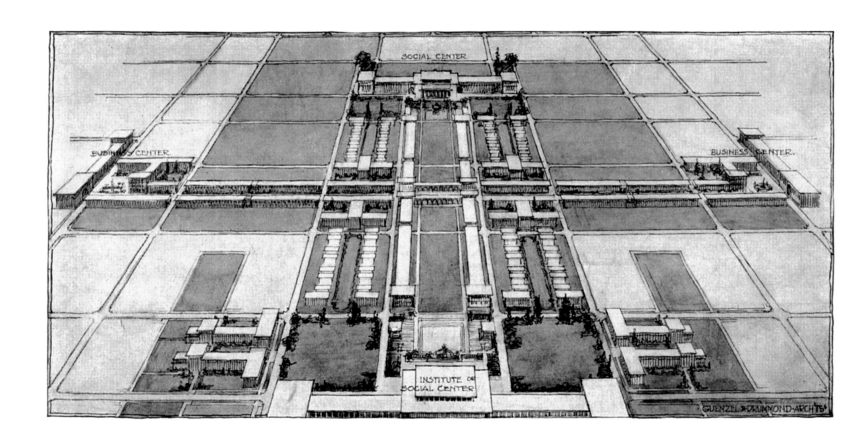

CHAPTER 10

PLANNING THE
INTERMEDIATE FABRIC

THE CHARACTER OF THE INTERMEDIATE FABRIC · THE CURRENT
STATE OF THE INTERMEDIATE FABRIC · THE FABRIC ALONG THE
EISENHOWER EXPRESSWAY · SHOULD WE PRESERVE THE FABRIC?
REAL AND IDEAL EXAMPLES FOR IMPROVEMENT · A NEW PLANNING
MODEL DESCRIBED · RULES FOR ARRANGING AND RELATING
BUILDINGS · IMPLEMENTING A NEW FABRIC

THE CHARACTER OF THE INTERMEDIATE FABRIC

The contemporary residential fabric of Chicago comprises what was the residential periphery prior to the introduction of the automobile. It begins at the edges of the central city, which encompasses the Loop and its extensions westward to the Kennedy Expressway and northward along Michigan Avenue to Oak Street. The fabric's outer edge largely coincides with the city limits, though in some places it extends beyond them, into nineteenth-century railway suburbs also planned on the grid, of which Oak Park and Evanston are the prime examples.[1] The fabric remains the primary residential zone of the city proper and contains most of its population and area. The City of Chicago divides this fabric into seventy-seven community areas or neighborhoods composed of multiple quarter sections that are half a mile on each side and house a diverse population at varying densities.[2] All share a pattern of streets and blocks that evolved alongside a transportation system based on mass transit, largely between the appearance of the railroad in the mid-nineteenth century and World War II.[3] Half-mile streets describe a large-scale grid of residential quarter sections, where smaller streets, sometimes one-way, typically define thirty-two blocks each measuring 660 x 330 feet. These are arranged in a pattern of 4 x 8 blocks that can run either east-west or north-south, allowing the grain of the fabric to vary from one quarter section to another (FIGURE 10.2).[4] A service alley bisects each residential block longitudinally and provides for parking, garbage pickup, and telephone and electrical wiring. Major streets, secondary streets, and service alleys organize various uses and building types that include multistory commercial or mixed-use structures along half-mile streets and multi-tenant apartment buildings, two- or three-flat detached houses, and single-family homes along residential streets. Service alleys typically separate commercial buildings from housing on the blocks along the half-mile streets.

Parks interrupt and enrich the fabric while conforming to the orthogonal boundaries of the quarter-section street pattern. With a variety of uses, scales, and characters, they constitute a complete program of recreation and natural exposure. These parks include the six large parks that comprise the original park systems, the medium-size parks like Sherman Park and Columbus Park incorporated in later peripheral expansions, and the scattered small parks and playgrounds that service individual neighborhoods.[5] Planners in the early twentieth century enlisted parks in larger plans for civic enrichment that would provide individual quarter sections with the same range of services and amenities one might find in a self-sufficient small town.[6] Piecemeal development eventually arranged schools, libraries, field houses, community centers, and churches more randomly, producing an enriched urban environment that was only implicitly ordered. For much of Chicago's history, the fabric represented the middle ground between town and country, where residents could enjoy the urban amenities of transportation, shopping, and community gathering places alongside the improved landscapes of parks. Moreover, the fabric served as a place where they could retreat from the public sphere that included these elements and into the privacy of their own homes.

Today this complex character is less apparent because automobile suburbs now occupy the middle ground between

Figure 10.1 Bird's-eye view of two adjoining quarter sections by William Drummond, 1913.

131

Figure 10.2 Figure-ground diagram showing the arrangement of streets, blocks, and buildings in a typical quarter section in the intermediate fabric.

Figure 10.2

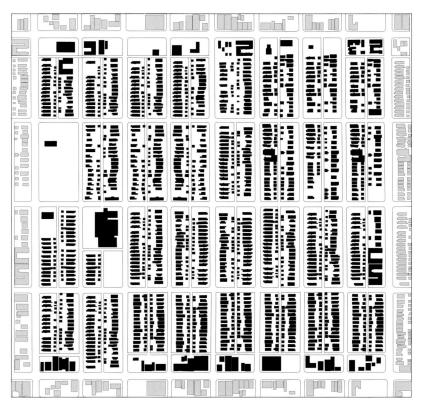

town and country. During the second half of the twentieth century, the middle class abandoned much of the old residential periphery for a new one farther from the center.[7] The automobile and limited-access highways provided access to larger lots in a natural landscape without sacrificing convenience to the central city. Suburbanization of housing was followed by suburbanization of shopping and work. The resulting larger, more-diffuse periphery, like its predecessor, combined a full range of program with a natural landscape, but the individual privacy and freedom it offered extended beyond the home to the personal automobile, which conferred on the driver both freedom of movement and freedom from a set schedule.

The emergence of a private transportation network has also affected the fabric more directly, altering its pattern both for better and for worse. The limited-access highways that bypass the fabric provide regular points of access, freeing half-mile streets to service local traffic and creating a more-efficient distribution of traffic in the fabric. But as an intrusive addition, the expressway has disrupted an established pattern at large and small scales. Channeled expressways present major obstacles to cross traffic and establish impenetrable barriers between once-contiguous neighborhoods. Their appearance has often coincided with the onset of blight in the adjacent neighborhoods, and in every case, it has compromised their restful character. On a smaller scale, those half-mile streets that have become

more local have also become less effective at insulating residential blocks from passing through traffic, as the demand for parking has literally broken down once-uniform street walls.

THE CURRENT STATE OF
THE INTERMEDIATE FABRIC

Though large parts of the intermediate fabric have remained stable and even prospered since the introduction of the automobile, its overall prognosis—owing to the combined effects of suburbanization, automobile transit, and proliferating social ills elsewhere—is gloomy; in Chicago this prediction is largely supported by metropolitan demographic statistics and trends.[8] Three primary divisions of the city's intermediate fabric correspond roughly to the original South, West, and North park districts; all are traversed by expressways. While the northern division, which is contiguous with affluent suburbs to the north and northwest, has largely retained its original character, the fabric's southern and western divisions contain some of Chicago's most blighted areas, places where the consequences of postwar suburbanization have coincided with advancing social ills borne of poverty and isolation. During the middle decades of the twentieth century, African Americans from the South, seeking employment in industry and escape from oppressive economic and social conditions, settled in

Figure 10.3 Site plan of Henry Horner Homes, Chicago, by Skidmore, Owings, and Merrill, 1952.

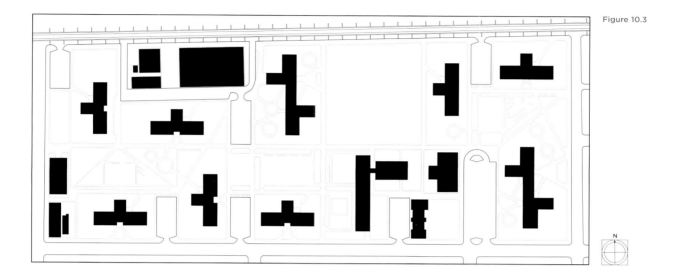

Figure 10.3

Chicago in large numbers. Economics, discrimination, and restrictive covenants confined them to historically African American neighborhoods in the southern and western fabric. These demographics expanded over larger portions of the fabric as the white middle-class residents of adjacent neighborhoods abandoned them for the periphery. A poorer population imposed a denser pattern of settlement on these areas, subdividing existing single-family homes (which were already becoming obsolete) into multi-tenant apartment houses.[9]

Attempts in the 1950s and 1960s to remediate the blight resulting from overcrowding, substandard living conditions that were the consequence of slumlord profiteering or symptoms of poverty, and diminishing tax revenues introduced peripheral planning strategies into the fabric on both the South and West sides. These occasionally stabilized, if not revived, the neighborhoods, though more often they were unable to arrest decline. In every case, they erased the existing street and block pattern in an effort to endow the fabric with the perceived benefits of the periphery.[10] Planners removed streets, combined blocks, and concentrated housing in high-rise towers that left a majority of these larger sites available for public open space, the lack of which was considered a contributing factor to neighborhood blight (FIGURE 10.3). This open space remained, however, largely undefined, without a clear purpose or program. Street-side retail also disappeared when blocks were consolidated and streets were removed. The nonurban character of high-density housing developments, planned for peripheral requirements of maximum natural light and ventilation, thereby opened holes in the intermediate fabric. Chicago's inability to annex new peripheral growth threw the plight of the fabric into greater relief.[11] Suburbs incorporated to resist annexation; small, affluent, often racially homogeneous, and politically self-contained,

they did not need to tax residents for social services, and their lower property taxes constituted an additional peripheral draw.

More-recent population trends and projections indicate that the decline of much of the fabric will continue.[12] The postwar cycle of abandonment by residents who have attained affluence and the repopulation of their neighborhoods by other ethnic groups has not significantly changed, with new populations leaving for the periphery as soon as they are able. Regional unemployment remains highest and per-capita income lowest in the southern and western fabric. Much of the fabric has either become a revolving door for arriving immigrants or remains chronically blighted. Population forecasts predict that the outer fabric will eventually merge with the older, denser settlements of early suburban communities of the post-automobile periphery to create a zone of terminal decline between an expanding outer periphery and an inner fabric of increasing density contiguous with the central city.[13]

THE FABRIC ALONG THE EISENHOWER EXPRESSWAY

From the edge of the central city to the city limit at Austin Boulevard, the Eisenhower Expressway traces a seven-mile path through the western fabric that exhibits both its characteristic features and its recent problems. It runs parallel to Madison Street, half a mile to the north, a primary spoke in the fabric's original mass-transit network. Madison Street remains the most important half-mile street in the western fabric, convenient to a range of transportation connections and public open space. The former include two sets of rail lines: one running along Lake Street, half a mile to the north; and the other along the Eisenhower Expressway, half a mile to the

Figure 10.4 Existing arrangement of streets, blocks, buildings, and open space along the Eisenhower Expressway, from the Circle Interchange west to Ridgeland Avenue, and from Madison Street south to Roosevelt Road. Buildings noted in the text are shown in gray. Moving west, the campus of the University of Illinois at Chicago and the Illinois Medical District are south of the expressway. North of the medical district are Malcolm X College, the United Center, and the site of the Henry Horner Homes, outlined in red. The North Lawndale campus of Sears, Roebuck and Company is further west, also outlined in red. Austin Boulevard, west of Columbus Park, marks the city limit of Chicago, beyond which is Oak Park, whose buildings are shown in gray.

Ridgeland Avenue

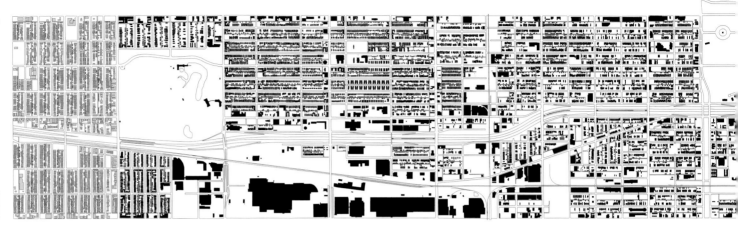

N

south—each of which includes routes for commuter and intra-city rail—and five bus routes centered on the half-mile area between Madison Street and the expressway.[14] This stretch of the fabric is also well endowed with a range of parks, including Garfield Park, its boulevard connection to Douglas Park, Columbus Park against the western city limits, and multiple neighborhood parks and playgrounds. Madison Street was the main street of one of Chicago's two original African American communities around Western Avenue, and blight in the western fabric spread from there.[15] Until 1974 Sears, Roebuck and Company was headquartered just south of the expressway in a vast complex on multiple blocks in North Lawndale. Its relocation to the Sears Tower in the Loop (and later to a suburban headquarters) resulted in a significant loss of employment and revenue for the adjacent community.

The impenetrable boundary of the expressway, special zoning designations, and protective political boundaries have situated a wide range of demographic groups in close proximity to one another in the western fabric. An institutional zone just west of the Eisenhower's junction with the Kennedy and Dan Ryan expressways includes the Illinois Medical District—which classifies itself as the largest urban medical district in the United States—the University of Illinois at Chicago, and Malcolm X College. All were explicitly planned or aggressively expanded with government support to remedy urban blight, and a continuing program of renewal in the adjacent blocks has partially remade the fabric without sacrificing its street pattern. The United Center, surrounded by sixteen blocks of parking, more seriously disrupts the fabric to the north and isolates the adjacent Henry Horner Homes (FIGURE 10.4). Here combined blocks, high-rise apartment buildings, and extensive open spaces once presented a typical example of peripheral planning in the fabric, through which a utopian architectural program

sought to remedy the social ills of the slums that it replaced. The Chicago Housing Authority has partially demolished the project and is redeveloping its land as a mixed-income neighborhood that will reinstate the fabric's characteristic street pattern and building arrangement.

Moving west from the United Center and Henry Horner Homes, the Eisenhower Expressway passes through five miles of largely intact fabric that exhibits characteristic problems in an advanced state. A neighborhood analysis undertaken by the University of Chicago Library in 2002 classifies the neighborhoods of East and West Garfield Park, North Lawndale, and most of Austin as "very urban, impoverished, English-speaking, with many female-headed families and numerous children."[16] The median income for this area, which remains a significant center for Chicago's urban African American population, is among the lowest per capita in the city; its unemployment rate is among the highest. The former Sears plant has been partially demolished and is currently the focus of an area renewal plan, which is restoring the surrounding fabric while incorporating activities more often associated with the periphery, such as organic farming. At the western edge of the city, the neighborhood of Austin surrounds Columbus Park and shares a border with the prosperous suburb of Oak Park, a physical extension of the urban fabric populated largely by professionals with families. Prior to postwar suburbanization, Austin shared Oak Park's demographic; today it more closely resembles the neighborhoods to the east. Whether it has succumbed less completely to the problems that plague those neighborhoods or is simply in an earlier stage of decline is unclear. Columbus Park is now a cushion and a barrier between the demographic groups of Austin and Oak Park.[17] Meanwhile, the fabric of Berwyn and Cicero, across the expressway from Austin and Oak Park, houses a growing Hispanic population. The former is classified

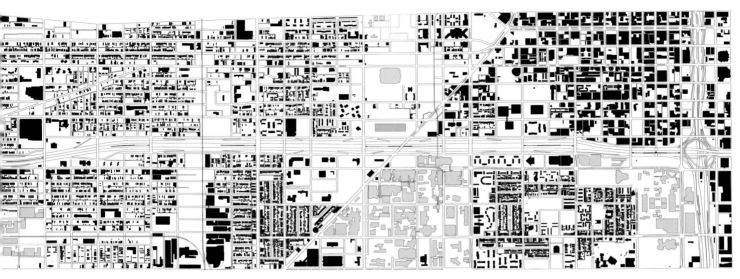

Figure 10.4

Madison Street

Circle Interchange

Roosevelt Road

in the neighborhood analysis as "somewhat linguistically isolated" and "mostly blue-collar," the latter as "impoverished and very linguistically isolated."[18]

SHOULD WE PRESERVE THE FABRIC?

The disruption of the Eisenhower Expressway produces jarring adjacencies between the radically different socioeconomic groups housed in the surrounding fabric, whose examples of advanced urban blight also appear to portend a larger pattern of decline. A new periphery has replaced and improved upon the attractions of the old one. In light of these circumstances, the viability of the fabric's basic pattern of settlement must be investigated before any specific improvements can be proposed.

Chicago has already acted on the impulse to remake the fabric. The introduction of peripheral planning strategies such as isolated, high-rise housing and suburban-style enclaves has, at best, achieved a limited success; more often it has accelerated blight in the affected neighborhoods. Even isolated successes have undermined the fabric by emphasizing their own distinctiveness. These interventions to improve the fabric have also ignored some of its original benefits, which stem from its character as a middle ground between town and country. A resident of the fabric can choose from a greater range of transportation modes and routes than his peripheral counterpart. A relatively small scale and compact arrangement, which accommodates a more-diverse program within a given space, makes walking convenient. Civic amenities and parks are typically also close at hand.

Despite multiple disruptions, the fabric remains largely in place. It is not a blank slate; past efforts have already enriched it in places. Parks and public buildings may need to be refurbished, but they stand as community landmarks.

Boulevards still offer a compelling example of circulation integrated with park space. The relatively low density and piecemeal character of the fabric allows individual buildings and blocks to be replaced without disturbing a larger pattern. More than either the central city or the periphery, the fabric can be gradually improved through a series of small steps. It can also accommodate the denser settlement that will entice public and private investment. Higher-density populations produce a more-robust tax base and greater potential return on private investment than the low densities that suburban-style models would support. Moreover, blocks of the fabric in many instances can now be acquired and improved cheaply. These innate advantages have been obscured in the recent past by entrenched patterns of land development, which concentrate new investment on either the central city or the outer periphery. Rehabilitation of the fabric is further discouraged by an implicit notion that its rail-based urban pattern is obsolete. A growing awareness of the costs of peripheral sprawl, however, intimates that this attitude could change.

The prohibitive cost of replacing an extensive fabric, its access to transportation and civic amenities, and its consonance with public and private goals all argue for preserving and improving the existing fabric. Enhancing its inherent attractions will draw investment and growth. A model for improving the fabric must offer convenient access to multiple transportation routes and modes, parks, and civic amenities. It must preserve a small-scale environment that is suitable for walking and a piecemeal character that will allow it to be implemented in a partial or modified form wherever specific aspects of this program are deficient. A model for improvement must also repair the damage caused by the automobile transportation network by reestablishing continuity across the expressway and along the half-mile streets.

Figure 10.5 Diagram showing the proposed arrangement of buildings, streets, and open space in a typical quarter section along the Eisenhower Expressway by Aric Lasher, 2009.

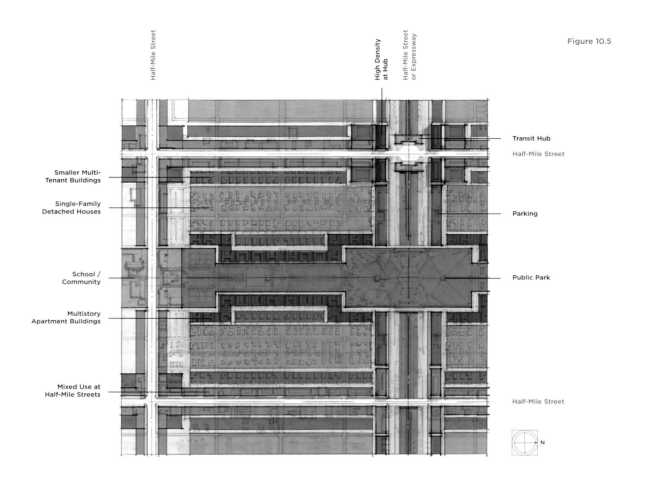

Figure 10.5

REAL AND IDEAL EXAMPLES FOR IMPROVEMENT

Existing examples demonstrate that these goals can be satisfied within the limits of the quarter section. A cohesive arrangement of public open space and a diverse assortment of commercial and residential building types, parks, and transit converge in a recognizable neighborhood unit in the area around Damen and Milwaukee avenues in Wicker Park. There a transit station is situated close to a neighborhood park and an intersection of secondary thoroughfares, which have generated a local cluster of high-density commercial buildings, with single- and multi-tenant residential buildings situated on adjacent side streets. Similar arrangements can be found elsewhere within the intermediate fabric, the most complete examples of which have shown remarkable resilience and an ability to attract residents and businesses.

Drummond and Jensen addressed these goals through planning models that took the existing periphery as a point of departure (FIGURE 10.1; SEE FIGURES 5.1 and 6.1). Both emphasized the quarter section as an introverted unit that nevertheless remained part of a larger uniform fabric, with a protected central park that served residents, schools, and community facilities. Such parks improved real-estate value, organized single- and multi-tenant housing in the adjacent blocks, and fostered a social program that allotted certain buildings to single laborers, local businesses, and community centers. Utilizing natural block divisions, these neighborhood units could be implemented gradually or partially; they could also provide a singular focus for surrounding quarter sections that remained unimproved, or join to create (as in Jensen's plan) continuous park space through multiple quarter sections. Drummond and Jensen proposed a basic style of architecture, in their case derived from the Prairie style, which provided suitable models for a range of building types and thus a strong community image. In what at the time would have been considered an inversion of conventional attributes of urban architecture, this regional idiom emphasized continuity between interior and exterior spaces and, through engagement with a naturalized urban landscape of private gardens and public parks, promised the benefits of an environment that incorporated idealized aspects of the midwestern prairie.

Overleaf:
Figure 10.6 Plan of two adjoining typical quarter sections along the Eisenhower Expressway by Aric Lasher, 2009.

A NEW PLANNING MODEL DESCRIBED

A model that combines Drummond's and Jensen's plans places equal and opposite emphasis on protecting the interior and reinforcing the boundaries of a typical quarter section. This proposal takes the existing grid as a framework for arranging commercial, residential, recreational, and service program around public space. Boundaries and corners reinforced with intensive mixed-use program elements define and protect residential quarter-section interiors whose buildings are arranged around linear parks (FIGURE 10.5).

Clearly delineated edges and an open center organize a basic pattern of use and density for the rest of the quarter section. Commercial buildings along the half-mile thoroughfares might have offices or townhouses located on their upper floors. Mixed-used buildings on major streets augment a local market for shops, encourage more activity on sidewalks, and constitute an effective screen for the quieter quarter-section interiors. A transitional program of two- and three-flat houses, attached or detached, occupies the interior half of these outer blocks. The protected blocks between these and a central park contain detached single-family homes, which may be built upon single or multiple city lots. The central park can attract higher-density housing development by providing an adjacent amenity for dwellings that lack private open space and can elevate real-estate values for properties convenient to a landscaped public space. The park is shown lined with the three- and four-story U- or H-shaped courtyard apartment buildings that are common fixtures of the Chicago fabric. These effectively define the park's edges and provide views and open space for units lacking private yards. The central park itself occupies the position of a vacated street and the longitudinal halves of the blocks to either side, the other halves of which are occupied by the court-yard apartment buildings. The park is a site for local recreation and community amenities that might include facilities for active and passive recreation, community centers, field houses, day care, community gardens, or, at locations where open space meets major streets, compatible commercial or retail program. Schools and community buildings might also occupy the inter-sections of park space and major streets, with easy access to transportation routes and recreational amenities. Existing schools, parks, and community buildings suggest specific sites for implementing further improvements. If comprehensively ordered, they can both reinforce and be reinforced by a stronger civic image.

Service program supports the larger program arrange-ment, further strengthening edges and helping to preserve an open interior. Surface parking behind commercial buildings on major streets allows them to maintain a uniform street wall. If required or supported by land values, structured parking also serves to reinforce corner locations, where it acts as a platform for taller buildings. Parking for two- and three-flat buildings, single-family homes, and courtyard apartment buildings is accessed from the service alleys behind them, keeping residential streets clear and separating buildings of different use and density that share the same block.

Creating connections between adjacent quarter sections that conform to these basic principles of arrangement can help repair the damaged fabric on either side of the expressway, which is incorporated as a large half-mile street with reinforced corners and edges (FIGURE 10.6). Though it remains separated by grade, the intersection of a half-mile street and the express-way seeds intensive activity in the adjacent quarter sections. Public plazas provide access to the rapid transit and commuter rail lines running between and alongside the lanes of the expressway. These transit plazas serve as a platform for multiuse corner developments that accommodate shopping, offices, and housing around and on top of structured parking. These nodes do not occur at every intersection with the expressway or at every transit stop, but rather where latent need or ease of implementation suggests their realization.

The area where the quarter section abuts the expressway constitutes another reinforced zone of intensive activity. There structured parking accommodates cars for area drivers using mass transit, serves as a protective barrier against the express-way, and creates a platform for residential buildings, particularly near transit plazas or busier commercial zones. Such reinforced nodes and edges adapt the normative model to accommodate a special condition and enforce urban continuity across the expressway without covering it. They are also potential sites for an additional program that might be added later. For example, light industry, warehouses, or even lateral expansions of the expressway can be enlisted in addition to structured parking to reinforce the edges of the quarter sections. Parallel service streets can also be augmented with bicycle routes and landscape elements to link intermittent open-space connections across the expressway. These connections ensure the continuity of the quarter section's natural as well as urban character. The edges of landscaped park overpasses, where they abut the expressway channel, are enclosed by walls or arcades that screen traffic noise and sights and reinforce their character as contiguous with the linear parks on either side. By engaging the expressway and using it as a platform for an integrated system of transit and open space that serves both the fabric and those passing through it, the proposed neighborhood unit integrates regional infrastructure with local amenities in a manner that mitigates the currently disruptive presence of the channeled motorway. This strategy for rehabilitating the fabric

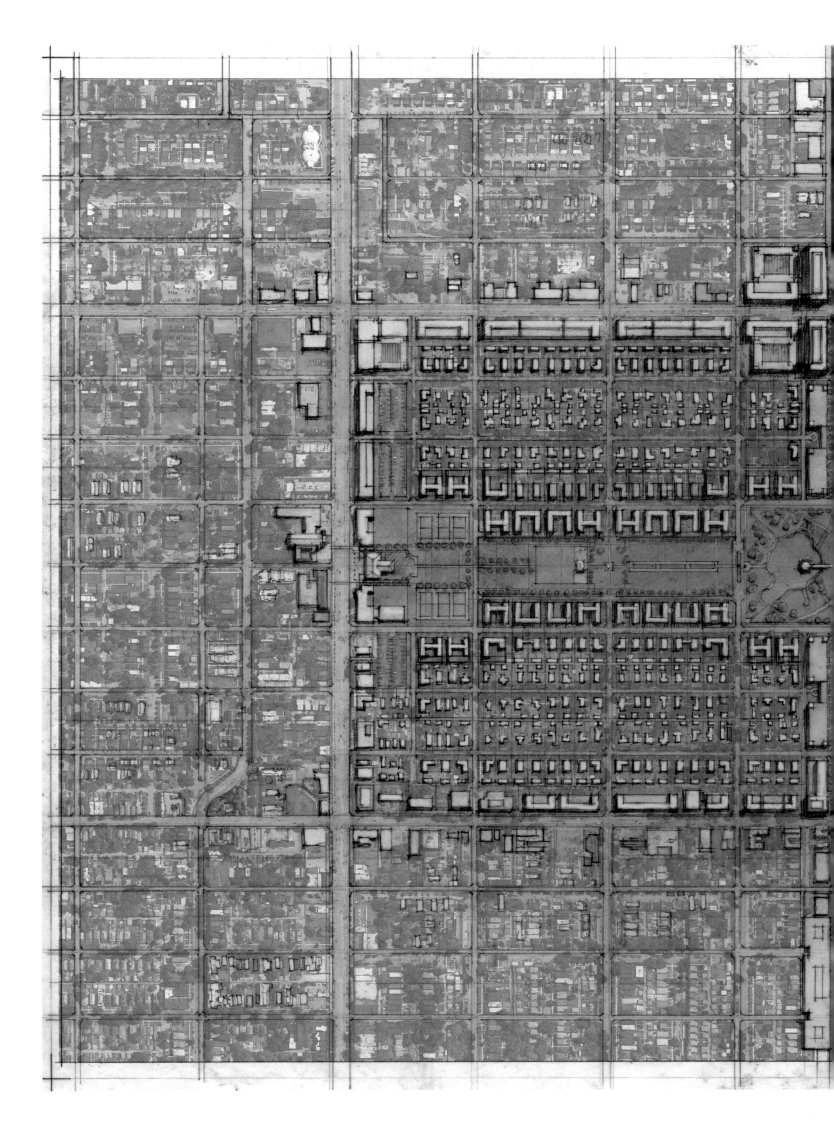

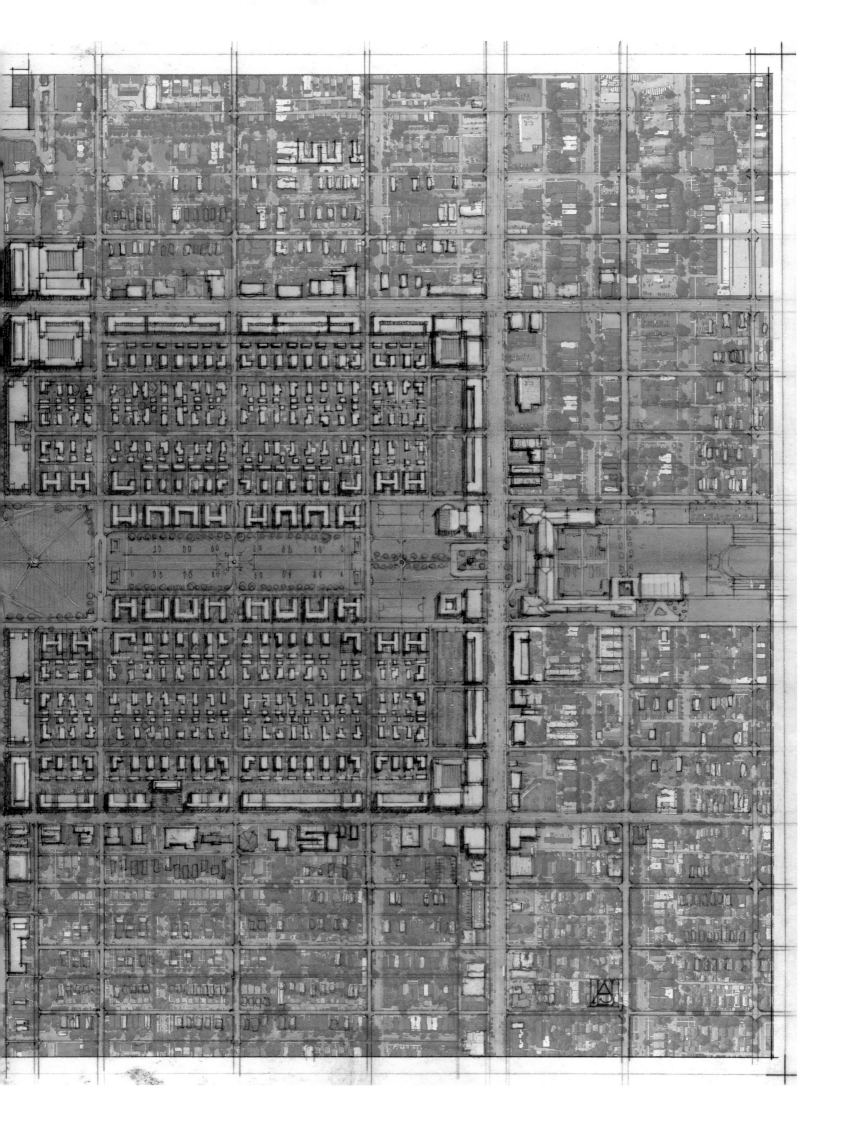

can also incorporate the current model of public housing, which eschews an identifiably institutional appearance in favor of closer integration with the surrounding community. As a physically continuous, medium-density urban environment, the intermediate fabric is capable of housing a diverse and integrated population while preserving the subtle but clear boundaries that define distinct neighborhoods.

RULES FOR ARRANGING AND RELATING BUILDINGS

Building codes reinforce a building's role in the quarter-section plan by establishing an appropriate relationship between the structure and the street. Where buildings insulate and protect, they are built out to their property lines, which establishes a unified public environment on major streets. This can be further reinforced by structured parking built behind street-level program. Buildings for parking and commerce can also support other functions above their parking decks. While buildings conform to the property boundaries at street level, they can be manipulated at upper floors to maximize their residents' exposure to direct sunlight or raised open space, which might include balconies or landscaped roof surfaces.[19]

In keeping with established practice, single-family homes and two- and three-flat dwellings follow conventional setbacks that allow them to receive light on all four sides. Courtyard apartment buildings along the central park space also adhere to established types, and are partially built out to lot lines to define and reinforce park and street boundaries. Enlisting established building types and densities allows improvements to be integrated into the existing fabric with minimal disruption.

Specific rules for relating these building types to one another reiterate larger urban relationships. In general, these relationships are considered in three dimensions, with vertical adjacencies equally as important as horizontal ones. The quarter section has two primary public spaces: the half-mile street and the interior park. Its public program is adjacent to and on the same level as these. Retail buildings front on the more-intensive public space of the half-mile street, where foot traffic and local or through vehicular traffic optimize their exposure to potential customers. The half-mile street sometimes expands to include public plazas or covered arcades at major transportation connections. Housing faces other housing, and where combined with different uses, it occupies floors above street level. Form-based coding has emerged in recent decades as a strategy for promoting the variety of scale and use and public engagement associated with traditional urbanism through the prescription of appropriate building envelopes, program distribution, relationship of buildings to streets, and traditional building

elements such as front porches, punched window openings, and roof profiles. Form-based coding can be incorporated into this planning model, which, however, focuses on the use and location of buildings with regard to streets and open space, rather than on their specific architectural character, to achieve compatible goals, which are appropriate for the urban pattern of the fabric.

No prescribed architectural expression for this model is suggested here. The symmetrical distribution of elements on the site is derived from original Prairie-school proposals, which elaborated the grid's existing character of regular emphasis. The model's diagrammatic symmetry provides a clear and legible point of departure for the incorporation of local asymmetries, the relocation of central elements, and the accommodation of existing or desired deformations or other design languages as circumstances call for them. Thus, this plan avoids a common problem encountered by earlier proposals, which were often strongly identified with a privileged architectural expression that was either embraced or, more often, rejected as inflexible and undemocratic.

IMPLEMENTING A NEW FABRIC

Earlier planning models for the fabric were not implemented because they rejected the methods and objectives of the private real-estate speculator. The opportunity to build high-density, mixed-use buildings along improved lines of transportation and new public park space constitutes a major inducement for private development in this proposal. The public sector's participation can theoretically be limited to improving the transportation network, originating and enforcing new zoning guidelines, and erecting public buildings. The opportunity to develop high-density housing along park edges can be tied to an obligation to build or finance the construction of a portion of the adjacent park. Redevelopment of half-mile streets need not require any special site preparation or alteration, though it might include guidelines for planting, paving, lighting, or other enhancements. Indeed, responsibilities can be realistically divided between the public and private sectors at any point. The public sector might clear the required blocks or build park infrastructure over the interstate, for example; or the private sector might erect a public building in exchange for the right to build along the central park space. The quarter section's ability to be divided into a boundary and an interior, and thence into smaller building lots, can promote public and private partnership and private speculation on a range of scales.

A plan that takes the pattern and components of the existing fabric as a point of departure can, like its precedents, be implemented partially or gradually. Deployment of familiar building types and densities ensures that implementation will not disrupt existing activity or character. Variations based on this model might include larger divisions of the half-mile grid, smaller park spaces, modified bridge elements, or any combination of these. The center of the quarter section might be improved while its boundaries are left untouched, or vice versa. Adjustments to accomodate changes in the prevailing orientation of blocks represent another possible variation. The blocks along the Eisenhower Expressway, for example, run primarily east-west (FIGURE 10.4).[20]

Quarter-section improvement should commence where it is most likely to attract speculative development. A unit such as the one proposed here can be placed at an existing transit stop, where current community needs and desires invite a shared open space or where conditions suggest a greater density of development. Along the Eisenhower Expressway, the areas around the Illinois Medical District and Oak Park are considerably more stable and affluent than the five-mile stretch of fabric between them and might therefore better attract private development. Alternately, larger parcels of blighted and sparsely populated fabric can provide opportunities for large-scale community improvement with less disruption of existing in-place fabric. Suburban residents at the western end of the city may prefer the expressway as an impenetrable barrier, which separates them from neighborhoods occupied by lower socioeconomic groups; Oak Park may not want to be reconnected to Austin or Berwyn. On the other hand, Columbus Park, renovated in 1992, presents a point of departure for improving the surrounding fabric while leaving existing neighborhood boundaries intact. At the eastern end of the expressway, institutions that have already invested in urban renewal, such as the Illinois Medical District and the University of Illinois at Chicago, still have a vested interest in improving their immediate surroundings. The prospect of a coordinated program of implementation and other incentives might further encourage them to partner with private interests.

The fact that the suburbs of the automobile era have replaced the original periphery as the source for a dominant pattern of new residential settlement should not blind us to the promise of a well-balanced urban environment that is the fabric's main advantage over both the urban core and the periphery. Suburban residents exchanged convenient public program and transportation options for larger private lots with better access to a natural landscape. Those seeking the former are better served by the fabric, and a growing population of unmarried service-sector employees and professionals in the northern fabric indicates that there is a viable market for such a lifestyle in Chicago.[21] The city's economic growth and prosperity will continue to rely on attracting these types of residents, as well as providing stable neighborhoods and better access to public amenities to those of lesser means. Even in its current state, the fabric presents a ready system for accommodating a range of activities at the higher density that could be most profitable for the City of Chicago and private developers. A coordinated approach to planning the fabric can evenly and fairly distribute public program and community and open-space amenities, and reinforce existing transportation and service infrastructure, while providing for its future enhancement and expansion. Where conditions suffer from the unresolved intrusion of expressways, such an approach can incorporate measures to correct these disruptions. The enhancement of underdeveloped transit corridors additionally suggests the foundation for the further coordination of regional systems of infrastructure, including water supply and drainage systems, as well as emerging ecological infrastructure. By providing a flexible model for implementation, the quarter-section plan allows for a tremendous amount of variation while ensuring a more-coherent overall fabric. As such, it represents a mid-scale manifestation of the objectives of a coherent metropolitan plan (FIGURE 10.7).

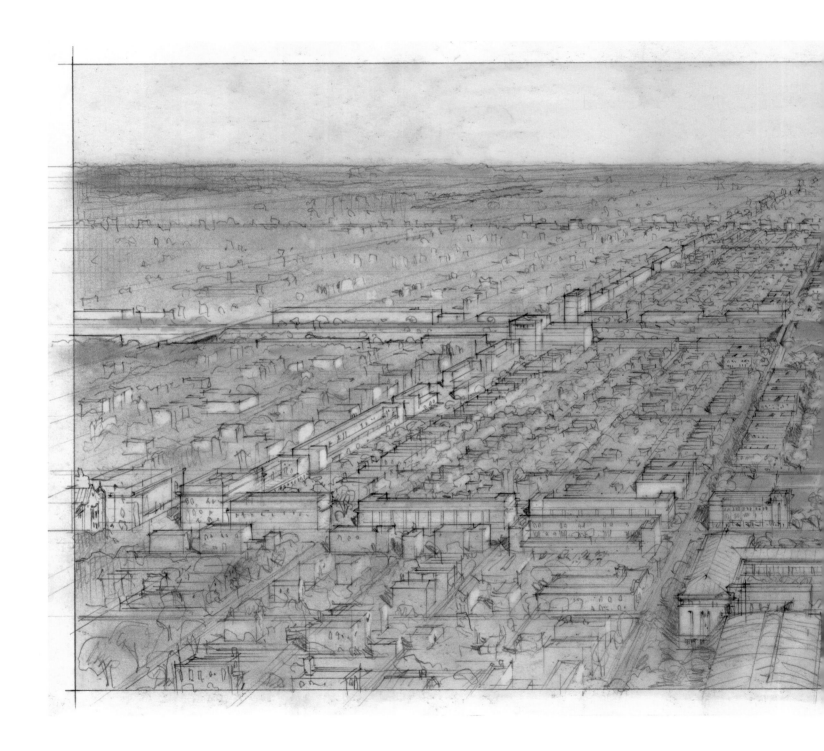

Figure 10.7 Perspective view of two adjoining typical quarter sections by Aric Lasher, 2009.

CHAPTER 11

PLANNING THE PERIPHERY

THE CHARACTER OF THE PERIPHERY AND ITS CURRENT STATE
THE GOALS OF PERIPHERAL EXPANSION AND THE POINTS OF DEPARTURE
FOR A PERIPHERAL PLANNING MODEL · A PERIPHERAL PLANNING MODEL
DESCRIBED · RULES OF ARRANGEMENT · IMPLEMENTATION

―

THE CHARACTER OF THE PERIPHERY AND ITS CURRENT STATE

Chicago has possessed an open and theoretically limitless periphery since its founding. In practice, the limits of the periphery have been fixed only by those of transportation connections. Indeed, the automobile has brought an area extending to thirteen counties in three states within easy commuting distance of Chicago.[1] Given the convenience of its transportation connections, the periphery's larger home lots, lower taxes, and equal accessibility to town and country exercise a persistent appeal. The periphery will likely continue to attract residents who seek an alternative to the denser, primarily man-made environment of the city.[2]

Chicago's current peripheral pattern shares with its predecessor—what has become the city's intermediate fabric—a dependence on transportation networks, a composition of semi-autonomous cells arranged in a grid, and a basic separation of building types by use. As in the fabric, a network of streets separates through traffic from local traffic, and more-intensive uses from less-intensive ones. A network of expressways has succeeded and mostly replaced the older railroad network as a conveyor of passenger and freight traffic. Like its predecessor, this network conforms to the overall radial pattern of the metropolitan area, and its spokes attract easily accessible concentrations of retail and office space, particularly near their intersections with other expressways. These major freight arteries also attract the light industry that is serviced by interstate trucking; light industry serviced by rail continues to cling to the lines of a peripheral railroad network that occasionally intersects or parallels the expressways. Smaller through-traffic circulation routes, which follow the regular demarcations of the surveyor's grid, though at larger intervals than in the fabric, are the peripheral analogues of the half-mile streets. They connect the expressways with the towns and neighborhoods of the periphery, which they divide and arrange into a matrix of cells with little relation to one another. Some of these cells contain railroad suburbs that were planned on the grid. Many include automobile suburbs, however, with curving street plans that recall Riverside. All are comprised primarily of single-family homes. Such cells occupy most of the periphery and house the majority of its population. They ensure that, despite changes in zoning that have made the periphery more self-sufficient, it retains a mostly residential character, like its predecessor.

A pattern of settlement that evolved from the automobile-based transportation network naturally reflects the particular character and requirements of the automobile. These have produced a periphery with a larger scale and a wider extent than the fabric. The current periphery is also physically less continuous, legally more private, and politically and functionally more autonomous than its predecessor.

Theoretically, the scale and diffusion of automobile-based settlement foster the constant contact with the natural landscape that, along with lower per-capita land costs, is the periphery's major attraction. Landscape elements can fill the interstices of the circulation web at every scale, separating zones of different use from one another, and buildings from routes of circulation. Placing buildings in the center of large lots, isolated from other buildings and tethered to the circulation network by slender service roads, is the primary strategy for maximizing individual exposure to the natural landscape for both residential and commercial use (FIGURES 11.2 and 11.3). The automobile promotes this strategy at both the large scale of shopping malls and office parks and the small scale of individual homes. The automobile also aggravates the resulting physical discontinuity

Figure 11.2 Site plan of McDonald's Corporate Campus by Lohan Associates, 1979.

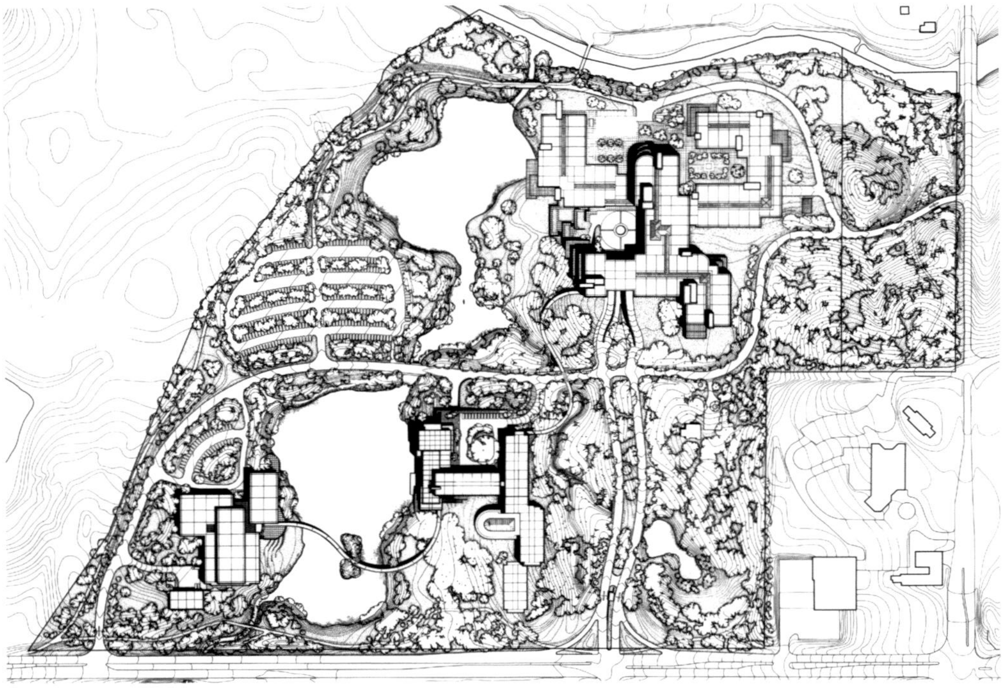

of zones and buildings. At a large scale, through-traffic circulation routes isolate the interstices of the peripheral grid by inhibiting movement between them. At a smaller scale, the demands of parking isolate commercial and residential buildings on their lots but also insulate them from the adjacent through-circulation routes.

The physical isolation of its buildings and the individual nature of automobile travel determine the private character of the periphery, though it does not lack public space. Both streets and the landscaping along them technically belong to the public; however, the former are experienced privately by individual drivers moving at high speeds, and the latter serve only to insulate the noisome effects of through circulation. The commercial buildings along the secondary through streets may, like their predecessors on the half-mile streets of the fabric, draw users from the residential areas on either side, but their physical remoteness and the constant mediation of the automobile prevent them from serving a public purpose. The periphery does harbor plenty of privately owned public space, which either lures potential customers to adjacent shopping or is restricted to certain users; much of the peripheral natural landscape falls into this latter category. The remainder, apart from the margins of circulation and the small municipal parks that emphasize active recreation, has been preserved in contiguous tracts that are the successors to earlier peripheral parks and represent the periphery's only truly public spaces.

Compared with the earlier parks, the Cook County Forest Preserve offers more opportunities for passive recreation and fewer for active recreation. Public space on the periphery focuses on an individual experience of the natural landscape rather than on collective recreational activities.

The automobile has also supplied the periphery with a greater political and functional autonomy than the fabric. New and existing settlements have preserved the political independence that allows their residents to avoid paying the taxes that support city-wide services. The physical remoteness of much of the periphery from the central city, and its ability to harbor different activities in relative isolation, have produced concentrated nodes of office, hotel, and retail space at some major expressway intersections. The commercial program of these peripheral nodes, the presence of tall buildings and thus particularly valuable real estate, and their functional interdependence with the surrounding residential zones recall the central city, but their physically isolated buildings and privatized public space identify them as elements specific to the peripheral pattern of settlement.

Though theoretically the automobile-based pattern of peripheral settlement can incorporate more of the natural landscape than its rail-based predecessor, the actual circumstances of peripheral expansion have prevented it from doing so. The surveyor's grid precludes an experience of the landscape as an unbounded continuum by dividing it into discrete parcels that

Figure 11.3 Site plan of Farnsworth House by Ludwig Mies van der Rohe, 1951.

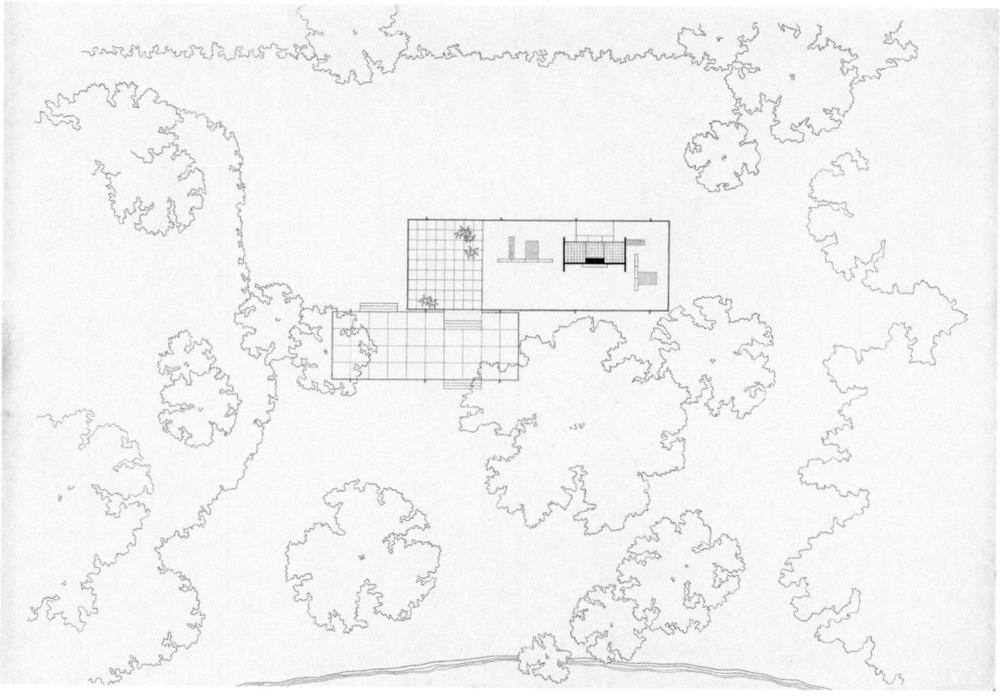

Figure 11.3

developers have a financial incentive to develop with the maximum density, and thus the minimum natural exposure, that the market will bear. In this context, they have little incentive to consider either their own parcel's larger context or the periphery's collective requirements for access to the natural landscape. As on the earlier periphery, natural public space is gradually pushed away from already-settled areas, while the promise of an unspoiled continuum continues to lure new arrivals. This process gradually transforms the peripheral landscape into a fabric that is both more extensive and less cohesive than its predecessor (FIGURES 11.4 and 11.5).

The increase in population that attends this creation of a new peripheral fabric compromises the efficiency of the network of expressways on which peripheral settlement relies. Newer residential settlements in the interstices of this radial system are more remote from these arteries than their predecessors, and the secondary routes of through traffic that connect them can therefore become congested as well.

The flaws in the established peripheral pattern have never prevented peripheral expansion, however, and the traditional seeds of further expansion are already in place in Chicago. A natural landscape, existing transportation connections, and new transportation facilities promise less congestion, more autonomy, and more natural exposure beyond the existing periphery. Two elements of a continental, intermodal freight-distribution network, which can seed an autonomous peripheral

economy, are already in place along the anticipated path of Chicago's westward peripheral expansion. In 2003 the Union Pacific Railroad opened the Rockford Global III Intermodal Terminal outside of Rochelle, Illinois, at the intersection of Interstates 88 and 39; and Chicago Rockford International Airport, a major hub for United Parcel Service, is located twenty-five miles north of this intersection, on Interstate 39, outside of Rockford, Illinois. The warehouses and distribution centers on which the intermodal freight network relies seek, like their predecessors in heavy industry, cheap peripheral land along transportation routes. The enclosure of the existing periphery and the lure of inexpensive, strategically located land beyond it will likely initiate the first steps of a peripheral expansion that will be relatively independent of the growth of Chicago itself.

THE GOALS OF PERIPHERAL EXPANSION AND THE POINTS OF DEPARTURE FOR A PERIPHERAL PLANNING MODEL

Further peripheral expansion should avoid the congestion and cellular isolation of the current periphery, while providing more-consistent access to the natural landscape, not just on the periphery's leading edge but also wherever settlement follows the peripheral pattern. More specifically, a peripheral pattern that is more consistently engaged with the natural landscape

Figure 11.4 View looking east along Interstate 88/Route 59, near Naperville, 1989.

Figure 11.4

should arrest the process of enclosure that currently sacrifices this landscape parcel by parcel; this change will require the development of some kind of continuous public space.

An improved peripheral pattern should, however, reinforce both the periphery's emerging autonomy and the existing practice of dividing and developing individual sections of the surveyor's grid. It should accommodate a full range of uses—including housing, commerce, and industry—across a range of densities. The continuous natural landscape these inhabit should not hamper the circumferential circulation that allows through traffic to bypass Chicago or travel between different parts of the periphery.

The continuous linear development model proposed by Hilberseimer can expand the periphery along existing expressways without consuming the natural landscape. While maintaining the regular divisions and cellular arrangement of the peripheral grid, Hilberseimer turned the typical process by which it divided land into bounded parcels inside out. Houses did not occupy the interiors of blocks but rather the exteriors of closed-end street networks projecting into a continuous natural landscape. On one side, these houses were served by vehicular streets; on the other, they opened onto landscaped paths, along which residents could walk to work or school. Residential streets shared a single common connection to the expressway, which also passed through a local commercial zone. Settlement units were relatively isolated from one another

but, in their range of uses and their balance of public and private space, highly integrated within themselves. They retained the clear definition and interchangeable character that made the traditional sections and quarter sections of the surveyor's grid appealing to speculative developers.

Hilberseimer's planning model reflected his interest in a universal settlement pattern ultimately based on social concerns for maximum and equivalent exposure to light and air for every resident. A uniform low density was central to those concerns, and thus his model did not incorporate the more-intensive uses also found on the current periphery. Hilberseimer's plan is indelibly associated with a modern architectural vocabulary that is not typical of peripheral residential development. Adjusting it to accommodate high-density as well as low-density land use, and removing any constraints related to architectural expression, will eliminate the major practical impediments to adapting this model to Chicago's expanding periphery.

A PERIPHERAL PLANNING MODEL DESCRIBED

An intensively developed transit corridor along the existing expressway, a typical neighborhood unit along a perpendicular "branch," and a continuous natural landscape accessible to all building users are the primary elements of the proposed planning model. The major through-circulation conduit, recognizable as

Figure 11.5 View looking east along Interstate 88/Route 59, near Naperville, 2007.

Figure 11.5

a stretch of expressway, functions as an inverse boulevard, a circulation route that carries buildings through a natural landscape rather than landscape elements through built surroundings. Such a boulevard gathers automobile and local and regional rail traffic along a common path, which confines the more-intensive activities of the periphery to the routes of concentrated through circulation on which they depend. Within this clearly bounded zone, intensive multi-tenant residential and commercial development, structured parking for local drivers using mass transit, and facilities for light industry can develop according to the traditional rules of the peripheral grid, with through streets separating incompatible uses and pedestrian circulation largely internalized within individually planned, self-contained parcels. Such zones are concentrated along one-mile-long, hairpin-shaped nodes with expressway exits at each end.[3] These occur at approximately three-mile intervals, a distance that can be modified as necessary but which, as shown, supports the proposed elements in an efficient arrangement (FIGURES 11.6 and 11.7).[4]

The perpendicular branches of independent neighborhoods extend in opposite directions from either end of these elongated nodes. A half-mile-wide greenbelt separates the clusters of single-family homes in these neighborhoods from the transit corridor. Within this belt, medium-density, low-rise residential clusters and the local stores, churches, and civic buildings used by neighborhood residents are situated along the secondary through streets. The neighborhoods themselves can be modified for greater or lesser density or a more picturesque organization. Self-contained, planned housing units can also be placed at the ends of secondary through streets, within the greenbelt on the opposite side of the transit corridor. Taller apartment buildings in this location can provide neighborhoods with an identifiable marker and their residents with a view over the natural landscape. These locations can alternately accommodate hotel or office program in mid-rise or high-rise buildings of similar scale and density.

A continuous natural landscape—accessible through a network of paths between residential streets that are in turn joined to a common greenbelt between neighborhoods—is the primary bond between adjacent neighborhoods and adjacent streets within each neighborhood cluster. A continuous watercourse within these greenbelts suggests a location and means for comprehensive watershed management, a shared amenity, and an alternative pedestrian or bicycle connection to streets and paths. Schools and recreational facilities placed within this natural landscape join adjacent neighborhoods through common use.

RULES OF ARRANGEMENT

Neither the periphery's diffuse physical character nor its history of privately financed implementation favors an overarching or specific mode of architectural expression. The periphery can equally well accommodate corporate modernism, postmodern or debased examples of vaguely historical styles of building, clusters of "Mediterranean" villas, or landscaped and walled enclaves whose only visible features are house rooftops and shrubbery. The vast scale and overall low density of the proposed peripheral model, the pervasive presence of the natural landscape, and the confinement of large-scale buildings to the transit corridor render the general impact of any architectural "statement" relatively insignificant.

This planning model can sustain a high degree of deformation without losing its essential coherence. It can be altered to accommodate specific functional requirements, existing landscape features, or existing settlement patterns. A cluster of residential development could, for example, take the form of a programmatically diverse and architecturally compact village based on models promoted by the New Urbanists. Similarly, the function, density, and size of the cluster could be modified to accommodate an office park or enclave of larger properties, provided that the ensemble was enclosed by the contiguous open space that defines the typical cluster and that it engaged the transit corridor by the specified means. The flexibility and scale of the peripheral planning model and the wide margins around the transit corridor can also incorporate the shifting and sometimes-undulating path of the expressway. Secondary roads between neighborhood clusters, or, at a larger scale, transportation connections between peripheral spokes, might even impose a large-scale grid, provided these are crossed by pathways of public open space.

IMPLEMENTATION

Because the seeds for further peripheral growth are already in place, an improved planning model should be undertaken where this growth is most likely to occur and in the order that development is most likely to proceed. The current and established presence of this model's individual elements in the existing periphery, combined with its overall low density and the relative autonomy of its parts, suggests that improvement might also be undertaken there on a less-systematic basis. Unlike improvements to the typical fabric, this will involve clarification of existing conditions rather than repairs to a damaged pattern. The implementation of this order will satisfy what appears to be a historically persistent impulse for peripheral expansion, while preserving the essential characteristics of

a continuous open landscape. This model will additionally reframe the relationship between peripheral development and the larger metropolitan area by incorporating an efficient and robust intermodal transportation system that can mitigate the dependency on the personal automobile that currently characterizes the suburban or exurban lifestyle.

A relatively large scale and a wide range of uses within each basic planning module constitute the major impediments to implementing this model on undeveloped land. Pullman, Illinois, and Gary, Indiana, offer clear precedents for autonomous industrial towns with similarly complete programs. The owners of intermodal transit terminals, railroads, or regional transit authorities may find it in their best interests to attract related industrial, residential, and commercial development based on such a model. The location of sizeable commercial, research, or industrial facilities on adjacent land would also encourage the establishment of such community units.

Responsibility for implementing this planning model can be logically divided among multiple entities at multiple scales. The development of a pair of neighborhood units might be initiated by the federal or state and local governments, which would make necessary improvements to infrastructure and build new streets; an industrial developer would build within the transit corridor; and a residential developer would be responsible either for an entire neighborhood unit or for a section thereof. This tripartite division also suggests a logical sequence of development, in which the residential development that follows transportation improvements and new commercial and industrial facilities would encourage additional programmatic diversity.

Through its various historical iterations, the periphery has provided an alternative model to the compact city for the assignment and experience of settled land, one that continues to offer to many a compelling promise of coexistence with the natural landscape. The benefits of this landscape are compromised, however, by the uncoordinated patterns of development that continue to shape peripheral expansion. A model that addresses the unintended consequences of suburban settlement can suggest a direction that would allow continued peripheral growth while preserving the integrity and characteristics of the landscape that are its principal component and attraction (FIGURE 11.8).

Figure 11.6 Diagram showing the proposed arrangement of buildings, streets, and open space in the peripheral expansion model by Aric Lasher, 2009.

Overleaf:
Figure 11.7 Plan of the proposed peripheral expansion model by Aric Lasher, 2009.

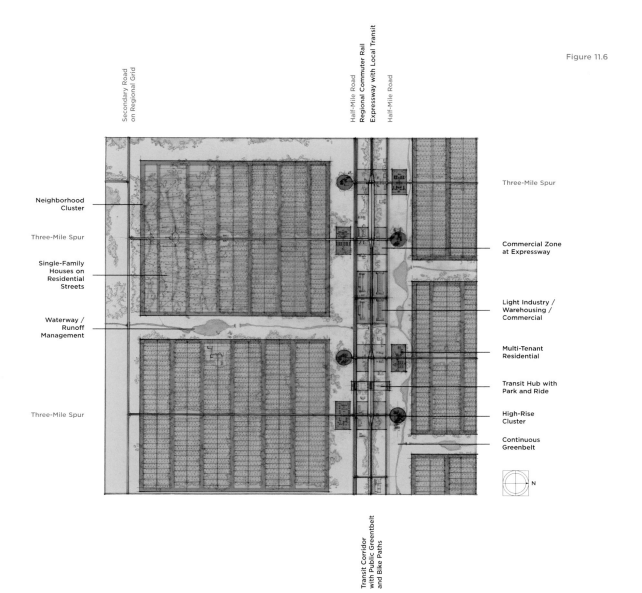

Figure 11.6

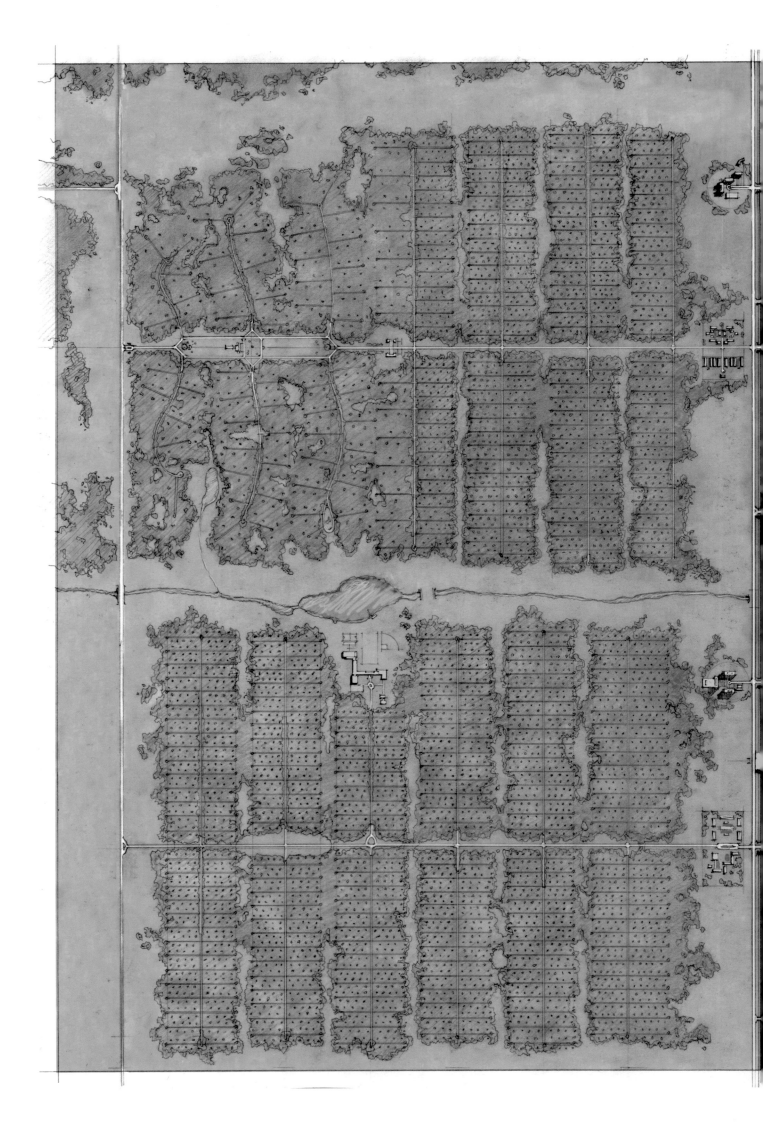

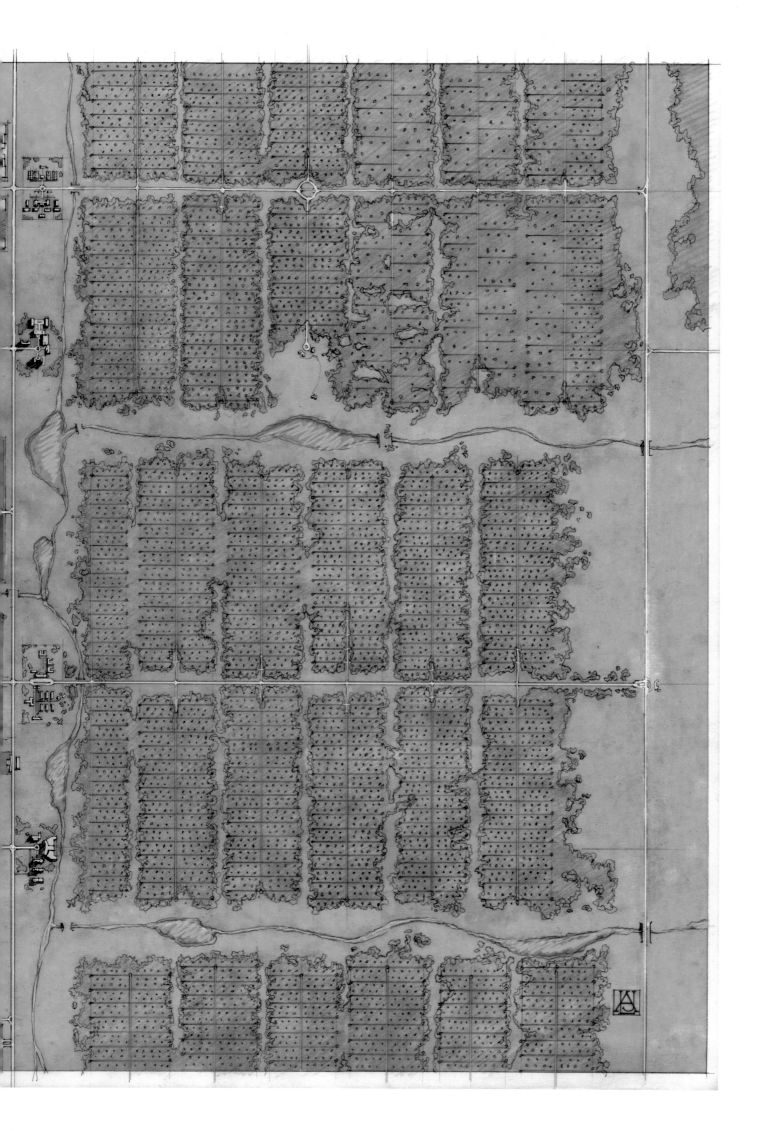

Figure 11.8 View looking to the west of the proposed peripheral expansion model by Aric Lasher, 2009.

CHAPTER 12

IMPLEMENTING AN IMPLICIT PLAN

THE PROBLEM OF IMPLEMENTATION · IMPLEMENTING THE
PLAN OF CHICAGO · BUILDING HAUSSMANN'S PARIS · BUILDING
BATTERY PARK CITY · IMPLEMENTING A NEW PLAN

THE PROBLEM OF IMPLEMENTATION

The partnership between public and private interests is a persistent feature of urban development in Chicago. It can be discerned in the city's original program of settlement, in which sections of the surveyor's grid, established by the federal government, were deeded, sold, and gradually settled through a process of speculative development. The partnership is also evident in the subsequent creation of a metropolitan park system as a spur to private investment on the periphery. The *Plan of Chicago* tied public and private interests together in the service of a specific vision of unprecedented scope. These interests are in fact represented in most urban improvements because the public and private spheres intersect most palpably in the city. Owing to the complex relationship between public and private interests, the varied scope of possible urban improvements, and the laws to which these improvements are subject depending on their location, there are virtually as many paths to implementation as there are proposals. The formulation of a specific path for the plan proposed here is the proper concern of those policy makers and private developers who choose to enact it and is therefore beyond the scope of this book.

This chapter will supply these potential participants with a few useful points of departure. It will identify possible forms that a partnership between public and private interests can take, as well as obstacles to their coordination through a comparative analysis of three historical precedents: Burnham and Bennett's proposal to implement the *Plan of Chicago* through existing public and private channels and relationships; the nineteenth-century reconfiguration of Paris, which utilized private speculation to implement urban improvements dictated by a centralized authority; and the creation of Battery Park City in New York according to a plan with a clear division of public and private responsibility that could be gradually implemented through established methods of speculative development.

IMPLEMENTING THE *PLAN OF CHICAGO*

The scope of Burnham and Bennett's plan presented tremendous obstacles to its successful implementation. Full realization demanded enormous sums from public and private sources. The introduction of new roads, transportation networks, industrial infrastructure, and shoreline improvements required logistical strategies that would avoid disrupting daily activity in an expanding metropolis. The political consensus needed to gain public financing for a comprehensive plan seemed all but impossible to secure, as the state legislature limited the amount of such financing available through established public channels.

Burnham and Bennett nevertheless proposed to implement the *Plan of Chicago* through existing public and private sources. They divided the responsibility for realizing its four central components—parks, transportation and street systems, and the Civic Center—between the public sphere and the consolidated private interest of the railroads. The planners expected the railroads to institute the rail loops of a more-efficient transportation system, as well as a portion of the proposed rapid-transit system, solely on the basis of their collective long-term commercial interests; these components of the plan were therefore removed from further financing considerations, which focused on the park and street systems, the Civic Center, and the portion of the transit system for which the public was responsible. In implementing these, the public would ultimately be acting in its own economic self-interest, for the future increase in revenue, both from visitors and taxes derived from higher-value property, would make Chicago a richer and more-beautiful city. Indirectly, and over a long period of time, these public improvements would therefore pay for themselves.[1]

Assuming that the logic of economic self-interest could command public support over a long period of time, Burnham and Bennett proposed that its components be financed and put in place individually through voter-approved bonds, for which lasting public support would be necessary. The planners therefore conceived their scheme as the opening salvo of a campaign of public promotion. In 1911 the Chicago Plan Commission published the *Wacker Manual*, an abridgement of the plan that was eventually introduced into Chicago public schools as an eighth-grade civics textbook.

In retrospect, a plan that depended to a large degree on the collective effect of separate though related proposals seems bound to have suffered from piecemeal implementation, no matter how enthusiastic the initial public support. The *Plan of Chicago*'s gradual progress was ultimately arrested by flagging public enthusiasm and the delaying effects of outside events such as the Great Depression.[2] Two existing legal obstacles, however, also stood in the way of a more-systematic approach to improvement. The Illinois state constitution limited the amount of debt a municipality could incur to five percent of the assessed value of its taxable property, and the time in which this debt could be repaid to twenty years. This debt ceiling helped keep cities solvent but prevented municipal funding of the kind of comprehensive improvement suited to Burnham and Bennett's plan. The state's powers of eminent domain — its primary means of repossessing private land for public improvement — were also limited. The state or its agents (municipalities, for example) could not knowingly condemn more land than was required for improvement and then resell the leftover land at a higher price; the government could not, therefore, finance public improvement through the sale of condemned private land.

These obstacles were the subject of a legal analysis appended to the plan, written by Walter L. Fisher, the legal counsel of the Plan Committee of the Commercial Club.[3] His conclusions on both counts were strictly provisional and, for practical purposes, indeterminate. He proposed that public agencies responsible for a specific improvement might be consolidated and their debt ceiling thereby raised, or that the measure by which the city's total taxable property value was assessed might be altered to raise the real value of the debt ceiling. His proposal regarding the problem of eminent domain was limited to the observation, made after summarizing recent cases in several state courts, that the issue of the public improvement of private land remained an open one. Beyond these tentative conclusions, the *Plan of Chicago* did not offer a new approach to implementation. Indeed, its authors largely staked the prospect of realizing the plan on sustained public enthusiasm and the logic of economic self-interest.

BUILDING HAUSSMANN'S PARIS

Burnham and Bennett did not specifically recommend enlisting private enterprise to realize their program of public improvement. However, such a reciprocal arrangement formed the backbone of the reconfiguration of Paris undertaken by Emperor Napoleon III and his prefect, Baron Haussmann, between the early 1850s and 1870. Paris was the *Plan of Chicago*'s primary model in terms of program, scope, and style, though ironically not in terms of implementation. Like Burnham and Bennett, the emperor and his prefect faced the problem of forging a modern, commercial capital from chaotic existing conditions in an industrial age. Though Paris, unlike Chicago, was a political capital as well, commercial interests were the ultimate source of its growing population, which virtually doubled between 1815 and 1848, and they were the primary authors and beneficiaries of its improvements. The motivation for these improvements is popularly attributed to the emperor's grandiosity and ability as monarch to channel vast resources into a pet project whose surreptitious role was to provide an efficient means of moving troops through the capital.[4] In fact, the emperor considered the improvements to be a vehicle for the well-being of the urban professionals who were his primary constituents and the artisans and tradesmen who depended on them, as well as a means of ameliorating urban poverty.[5] Like the business leaders of Chicago, the emperor and Haussmann sought to endow a public-works program of updated systems of circulation, transportation, sanitation, water supply, port facilities, and open space with the physical monumentality that the status of their city demanded. Though the character of Chicago's existing urban fabric differed markedly from that of Paris, the planners in both cities expressed a similar willingness to sacrifice existing conditions where these could not be enlisted to achieve the desired final effect. Like Napoleon III and Haussmann, Burnham and Bennett sought to create a functional and beautiful urban whole that would increase tax revenue by raising property values and attracting visitors and investment from elsewhere.

The successful reconfiguration of Paris according to these aims was the product of an innovative strategy of implementation that enlisted private capital to build public works. This combined the government's power to condemn private land for public benefit with the capital resources of private development. The limited availability of municipal funds for improvement projects, and the emperor's stipulation that such projects not be financed through additional taxes on the urban middle class, forced Haussmann to design a mechanism for implementation that allowed improvements to pay for themselves.[6]

Figure 12.1 Panoramic view of the place de L'Opéra, Paris, 1909. The public Opéra is on the left, flanked on both sides by private apartment buildings with shops on the ground floor.

Figure 12.1

An existing municipal budget surplus and additional revenue generated by the *octroi* (duties gathered from the importation of all foodstuffs and building materials into Paris) were insufficient in themselves to cover the proposed improvements, whose cost, in equivalent 2009 dollars, amounted to upwards of 500 billion.[7] Instead, Haussmann used these funds to secure private financing, and he contracted with private developers to execute all aspects of improvements planned and awarded by the city. These included the compensation of those whose property had been condemned and the construction of new streets, infrastructure, and buildings; in assuming responsibility for these, private contractors incurred all costs and risk as well. In return, the city promised to reimburse them upon completion for the streets, sewers, sidewalks, plantings, and fixtures that were the public component of this work. For those with adequate resources, the potential profit of building for the city outweighed the risk.

Transactions between the city and contractors were managed by the Caisse de Travaux, a city-administered clearinghouse that, because it dealt with private sources of revenue rather than tax receipts, operated largely without public oversight. The Caisse accepted deposits from lenders and private contractors guaranteeing completion and issued bonds for new projects; these were the primary sources of income for further improvements, and they were supplemented by the sale of building materials from demolished properties and the resale of portions of condemned buildings that remained intact.[8] In this way, private contractors were reimbursed for completed improvements with the deposits for new ones.[9] In accordance with this process, proposed improvements were divided into three successive stages known as *réseaux* (networks). The later *réseaux* resorted to increasingly elaborate financial machinations to compensate for the unforeseen consequences of earlier successes. As the improvements increased in scope, they in turn generated a lucrative secondary market in bonds issued for their completion.[10] Financial arrangements initially made to avoid contractors' defaults on several projects, resulting from contraction of credit markets, became another means of providing funds for the *réseaux* when their scope exceeded the resources of contractors.[11] Under this system, the city declared a project complete prior to commencement so that repayment of the deposited funds could begin immediately. This guarantee ensured that contractors had necessary access to private credit, which in turn was used by the Caisse to initiate new work.[12] The promise of eventual rewards, inspired by the impressive scope and results of the completed work, led to profiteering by owners of condemned properties and aggressive speculation in bonds, contributing to escalating costs and fluctuations in the currency markets. These developments consequently demanded further elasticity in previously accepted lending practices to ensure that unanticipated sums would continue to be made available for remaining phases of work.

An increasingly volatile financial climate was accompanied by rising political costs. The instability of the overheated system eventually caused cracks to appear in Haussmann's financial apparatus, and the scale of the debt that the city needed to service, as well as the irregularities suggested by unorthodox methods, ultimately brought the shadow system under public scrutiny. Political opponents of Haussmann and the emperor attacked the Caisse on grounds that it improperly or illegally committed the city to vast amounts of unauthorized debt.[13] Parochial interests saw no benefit in the embellishment of the capital.[14] Future support for the *réseaux* was all but withdrawn, and Haussmann's tenure as prefect concluded. His downfall occurred as most of the projects he had implemented were nearing completion, and the onset of war with Prussia definitively ended his work, as well as the extraordinary growth and benefits that it had generated.

Figure 12.2 Site plan of Battery Park City by Cooper Eckstut, 1979.

Though certainly a cautionary study in the potential hazards of elaborate debt financing, the improvement of Paris under Haussmann forged an exceptionally successful partnership between public and private interests. Haussmann succeeded in directing private resources toward public improvement on an unprecedented scale with the promise of future profits. In pursuit of those profits, private developers were willing to take on extraordinary risk and provide public streets and infrastructure. The municipal government, for its part, eschewed potentially unpopular direct taxation by incorporating the incentives and efficiencies of the private sector.

The impressive spectacle of these improvements, and the tangible physical and economic effects of projects still under way, inspired greater confidence in the city as a reliable site for investment. The projects attracted residents seeking work and generated public and private revenue and additional investment while freeing the city from the encumbrances of its chaotic, preindustrial past. The final product of a well-coordinated plan of implementation was an equally unified physical environment (FIGURE 12.1). This conferred on Paris an indelible place in the public imagination and consequently ensured a steady source of revenue derived from tourism, which has persisted since the *réseaux* were put in place.

BUILDING BATTERY PARK CITY

Haussmann's improvements amounted to a total urban reconfiguration that was planned and implemented in a relatively short time. In contrast, Battery Park City, a smaller-scale urban extension of lower Manhattan in New York, with an equally inclusive program of infrastructure, buildings, and open space, was planned and built gradually over a similar length of time. This gradual process of implementation, based on a clear division between public and private interests, acknowledged the established character of urban development in the United States.

A largely residential westward extension of lower Manhattan was proposed in 1963 as part of a comprehensive plan for developing the Hudson River waterfront from the southern tip of Manhattan to West 72nd Street. This proposal was further developed in 1966, when Governor Nelson Rockefeller announced plans for a mixed-use community between Battery Park and Chambers Street, to be built on a landfill extension into the Hudson River. This would be jointly financed by public and private interests—the state would be responsible for subsidized housing and public facilities, and private developers would build the office space. The creation and improvement of the site and the project's planning, administration, and debt service were financed by an initial bond

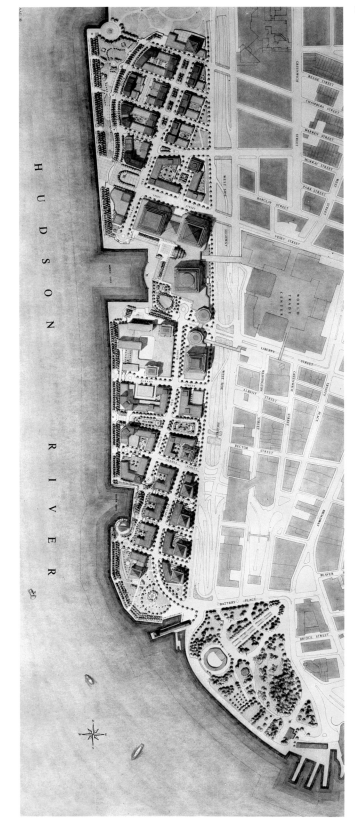

Figure 12.2

issue. As the city became involved, the plan underwent multiple iterations, which collectively undermined its initial focus on subsidized housing. All of these versions shared a characteristically modern configuration, with few streets, large blocks, and a multilayered, intensively developed transportation and service infrastructure. When a fiscal crisis in the state and local governments stalled further development in 1976, only the site was complete.[15]

A new master plan was commissioned by the responsible state development agency in 1979, primarily to avoid a looming default on the initial bonds (FIGURE 12.2).[16] Timely development was therefore of the utmost importance. The planners, Cooper and Eckstut, dispensed with the intensive infrastructure that would otherwise have had to be put in place before income-producing buildings could be constructed. They consolidated all proposed office space at the point where the main utility lines entered the site and thereby minimized the cost of new service infrastructure. They extended the existing urban pattern of streets and blocks in lower Manhattan westward across the site, dividing up the proposed consolidated blocks into smaller parcels that could be developed by separate interests in the manner of typical urban streets. The planners thus proposed two methods for implementing their plan: the smaller, primarily residential lots could be developed gradually, while the consolidated commercial lots could be developed at once. The latter occurred when the developer Olympia and York bid successfully to develop the World Financial Center as an integrated complex of four office towers.[17]

Battery Park City was largely completed along the lines indicated in the Cooper and Eckstut plan. It introduced a multiuse program into a district previously dominated by office space and thereby took advantage of existing improvements to transportation infrastructure and expanded and enhanced previously underutilized public amenities such as the waterfront. The neighborhood's gradual development replicated the organic growth of the older city around it and demonstrated how large-scale urban improvements can be integrated with their surroundings over time. These objectives were accomplished by a plan that built on both established urban patterns and methods for implementation.

IMPLEMENTING AN IMPLICIT PLAN

The examples of Chicago, Paris, and Battery Park City suggest a possible approach to implementing the plan proposed in this book. Such an approach could directly incorporate and synthesize relevant aspects of each example, or, through closer examination of each proposal, consider strategies that a strictly conventional course of implementation would leave unexplored.

Whether they cultivated public enthusiasm, encouraged private speculation, or revived established but overlooked development practices, all these plans demonstrated that creative approaches to physical planning and implementation are inseparable. The physical characters of the Paris and New York improvements, for example, are difficult to separate from the procedures that put them in place.[18]

The *Plan of Chicago* provides an example for generating political support through public presentation, which, in the case of Burnham and Bennett, began with the creation of the planning document itself. The plan also offers a framework for addressing the legal structure that must guide the implementation of any large-scale plan in Chicago. Following the plan's adoption, the development of special improvement districts and the formation of public and private partnerships provided means of avoiding the debt limit and the strictures on the use of eminent domain that existed when the plan was drafted. The former was relaxed in 1970 by the Illinois State Legislature, which also allowed Chicago to begin issuing bonds for up to three percent of the assessed value of its property without holding a referendum, and extended the deadline for paying these off to forty years.[19] Recent developments in eminent-domain law have acknowledged the close relationship between public and private interests in the process of urban improvement, though the involvement of private entities in improvement that involves the condemnation of private property remains controversial.[20]

Haussmann's exploitation of this inevitably murky relationship demonstrates both the costs and the benefits of enlisting private capital to build public improvements administered by a central authority. However, an awareness of these costs should not obscure the fact that both interests ultimately benefited immeasurably from this method of implementation. Through it, Haussmann was able to realize his goal of producing a functionally efficient city whose physical beauty laid the foundation for increased public revenue from the residents and visitors it attracted.

The Battery Park City project demonstrates how a similarly comprehensive urban improvement could be implemented in an American city. An implicit plan without a prescribed architectural style was gradually realized through piecemeal expenditures of a limited and manageable scale. This approach successfully incorporated and extended existing infrastructure, familiar building types, and street and block configurations, thereby creating a physical environment that was both distinct from and contiguous with its surroundings. Design guidelines sought to convey this quality at the level of architecture. These specified a common cornice height for visual continuity between buildings, as well as varied rooflines that would establish buildings as individual elements on the skyline.[21]

The plan we have presented here attempts to incorporate and combine some of the characteristics of these precedents. Its related parts can be implemented together or singly. Their common basis in typical existing conditions suggests that they can be gradually integrated with their surroundings. Their proposed introduction along high-volume traffic conduits can accommodate multiple growth scenarios, for in any circumstances, these dedicated channels represent the most efficient means of moving people across large cities. The concentration of population along these heavily trafficked connections will therefore always represent an efficient allocation of resources.

A plan that incorporates both public systems of circulation and open space and private buildings suggests a clear division of responsibility for these components. Interstates can be imagined as partially implemented Parisian boulevards, awaiting the appropriate sleeve of private buildings to integrate them with their surroundings. Public investment in this existing network of federally administered and funded infrastructure can encourage private developers to put these buildings in place. Such an integration may initially be undertaken in those areas where the traumatic introduction of modern-scale infrastructure has most notably compromised the preexisting relations between buildings, streets, and open space. The intermediate fabric, for example — with its parity of private and public, and built and natural space — presents an efficient urban model with a potentially broad appeal, capable of sustaining a range of densities. The present urgent call to address the inadequacies of the transportation network and the emerging consensus regarding the need to reduce energy consumption and harmful emissions suggest the introduction of environmental infrastructure along these corridors as another possible spur to private development.

Such initiatives will advance the development of healthier communities, provide the short-term employment benefits of a large-scale public-works project, and encourage the flow of private capital. In the longer term, they may also advance Chicago's regional interests and perhaps, by introducing a model capable of more-general application, its national interests as well. The revenue that successful development may eventually draw from residents and visitors need not be guessed at, as Paris continues to provide proof of the economic benefit, both public and private, of a unified and integrated physical environment.

CONCLUSION

—

Most American cities share Chicago's grid-based plan and radial arrangement of distinct zones, as well as the historical patterns of development that produced these features. Chicago's geographic character and its transportation-based economy have exaggerated and simplified these spatial and historical patterns, so that the city has developed as a kind of laboratory for plans that proposed to improve on them. Together these plans—beneficiaries of a local tradition of practically minded architectural innovation—comprise a point of departure for investigating the persistent and evolving planning issues that confront the American city more generally.

Our investigation has revealed that planning approaches that proceed from either the periphery or the center are not in themselves adequate to address the complex character of American cities, which developed without the defensive requirements of their preindustrial predecessors, and consequently without their physical limits. The seemingly limitless possibility of peripheral expansion in American cities allowed different uses to seek dedicated zones that could be configured to their individual needs. Commerce concentrated around converging transportation connections. Industry developed farther out along these connections, where inexpensive land was available for expansion. Housing, not needing protection, sought communion with the natural landscape on the urban

periphery. Where such functional zoning was unaffected by geography, the practice produced a circular urban pattern with radial and concentric divisions. The displacement of some functions by others spread outward in waves and thereby reinforced this pattern.

Since organizing a city according to use produced constant movement between zones, the American city depended to a greater extent than its predecessors on internal transportation connections. Advances in transportation technology therefore set the course of the city's physical expansion, and patterns of circulation determined the arrangement of buildings and open space within its various zones. These arrangements were further influenced by advances in building technology, which serviced both the commercial concentration of the central city and the peripheral diffusion appropriate to an arcadian model of housing.

Functionally zoned, physically varied, and extensive in area, American cities developed with two separate but related sets of requirements. Zones of commerce, housing, and industry have distinct needs related to their purposes, but they also share a dependence on metropolitan systems of infrastructure and open space. The servicing of these common needs, along with their functional dependence on one another, binds these physically segregated zones together, abstract connections replacing defensive walls as a supplier of common identity. The American city consequently relies more fully than its forebears on a shared metropolitan idea.

Over time, the traditions of peripheral planning and planning from the center have addressed the functional requirements of distinct zones and their collective desire, both practical and ineffable, for strong connections. A planning approach that fully acknowledges the complex character of the American city should therefore synthesize these two traditions, seeking common ground wherever it can be found and recognizing that the objectives of both planning traditions are valid. Such an approach should take an opportunistic attitude toward history, looking for shared priorities and compatible planning strategies across time as well as space. It should accept the power of technological advancement to shape the specific character of urban development, while understanding the persistent impulses that such advancement serves. At the same time, it should acknowledge that even abstract connections can be made clear through common physical elements, and therefore accord a central role to the physical arrangement of streets, buildings, and open space in the larger enterprise of urban planning.

These attitudes are not always evident in contemporary planning practice, which is beset by anxieties about technological innovation and its effects. Planning discourse appears riven between the wholehearted embrace of such innovation by professionals who are willing to discard earlier urban patterns based on obsolete technology, and a nostalgic desire on the part of their opponents to re-create precisely those patterns, which they imagine to be free of the anomie that they ascribe to the urban pattern produced by current technology. Both attitudes imbue technology with the power to create or destroy urban life, and both assume that the current rampant pace of change is without historical precedent. In this context, history is a record of past events whose products are alternately entirely appropriated and passed over as obsolete, rather than a body of collective experience that is contiguous and relevant to our own.

The record of past events, however, shows that anxiety about the effects of technology is a regular historical occurrence. Such an attitude traditionally prepares the way for coordinated planning. Can such planning be based jointly on the application of historical lessons and the creation of physical connections? This book has suggested that it can be and has thus attempted to make use of those aspects of the *Plan of Chicago* that constitute its primary legacy.

AFTERWORD

STUART COHEN

———

This book has undertaken a reexamination of the impact and continued relevancy of the Burnham and Bennett *Plan of Chicago* on the centennial of its publication. As a part of this reexamination, we must ask why the *Plan of Chicago* was the most memorable of the plans made as a part of the City Beautiful movement. Does the *Plan of Chicago* contain any ideas about the physical characteristics of cities and strategies for planning them that still have value today? At a time when the formulation of a plan for the form and growth of a city seems anachronistic, and control over the development of cities has been ceded to zoning ordinances, we must also ask what purpose is served by the creation of a physical plan.

Many of the features of the Burnham and Bennett plan have been ignored since its publication, including its call for a city center of uniform building height. Burnham thought that this proposal would give scale, cohesion, and character to Chicago's streets, allowing commercial buildings of uniform height to act as a backdrop to civic buildings and public spaces. However, the idea of a uniform height for commercial buildings was ignored because it had no relationship to political reality nor to the desire to build at a high density that resulted from the city's land values and developmental pressures. Likewise, the most important location in the plan, as determined by the formal layout of city streets, was the site of Burnham's domed city hall, which is now occupied by a highway interchange. Despite these conflicts between theory and implementation, the plan was based on a concept of how we understand the importance of and difference between public and private buildings and spaces in our cities, and this idea is still relevant today. Because Burnham and Bennett's proposal was knowingly based on an idea of land acquisition incompatible with the reality of commercial cities, we must reconsider whether its purpose was to act as a literal blueprint for construction. Perhaps it was meant instead to serve as a guiding vision for Chicago, defining the city's relationship to the lake and, as Burnham put it, creating an image of Chicago that would have the "magic to stir men's blood."*

The Burnham and Bennett plan assumed that new ideas and images of cities could be understood and conceptualized by fitting them into a framework of existing knowledge, visualizing a scheme that did not yet exist through an analogy to something that did. Their text examined the physical characteristics of some of the great cities of the world. Paris was the inspiration for the civic spaces in the *Plan of Chicago*. Grant Park was designed to be like the gardens of the Tuileries, stretched out along the edge of the water; and Michigan Avenue was to be Chicago's rue de Rivoli. The value of this kind of visual analogy was that, for anyone who knew Paris, it was possible to envision the center of Chicago transformed into the "Paris of the Midwest." The relationship created between the plan's new elements and the existing city, particularly the proposed waterfront parks and boulevards, was intended to reconfigure Chicago in the manner in which Paris had been reconfigured in the nineteenth century.

Thanks to the brilliant promotion of the *Plan of Chicago* through the Wacker Manual, a public-school civics text that inculcated an entire generation of Chicagoans, the city defines its physical image in terms of its lakefront park system. It was the creation of this shared vision of Chicago—a city with a continuous lakefront park, an outer ring of forest preserves, and neighborhoods connected by landscaped boulevards—that made the *Plan of Chicago* memorable. This suggests that it was the creation of a shared vision that was the real lasting contribution of the *Plan of Chicago* and perhaps the most important contribution that any urban plan can make.

The difficulty of establishing such a shared vision lies in creating a plan at a scale that enables it to organize whole parts of a city, rather than just producing a "cityscape" through the addition of park benches and trees. Because we believe that planning requires predicting the future and that it rarely works to control change, we no longer trust in the relevancy of physical planning and urban design. We do not believe that we can meaningfully plan or design at anything but the smallest scale. Indeed, large-scale designs for cities that were put forward after the 1920s tended to be futuristic, based on unfounded assumptions about how people would live and move in cities in the future. While these modernist plans did create a vision for the city, they also inverted many of the characteristics of traditional urbanism that we identify with the city's physical form.

What were these elements of traditional urbanism that were inverted by modernism, and how did they figure into Burnham and Bennett's ideas about urbanism and their *Plan of Chicago*? With respect to both architecture and urban design, a plan is quite simply a scheme of arrangement. In buildings, architects arrange spaces, structures, and surfaces. In cities they do not design buildings; they design the spatial fabric, which locates buildings and gives shape to the public space we collectively use, occupy, and move through. It is this open space, the most public aspect of cities, that makes them memorable. That Burnham and Bennett understood this is evident in their plan for Grant Park. Open public space in the form of parks is bounded, but may not be defined, by physical edges of buildings or landscaping. In Chicago, Grant Park is edged on the west by the wall of buildings along Michigan Avenue. The importance of this distinct edge is so well recognized that it is doubtful that a design for any new building along Michigan

Avenue that violated this pattern would gain approval. On its east side, the park is bounded by Lake Shore Drive and Lake Michigan. Identifying the edges and boundaries of the park provides a clear understanding of its extent. In addition to parks, other kinds of public open spaces occur in cities, including the space between and around buildings. When this is defined by the faces of buildings, it, rather than the individual buildings, becomes the focus of our experience. We understand that we are in a space that is like an outdoor room, intentionally created for a ceremonial, recreational, or commercial purpose.

The open public space that is the most omnipresent in cities is the street. Where streets are memorable, they tend to have spatial definition and other physical characteristics that come to be associated with them, such as their paving materials, their landscaping, or the specific architectural character of their buildings. The space of the street is formed by the buildings that define its edges. Streets that are spatially defined seem to be memorable in ways that streets that are only paved paths are not. Streets are the primary location of both commerce and social interchange in cities. While they may no longer work as efficient carriers of mechanical transportation, as long as people walk in cities, streets will survive as important urban spaces.

The other most important and memorable spaces in cities are the defined open spaces in front of civic, institutional, or religious buildings—squares and plazas. These spaces are usually enclosed by the surfaces of adjacent buildings. When open public space in a city is visually continuous around a building, the building itself becomes the focus, an object standing in space. In cities built before the twentieth century, freestanding buildings, or buildings with three exposed sides, were usually understood as unique; this condition frequently corresponded to their civic importance. Initially, such freestanding buildings were constructed for religious or government purposes. By the nineteenth century, however, buildings that had this sort of physical prominence within the fabric of the city also included new kinds of public institutions: libraries, museums, opera houses, and other similar structures. Recognizing these buildings as public structures is dependent not only on their architectural expression but also on the fact that they are freestanding.

The significance of freestanding buildings was also based on a hierarchy of civic importance that related to a building's height. In older cities, churches and city halls were the tallest structures. Because they were taller than surrounding buildings, they also became locational landmarks that allowed people to understand and find their way through cities. In secular cities, this height-based prominence has been ceded to competing corporate office buildings. Indeed, when tall buildings become the norm, the identity and importance they try to establish for their respective institutions is lost. The buildings at the centers of modern cities are now so tall that they only have an identity at ground level and perhaps at the scale of the entire city's skyline. Along with the loss of an understood building hierarchy based on height, the contemporary secular commercial city no longer has a hierarchy of location. New public buildings are built on land that is commercially available, rather than land that occupies an important location in the city. The significance of the locations of new civic buildings was an important feature of the *Plan of Chicago*, though it proved impossible to implement.

When twentieth-century architects argued that tall buildings blighted streets by blocking light and air and that they needed to be set further apart, with space between and around them, they were also implicitly arguing for the greater perceived importance of these buildings. Freestanding in space, they represented a new order, replacing older structures that participated in the definition of public spaces. This new order was based on a vision of the "city of tomorrow" conceived by the French architect Le Corbusier and other early-twentieth-century modernists. The best example of the urbanism created by this new city form is demonstrated by the corporate towers and random plazas along Sixth Avenue in New York City, examples of mid-century modern design that produced a no-man's-land by destroying the definition of the street. Le Corbusier's city of towers in a park was also adapted as the model for the United States' post–World War II subsidized housing projects. Models of alienation and social dysfunction, these high-rise buildings eliminated defined public space as a designed urban element.

When architects and urban designers plan a city, or a part of a city, they create a scheme that locates building sites, parks, plazas, and streets. If design is the creation and ordering of spaces and three-dimensional objects, then cities should be designed with a perceptible system of order that will make them understandable and navigable. Nineteenth-century American cities had a strong system of order: the grid. But grid plans are lacking in hierarchy, a characteristic usually provided by the unique location, size, or shape of a building site. The *Plan of Chicago* used two devices to try to create important sites within the existing grid of Chicago streets. The first was the introduction of diagonal streets. Ostensibly employed to improve the flow of traffic, diagonal streets created unique intersections and distinctively shaped building sites as they crossed the streets of the grid. The second device was axial planning, the creation of a straight path with a significant element at either end. This is perhaps the most potent ordering device that can be used to create a logical arrangement of spaces and buildings. From the Renaissance to the nineteenth

century, axial planning was overlaid as a device of clarification for the picturesque chaos of medieval cities, usually to connect important locations or buildings within a city and to improve the movement of traffic. This planning device, one of the design methods of Burnham and Bennett's *Plan of Chicago*, provides for sequences that have a beginning and end, points of focus, and a hierarchy of importance for the elements it organizes. Although the belief in and use of axial planning is far from universal today, the attributes of this design method are elements found in many of the buildings and cities that are collectively admired in Western culture.

Perhaps the greatest value of reexamining the *Plan of Chicago* lies in its ability to remind us that cities are not just aggregates of buildings but rather are fabrics of defined, open public space; that there is a continuing significance to the strategies the *Plan of Chicago* used for organizing these spaces; and that urban design also needs to provide a vision that has the "magic to stir men's blood."

* This was the second half of Burnham's famous exhortation to "make no small plans," as reported by his biographer, Charles W. Moore, who also served as editor of the *Plan of Chicago*.

BIBLIOGRAPHY

Abalos, Iñaki, Juan Herreros, and Joan Ockman. 2003. *Tower and Office: From Modernist Theory to Contemporary Practice.* MIT Press.

Alonso Pereira, José Ramón. 1998. *La ciudad lineal de Madrid.* Fundación Caja de Arquitectos.

Alphand, Adolphe. 1873. *Les promenades de Paris.* Rothschild.

American Association of State Highway and Transportation Officials. 2002. *Transportation: Invest in America: Freight-Rail Bottom Line Report.* American Association of State Highway and Transportation Officials.

Anderson, G. W. 1917. *Atlas of Allamakee County, Iowa.* Anderson Publishing Co.

Anderson Publishing Company. 1917. *Atlas of Allamakee County, Iowa: Containing Maps of Townships of the County, Maps of State, United States and World, Farmers Directory, Analysis of the System of U.S. Land Surveys.* Anderson Pub. Co.

Andreas, Alfred Theodore. 1884–86. *History of Chicago from the Earliest Period to the Present Time.* 3 vols. Alfred Theodore Andreas.

Appelbaum, Stanley. 1980. *The Chicago World's Fair of 1893: A Photographic Record, Photos from the Collections of the Avery Library of Columbia University and the Chicago Historical Society.* Dover Publications.

Arnold, Bion J. 1905. *Report on the Engineering and Operating Features of the Chicago Transportation Problem.* McGraw Pub. Co.

Bach, Ira J. 1973. "A Reconsideration of the 1909 'Plan of Chicago.'" *Chicago History* 2, 3 (Spring-Summer), pp. 132–141.

Bachin, Robin Faith. 2004. *Building the South Side: Urban Space and Civic Culture in Chicago, 1890–1919.* University of Chicago Press.

Banham, Reyner. 1960. *Theory and Design in the First Machine Age.* Praeger Publishers.

Berube, Alan, and Ryan Prince. 2003. *Chicago in Focus: A Profile from Census 2000.* Brookings Institution Center on Urban and Metropolitan Policy/Living Cities, the National Community Development Initiative.

Beveridge, Charles E., Paul Rocheleau, and David Larkin. 1998. *Frederick Law Olmsted: Designing the American Landscape.* Universe.

Blackford, Mansel G. 1993. *The Lost Dream: Businessmen and City Planning on the Pacific Coast, 1890–1920.* Ohio State University Press.

Bluestone, Daniel M. 1991. *Constructing Chicago.* Yale University Press.

Braunfels, Wolfgang. 1988. *Urban Design in Western Europe: Regime and Architecture, 900–1900.* University of Chicago Press.

Brooks, H. Allen. 1983. *Prairie School Architecture: Studies from "The Western Architect."* Van Nostrand Reinhold.

Brooks, H. Allen and Donald D. Walker. 1981. *Writings on Wright: Selected Comment on Frank Lloyd Wright.* MIT Press.

Burke, Marcilynn A. 2006. "Much Ado about Nothing: Kelo v. City of New London, Sweet Home v. Babbitt, and Other Tales from the Supreme Court." *University of Cincinnati Law Review* 75, 2, pp. 663–724.

Burnham, Daniel Hudson, Edward H. Bennett, and Charles Moore. 1909. *Plan of Chicago.* The Commercial Club of Chicago.

Burnham, Daniel Hudson, Edward H. Bennett, and Edward F. O'Day. 1905. *Report on a Plan for San Francisco.* City of San Francisco.

Burnham Library of Architecture. 1979. *The Plan of Chicago, 1909–1979: An Exhibition of the Burnham Library of Architecture, the Art Institute of Chicago, December 8, 1979, through November 30, 1980.* Art Institute of Chicago.

Bushong, William. 1990. *Historic Resource Study: Rock Creek Park, District of Columbia.* United States Department of the Interior, National Park Service.

Cain, Louis P. 1978. *Sanitation Strategy for a Lakefront Metropolis: The Case of Chicago.* Northern Illinois University Press.

Caldwell, Alfred. 1948. *The City in the Landscape: A Preface for Planning.* Alfred Caldwell.

Cassell, Frank A., and Marguerite E. Cassell. 1983. "The White City in Peril: Leadership and the World's Columbian Exposition." *Chicago History* 12, 3, pp. 10–27.

Chicago Central Area Committee. 1983. *Chicago Central Area Plan: A Plan for the Heart of the City.* Chicago Central Area Committee and the City of Chicago.

Chicago Department of City Planning. 1958. *Development Plan for the Central Area of Chicago: A Definitive Text for Use with Graphic Presentation.* Chicago Department of City Planning.

Chicago Department of Planning and Development, Chicago Plan Commission, Chicago Department of Transportation, and Chicago Department of Environment. 2003. *The Chicago Central Area Plan: Preparing the Central City for the 21st Century, Draft Final Report of the Chicago Plan Commission, May 2003.* City of Chicago Department of Planning and Development.

Chicago Historical Society, Chicago Park District, and Morton Arboretum. *Prairie in the City: Naturalism in Chicago's Parks, 1870–1940.* Chicago Historical Society.

Chicago Metropolis 2020. 2004. *The Metropolis Freight Plan: Delivering the Goods.* Chicago Metropolis 2020.

Chicago Plan Commission. 1973. *Chicago 21: A Plan for the Central Area Communities.* Chicago Plan Commission.

City Club of Chicago. 1913. *The Railway Terminal Problem of Chicago: A Series of Addresses before the City Club, June Third to Tenth, 1913, Dealing with the Proposed Re-Organization of the Railway Terminals of Chicago, Including All Terminal Proposals Now before the City Council Committee on Railway Terminals.* City Club of Chicago.

City of Chicago. 2007. *Census Maps.* City of Chicago.

Cohen, Stuart Earl. 1976. *Chicago Architects: Documenting the Exhibition of the Same Name Organized by Laurence Booth, Stuart E. Cohen, Stanley Tigerman, and Benjamin Weese.* Swallow Press.

Collins, George R. 1959. "Linear Planning throughout the World." *The Journal of the Society of Architectural Historians* 18, 3 (Oct.), pp. 74–93.

Commercial Club of Chicago. 1922. *The Merchants Club of Chicago: 1896–1907.* The Commercial Club of Chicago.

Condit, Carl W. 1964. *The Chicago School of Architecture: A History of Commercial and Public Building in the Chicago Area, 1875–1925.* University of Chicago Press.

———. 1973. *Chicago, 1910–29: Building, Planning, and Urban Technology.* University of Chicago Press.

———. 1974. *Chicago, 1930–70: Building, Planning, and Urban Technology.* University of Chicago Press.

Craig, Lois A., and the Federal Architecture Project. 1978. *The Federal Presence: Architecture, Politics, and Symbols in United States Government Building.* MIT Press.

Cronon, William. 1991. *Nature's Metropolis: Chicago and the Great West*. W. W. Norton.

Delano, Frederic Adrian. 1906. *Chicago Railway Terminals: A Suggested Solution for the Chicago Terminal Problem*. R. R. Donnelley and Sons Co.

Dickens, Charles. 1868. *American Notes for General Circulation*. D. Appleton.

Draper, Joan E. 1982. *Edward H. Bennett, Architect and City Planner, 1874–1954*. Art Institute of Chicago.

Evenson, Norma. 1970. *Le Corbusier: The Machine and the Grand Design*. 1969. Repr., G. Braziller.

Fein, Albert. 1972. *Frederick Law Olmsted and the American Environmental Tradition*. G. Braziller.

Fisher, Irving D. 1986. *Frederick Law Olmsted and the City Planning Movement in the United States*. UMI Research Press.

Fishman, Robert. 1977. *Urban Utopias in the Twentieth Century: Ebenezer Howard, Frank Lloyd Wright, and Le Corbusier*. Basic Books.

Florida, Richard. 2009. "How the Crash Will Reshape America." *The Atlantic Monthly* 303, 2 (Mar.), pp. 44–55.

Fogelson, Robert M. 2001. *Downtown: Its Rise and Fall, 1880–1950*. Yale University Press.

Ford, Frederick Luther. 1904. *The Grouping of Public Buildings*. Municipal Art Society (Hartford).

Ford, Henry, and Samuel Crowther. 1922. *My Life and Work*. Doubleday, Page and Co.

Frampton, Kenneth. 1980. *Modern Architecture: A Critical History*. Thames and Hudson, Ltd.

Fuchs, Ester R. 1992. *Mayors and Money: Fiscal Policy in New York and Chicago*. University of Chicago Press.

Garvin, Alexander. 2002. *The American City: What Works, What Doesn't*. 2nd ed. McGraw-Hill.

George A. Fuller Company. 1910. *Prominent Buildings Erected by the George A. Fuller Company*. G. A. Fuller.

Giedion, S. 1967. *Space, Time, and Architecture: The Growth of a New Tradition*. 5th ed. Harvard University Press.

Gordon, David L. A. 1997. *Battery Park City: Politics and Planning on the New York Waterfront*. Gordon and Breach.

Grese, Robert E. 1992. *Jens Jensen: Maker of Natural Parks and Gardens*. Johns Hopkins University Press.

Grossman, James R., Ann Durkin Keating, and Janice L. Reiff. 2004. *The Encyclopedia of Chicago*. University of Chicago Press.

Guiton, Jacques. 1981. *The Ideas of Le Corbusier on Architecture and Urban Planning*. Translated by Margaret Guiton. G. Braziller.

Gutheim, Frederick Albert, and Antoinette J. Lee. 2006. *Worthy of the Nation: Washington, D.C., from L'Enfant to the National Capital Planning Commission*. Johns Hopkins University Press.

Handlin, David P. 1979. *The American Home: Architecture and Society, 1815–1915*. Little, Brown.

Harris, Richard. 1994. "Chicago's Other Suburbs." *Geographical Review* 84, 4 (Oct.), pp. 394–410.

Hegemann, Werner, and Elbert Peets. 1922. *The American Vitruvius: An Architect's Handbook of Civic Art*. Architectural Book Pub. Co.

Hilberseimer, Ludwig. 1944. *The New City; Principles of Planning*. P. Theobald.

———. 1955. *The Nature of Cities; Origin, Growth, and Decline, Pattern and Form, Planning Problems*. P. Theobald.

———. 1963. *Entfaltung einer Planungsidee*. Ullstein.

Hines, Thomas S. 1974. *Burnham of Chicago, Architect and Planner*. Oxford University Press.

———. 1988. "No Little Plans: The Achievement of Daniel Burnham." *Art Institute of Chicago Museum Studies* 13, 2, pp. 96–105.

Hitchcock, Henry Russell. 1944. "Frank Lloyd Wright and the 'Academic Tradition' of the Early Eighteen-Nineties." *Journal of the Warburg and Courtauld Institutes* 7, 1 and 2 (Jan.–June 1944), pp. 46–63.

———. 1973. *In the Nature of Materials, 1887–1941: The Buildings of Frank Lloyd Wright*. 1942. Repr., Da Capo Press.

———. 1977. *Architecture, Nineteenth and Twentieth Centuries*. 4th ed. Penguin Books.

Hitchcock, Henry Russell, and Edgar Kaufmann. 1970. *The Rise of an American Architecture*. Metropolitan Museum of Art/Praeger.

Hoffmann, Donald. 1988. *The Architecture of John Wellborn Root*. 1973. Repr., University of Chicago Press.

Holland, Robert A. 2005. *Chicago in Maps: 1612–2002*. Rizzoli.

Howe, Walter A., and Illinois Division of Waterways. 1956. *Documentary History of the Illinois and Michigan Canal: Legislation, Litigation, and Titles*. Illinois Department of Public Works and Buildings, Division of Waterways.

Hoyt, Homer. 1933. *One Hundred Years of Land Values in Chicago; The Relationship of the Growth of Chicago to the Rise in Its Land Values, 1830–1933*. University of Chicago Press.

Jackson, Kenneth T. 1987. *Crabgrass Frontier: The Suburbanization of the United States*. 2nd ed. Oxford University Press.

Jensen, Jens. 1920. *A Greater West Park System: After the Plans of Jens Jensen*. West Chicago Park Commissioners.

———. 1990. *Siftings*. Johns Hopkins University Press.

Johnson, Donald Leslie. 1990. *Frank Lloyd Wright versus America: The 1930s*. MIT Press.

Johnson, Elmer W. 2001. *Chicago Metropolis 2020: The Chicago Plan for the Twenty-First Century*. University of Chicago Press.

Jordan, David P. 1995. *Transforming Paris: The Life and Labors of Baron Haussmann*. Free Press.

Jordy, William H. 1976. *American Buildings and Their Architects, Volume 3: Progressive and Academic Ideals at the Turn of the Twentieth Century*. Anchor.

———. 1976. *American Buildings and Their Architects, Volume 4: The Impact of European Modernism in the Mid-Twentieth Century*. Anchor.

———. 2005. *"Symbolic Essence" and Other Writings on Modern Architecture and American Culture.* Yale University Press.

Knight, Robert, and Lucius H. Zeuch. 1928. *The Location of the Chicago Portage Route of the Seventeenth Century.* Chicago Historical Society.

Kohler, Sue A., Pamela Scott, and United States Commission of Fine Arts. 2006. *Designing the Nation's Capital: The 1901 Plan for Washington, D.C.* United States Commission of Fine Arts.

Kostof, Spiro. 1992. *The City Assembled: The Elements of Urban Form through History.* Little, Brown.

Kunstler, James Howard. 2001. *The City in Mind: Meditations on the Urban Condition.* Free Press.

Lambert, Phyllis, Ludwig Mies van der Rohe, et al. 2001. *Mies in America.* H. N. Abrams.

Lang, Robert E. 2000. *Office Sprawl: The Evolving Geography of Business.* Brookings Institution, Center on Urban and Metropolitan Policy.

Larkin, Oliver W. 1966. *Art and Life in America.* 1960. Repr., Holt, Rinehart, and Winston.

Leinbach, Thomas R., and Christina Capineri, eds. 2007. *Globalized Freight Transport: Intermodality, E-Commerce, Logistics, and Sustainability.* Edward Elgar Publishing.

Lillibridge, Robert M. 1953. "Pullman: Town Development in the Era of Eclecticism." *The Journal of the Society of Architectural Historians* 12, 3 (Oct.), pp. 17–22.

Linklater, Andro. 2002. *Measuring America: How an Untamed Wilderness Shaped the United States and Fulfilled the Promise of Democracy.* Walter and Co.

Lombardi, Britton, and Martin Lavelle. 2009. "Fresh Water and the Great Lakes Economic Future—A Conference Summary." *Chicago Fed Letter* 259a (Feb.), n.pag.

Macdonald, William L. 1986. *The Architecture of the Roman Empire, Volume 2: An Urban Appraisal.* Yale University Press.

Malagón, Christian E., Timothy P. McInerney, and Sharon D. Panek. 2008. "Gross Domestic Product by Metropolitan Area: Newly Available Statistics for 2006 and Revised Statistics for 2004–2005." *Survey of Current Business Online* 88, 10 (Oct.), pp. 100–32.

Marquette, Jacques, Claude Dablon, and James H. Schultz. 2001. *Father Marquette's Journal.* Michigan Historical Center, Dept. of History, Arts, and Libraries.

Mayer, Harold M., and Richard C. Wade. 1969. *Chicago: Growth of a Metropolis.* University of Chicago Press.

McKim, Mead, and White. 1914–15. *A Monograph of the Work of McKim, Mead & White, 1879–1915.* Architectural Book Pub. Co.

McPhee, John. 2005. "Out in the Sort: UPS and the Art of Moving Everything." *The New Yorker* (Apr. 18), pp. 160–73.

Merriam, William R. 1901. *Twelfth Census of the United States, Taken in the Year 1900.* United States Census Office.

Moore, Charles, ed. 1902. *The Improvement of the Park System of the District of Columbia.* Government Printing Office.

———. 1929. *The Life and Times of Charles Follen McKim.* Houghton Mifflin Company.

Morris, A. E. J. 1979. *History of Urban Form: Before the Industrial Revolutions.* 2nd ed. Wiley.

Mumford, Lewis. 1955. *Sticks and Stones: A Study of American Architecture and Civilization.* 2nd ed. Dover Publications.

———. 1971. *The Brown Decades: A Study of the Arts in America, 1865–1895.* 1931. Repr., Dover Publications.

———. 1986. *The Lewis Mumford Reader,* edited by Donald Miller. Pantheon Books.

Nash, Tom E., and Milton E. Connelly. 1941. *Historical Register of the Twenty-Two Superseded Park Districts.* Works Progress Administration.

Newton, Norman T. 1971. *Design on the Land: The Development of Landscape Architecture.* Belknap Press.

Northeastern Illinois Planning Commission. 2004. *2030 Municipal Forecast Maps.* Northeastern Illinois Planning Commission.

Ochsner, Jeffrey Karl. 1982. *H. H. Richardson, Complete Architectural Works.* MIT Press.

Olmsted and Vaux. 1868. *Preliminary Report upon the Proposed Suburban Village at Riverside, near Chicago.* Sutton, Bowne, and Co.

Olsen, Donald J. 1988. *The City as a Work of Art: London, Paris, Vienna.* 1986. Repr., Yale University Press.

Perkins, Dwight Heald, and John J. Bradley. 1905. *Report of the Special Park Commission to the City Council of Chicago on the Subject of a Metropolitan Park System.* W. J. Hartman.

Perry, Marc J. 2001. *Population Change and Distribution, 1990 to 2000.* United States Department of Commerce, Economics, and Statistics Administration, United States Census Bureau.

Peterson, Jon A. 2003. *The Birth of City Planning in the United States, 1840–1917.* Johns Hopkins University Press.

Phelps, Barton. 1992. "Corridor: The Highspeed Roadway as Generator of New Urban Form." *Architecture California* 14, 2 (Nov.), pp. 54–59.

Pinkney, David H. 1955. "Napoleon III's Transformation of Paris: The Origins and Development of the Idea." *The Journal of Modern History* 27, 2, pp. 125–34.

———. 1957. "Money and Politics in the Rebuilding of Paris, 1860-1870." *The Journal of Economic History* 17, 1 (Mar.), pp. 45–61.

———. 1958. *Napoleon III and the Rebuilding of Paris.* Princeton University Press.

Pommer, Richard, David A. Spaeth, and Kevin Harrington. 1988. *In the Shadow of Mies: Ludwig Hilberseimer, Architect, Educator, and Urban Planner.* Art Institute of Chicago/Rizzoli International Publications.

Pope, Albert. 1996. *Ladders.* Rice School of Architecture/Princeton Architectural Press.

Ranney, Victoria Post. 1972. *Olmsted in Chicago.* Open Lands Project.

Rasmussen, Steen Eiler. 1973. *Towns and Buildings Described in Drawings and Words.* 1969. Repr., MIT Press.

Reps, John William. 1965. *The Making of Urban America: A History of City Planning in the United States.* Princeton University Press.

———. 1980. *Town Planning in Frontier America*. University of Missouri Press.

———. 1983. "Burnham Before Chicago: The Birth of Modern American Urban Planning." *Art Institute of Chicago Museum Studies* 10 (*The Art Institute of Chicago Centennial Lectures*), pp. 190–217.

Roper, Laura Wood. 1973. *FLO: A Biography of Frederick Law Olmsted*. Johns Hopkins University Press.

Roth, Leland M. 1983. *McKim, Mead, and White, Architects*. Harper and Row.

Rowe, Colin. 1995. *The Mathematics of the Ideal Villa, and Other Essays*. MIT Press.

Ruskin, John. 2003. *The Stones of Venice*. Da Capo Press.

Rybczynski, Witold. 1999. *A Clearing in the Distance: Frederick Law Olmsted and America in the Nineteenth Century*. Scribner.

Saalman, Howard. 1971. *Haussmann: Paris Transformed*. G. Braziller.

Schuyler, Montgomery. 1961. *American Architecture and Other Writings*. 2 vols. Belknap Press.

Scully, Vincent Joseph. 1988. *American Architecture and Urbanism*. H. Holt.

Seale, William. 1992. *The White House, the History of an American Idea*. The American Institute of Architects Press.

Sessions, Gordon M. 1971. *Traffic Devices: Historical Aspects Thereof*. Institute of Traffic Engineers.

Sinkevitch, Alice, Laurie McGovern Petersen, et al. 1993. *AIA Guide to Chicago*. Harcourt Brace.

Smith, Carl S. 2006. *The Plan of Chicago: Daniel Burnham and the Remaking of the American City*. University of Chicago Press.

Stamper, John. 1989. "The Galerie des Machines of the 1889 World's Fair." *Technology and Culture* 30, 2, pp. 330–53.

Stern, Robert A. M., Thomas Mellins, and David Fishman. 1995. *New York 1960: Architecture and Urbanism between the Second World War and the Bicentennial*. Monacelli Press.

Sudjic, Deyan, and Philip Sayer. 1992. *The 100 Mile City*. Harcourt Brace.

Sullivan, Louis H. 1956. *The Autobiography of an Idea*. Dover Publications.

Summerson, John. 1962. *Georgian London*. Penguin Books.

Sutton, S. B., ed. 1971. *Civilizing American Cities: A Selection of Frederick Law Olmsted's Writings on City Landscapes*. MIT Press.

Taylor, Robert M. 1987. *The Northwest Ordinance, 1787: A Bicentennial Handbook*. Indiana Historical Society.

Thomas, George E., and Michael A. Lewis. 1992. *American Architectural Masterpieces: An Anthology Comprising Masterpieces of Architecture in the United States and American Architecture of the Twentieth Century*. Princeton Architectural Press.

Treaty of Greenville, Aug. 3, 1795. Ratified Indian Treaty #23, 7 STAT 49.

Tselos, Dimitri. 1967. "The Chicago Fair and the Myth of the Lost Cause." *The Journal of the Society of Architectural Historians* 26, 4 (Dec.), pp. 259–68.

Tunnard, Christopher. 1950. "A City Called Beautiful." *The Journal of the Society of Architectural Historians* 12, 3 (Mar.–May), pp. 31–36.

———. 1970. *The City of Man*. 2nd ed. Scribner.

Tunnard, Christopher, and Henry Hope Reed. 1956. *American Skyline: The Growth and Form of Our Cities and Towns*. New American Library.

Turak, Theodore. 1981. "Riverside: Roots in France." *Inland Architect* 25 (Nov.–Dec.), pp. 12–19.

———. 1986. *William Le Baron Jenney: A Pioneer of Modern Architecture*. UMI Research Press.

University of Chicago Library Map Collection. 2001–06. *Chicago, Census 2000 Maps*. University of Chicago Library.

Van Brunt, Henry. 1969. *Architecture and Society: Selected Essays of Henry Van Brunt*, edited by William A. Coles. Belknap Press.

Waldheim, Charles, and Katerina Rüedi Ray, eds. 2005. *Chicago Architecture: Histories, Revisions, Alternatives*. University of Chicago Press.

West Chicago Park Commissioners. 1873. *Fourth Annual Report of West Chicago Park Commissioners, for the Year Ending February 28th, 1873*. Evening Journal Book and Job Printing House.

Wetmore, Louis B. 1966. *The Comprehensive Plan of Chicago*. Chicago Department of Development and Planning.

Willis, Carol. 1995. *Form Follows Finance: Skyscrapers and Skylines in New York and Chicago*. Princeton Architectural Press.

Wiseman, Carter. 1998. *Shaping a Nation: Twentieth-Century American Architecture and Its Makers*. Norton.

Wittman Hydro Planning Associates. 2008. *Water Demand Scenarios for the East-Central Illinois Planning Region: 2005–2050, Final Report*. Wittman Hydro Planning Associates.

Wright, Frank Lloyd. 1943. *Frank Lloyd Wright, an Autobiography*. Duell, Sloan, and Pearce.

———. 1958. *The Living City*. Horizon Press.

Yeomans, Alfred B. 1916. *City Residential Land Development: Studies in Planning; Competitive Plans for Subdividing a Typical Quarter Section of Land in the Outskirts of Chicago*. University of Chicago Press.

Young, Donald Ramsey. 1932. *The Modern American Family*. American Academy of Political and Social Science.

Zorbaugh, Harvey Warren. 1929. *The Gold Coast and the Slum: A Sociological Study of Chicago's Near North Side*. University of Chicago Press.

Zukowsky, John, ed. 1987. *Chicago Architecture, 1872–1922: Birth of a Metropolis*. Prestel-Verlag/Art Institute of Chicago.

———. 1993. *Chicago Architecture and Design, 1923–1993: Reconfiguration of an American Metropolis*. Prestel-Verlag/Art Institute of Chicago.

ENDNOTES

CHAPTER 1

1   In 1674 Joliet recounted his journey across the portage in an interview with Father Claude Dablon. See Marquette, Dablon, and Schultz 2001; a copy in translation is also available through the Wisconsin Historical Society. The portage that Marquette and Joliet crossed was a wetland six and a half miles long, stretching southwest from the present-day Damen Avenue at 31st Street to Harlem Avenue, which occasionally filled with the mingling waters of the Chicago and Des Plaines rivers. See Knight and Zeuch 1928, pp. 32–34.

2   See Treaty of Greenville 1795, p. 1.

3   Ibid.

4   The canal's sporadic construction, interrupted by a fiscal crisis brought on by rampant speculation in real estate, underlined the potential hazards of such a relationship.

5   See Bluestone 1991, p. 17, for a discussion of these public appropriations in the context of the larger parks movement in Chicago.

6   See Merriam 1901, p. 356.

7   Ogden chartered the railroad in 1836 and served as mayor of Chicago from 1837 to 1838. Construction of the Galena and Chicago Union Railroad was interrupted by the same financial crisis that stopped work on the canal; the project was revived in 1848 and completed in 1853; and the first stretch, from Chicago to Oak Park, opened on Oct. 25, 1848. William Cronon (1991, pp. 55–93) chronicled the gradual supplanting of waterborne commerce by the railroad and explored Chicago's simultaneous transformation into a national transportation hub.

8   See maps in ibid., p. 69; and Mayer and Wade 1969, p. 43.

9   See Cronon 1991, p. 83.

10 The Monadnock Block was constructed with a load-bearing masonry wall. See FIGURE 1.7.

11 See Jackson 1987, p. 140.

12 See Grossman, Keating, and Reiff 2004, p. 493.

13 See Jackson 1987, pp. 124–28; and Giedion 1967, pp. 281–88.

14 Jon Peterson (2003, p. 37) characterized this as the first comprehensive water-carriage sewerage system. See also Cain 1978.

15 See Bluestone 1991, pp. 27–35. A single metropolitan park system centered on the South Side was proposed to the Illinois General Assembly in 1869 but did not pass. Reconfigured as three separate systems, the plan garnered enough public support to be approved later that same year. Boulevards connected parks within each system to one another, as well as to the larger systems. The *Historical Register of the Twenty-Two Superseded Park Districts* (Nash and Connelly 1941) recounts the development of each system in detail, together with that of a host of smaller park districts.

16 The term *landscape architect* was first used officially in 1863 by the Central Park Commission in accepting the resignations of Olmsted and Vaux from their positions overseeing the implementation of their design. See Newton 1971, pp. xxi and 273.

17 Olmsted and Vaux were not the first American architects to practice in the romantic tradition. Both Andrew Jackson Downing and Alexander Jackson Davis were early proponents. See Fein 1972, pp. 74–75. Witold Rybczynski (1999, p. 168) listed Birkhead Park in Liverpool, Laurel Hill Cemetery in Philadelphia, and Greenwood Cemetery in Brooklyn as the major precedents for Central Park.

18 Vaux was Olmsted's design partner for Central Park and for Prospect Park in Brooklyn. Rybczynski (ibid., pp. 309–10) credited Olmsted alone with the plan for the Buffalo Park System. Olmsted was explicit about the shortcomings of the grid as a plan for residential neighborhoods. He characterized the New York brownstone, which evolved from the city's grid plan, as "really a confession that it is impossible to build a convenient and tasteful residence in New York, adapted to the general requirements of a single family, except at a cost which even rich men generally find prohibitory." Quoted in Jackson 1987, p. 75. On Olmsted as a planner, see Fein 1972, pp. 30–35; and Fisher 1986.

19 See p. 16 for a discussion of Olmsted's work at Riverside, one of the first planned suburbs and the major precedent for this component of the South Park proposal.

20 See Jackson 1987, pp. 3–19, for a discussion of the origin and definition of the term *suburb*. A cursory definition is given in relation to Olmsted's plan for Riverside on p. 16.

21 This was the core of the 1869 proposal for a metropolitan park system that did not pass. See n. 15.

22 Olmsted characterized the South Park plan in this way. See Sutton 1971, pp. 156–96.

23 Olmsted explained, "There is but one object of scenery near Chicago of special grandeur of sublimity, and that, the lake, can be made by artificial means no more grand or sublime" (ibid., p. 162).

24 Ibid., p. 167.

25 This is not evident in Olmsted's 1871 plan, which by the terms established by the state legislature addressed only the central park component of his scheme. The scheme is described at length in Olmsted's written proposal (see n. 22). This component of the plan was not realized.

26 Bluestone used the term interchangeably with *parkways*. See Bluestone 1991, p. 52.

27 Olmsted and Vaux called the boulevards planned around Prospect Park in Brooklyn parkways.

28 The Great Fire of 1871 and a national economic depression in the following years substantially curtailed development of the South Park. When it resumed, the South Park Commissioners omitted the Midway Canal. The Lower Park remained largely unimproved until it became the site for the World's Columbian Exposition, after which it was enhanced according to a revised plan made by Olmsted and Olmsted in 1895 (headed at the time by Frederick Law Olmsted, Jr.). A romantically planned residential suburb based on the model proposed by Olmsted, Sr., was never undertaken.

29 In 1884 he also designed the Home Insurance Building in the central city, the major precursor to the steel-frame tall office building.

30 For a discussion of Jenney's education and its influence on his work, see Turak 1986, pp. 40–47. Reuben Rainey suggested that Jenney's residence in Chicago and his treatise on architectural theory may have contributed to his selection. See Waldheim and Ray 2005, p. 368, n. 4.

31 Central Park was renamed Garfield Park in 1881 in honor of President James A. Garfield, who was assassinated that year.

32 The North Park District, which grew north along the lakefront from North Avenue, had its origins in Chicago's first cemetery. This meant that it was older than its counterparts (predating their 1869 charters) and that it had a genuine romantic pedigree. As the original improved natural landscapes, cemeteries were places of rest and escape for the living as well as the dead, and as such they were precedents for the parks that succeeded them (see n. 17). When the railroad opened up new cemeteries on the expanded periphery, the city cemetery was vacated, rededicated as public parkland, and named Lincoln Park in 1865. Lake Shore Drive developed from a park drive along the lakefront as a sort of internal parkway.

33 In 1853 Llewellyn Haskell commissioned Alexander Jackson Davis to lay out Llewellyn Park in West Orange, New Jersey, as a romantic residential enclave with convenient access to New York City. It was envisioned as a retreat for businessmen who shared Haskell's religious inclinations and, in that sense, was too exclusive to be considered a prototypical suburb. It was, however, a precedent for Olmsted and Vaux's work at Riverside, as was their 1866 plan for the College of California at Berkeley, which incorporated a romantically planned residential neighborhood. See Roper 1973, pp. 321–23.

34 The best summary of Riverside is Olmsted's own; see Sutton 1971, pp. 293–305. Other descriptions appear in Fisher 1986, pp. 136–48; and Jackson 1987, pp. 79–81.

35 Olmsted and Vaux 1868, p. 8.

36 Consequently, Pullman's working "center" was diffuse and its residential "periphery" dense.

CHAPTER 2

1   European precedent included picturesque landscape planning (see ch. 1, n. 17).

2   Paris presents the most notable and comprehensive example. Even where improvements were undertaken on the old or existing urban periphery, as in Vienna and London, respectively, they seeded urban rather than suburban growth. Improvements to Paris, Vienna, and London all used housing to shape and finance new public urban space, which in London's case had a picturesque character (see Summerson 1962, pp. 177–90). The peripheral parks that were also a part of these programs

were not primarily sites for suburban settlement but rather for urban excursions (see Olsen 1988). See ch. 4 for a discussion of metropolitan improvements to Paris.

3   See Hitchcock and Kaufmann 1970, pp. 51–112.

4   These were built on the periphery of the commercial center, often within or adjacent to parks that preserved their identification with nature. The Newberry Library, completed in 1893, faced Washington Square Park; and the 1892 Chicago Historical Society was located in the elite residential district north of the Chicago River. The Chicago Public Library was begun in 1891 on the lakefront parcel designated as public space in the 1839 federal addition to Chicago (see ch. 1, p. 7). The original Art Institute of Chicago was built in 1885 on the eastern edge of the Loop, facing the lake; it was replaced in 1892 by a new building in the park area across Michigan Avenue (the nucleus of the current Art Institute). The Chicago Symphony Orchestra's first home was the auditorium of Adler and Sullivan's Auditorium Building, finished in 1889, on Michigan Avenue facing the lake. Other cities also located major cultural institutions in or across from parks; the Metropolitan Museum of Art in New York, the Museum of Fine Arts in Boston, and the Philadelphia Museum of Art are representative examples.

5   See Cassell and Cassell 1983, pp. 10–27.

6   The Cassells estimated that twenty-eight million visitors passed through the fair's gates over a six-month period. A rough estimate suggests that 150,000 people visited each day (the fair was open on Sundays). See ibid., p. 11.

7   Congress designated Chicago as the host of the fair in Feb. 1890. President Harrison confirmed the Jackson Park site on Dec. 24, 1890. Jon Peterson noted that the planners of the 1889 Exposition Universelle had been a "full year ahead of the Americans at a comparable stage" (Peterson 2003, p. 64).

8   This was distinct from, but in the same tradition as, the École Centrale des Arts et Manufactures, from which Jenney graduated.

9   See Condit 1964, p. 83; and ch. 1, p. 15.

10 Charles Atwood, a classically trained architect working for McKim, replaced Root in Burnham's office and in his responsibilities at the exposition after Root died unexpectedly in 1891.

11 The designer of the Crystal Palace, Joseph Paxton, also designed Birkenhead Park (see ch. 1, n. 17). Prince Albert is credited with conceiving the exhibition, and he opened the Crystal Palace in 1851.

12 On the iron structure of the Galerie des Machines, see Stamper 1989.

13 See ch. 4.

14 The domed rotunda–identified in the Renaissance with sacred architecture and in antiquity with funerary monuments–had since the Enlightenment gradually taken on a secular character reserved for the most-exalted public program. The Church of Sainte-Geneviève in Paris, the city's major Neoclassical monument, was renamed the Panthéon and converted into a national shrine for the internment of great men during the French Revolution; it subsequently fluctuated between sacred and secular uses. National heroes were also interred in the Roman Pantheon and in St. Paul's Cathedral in London. The completion of the dome of the United States Capitol in 1863, followed by the construction of a spate of domed state capitols, confirmed the secular shift.

15 L'Enfant's plan for central Washington and the squares of Savannah (planned 1733), Philadelphia (planned 1683), Boston (Louisburg Square [completed 1848] and Franklin Place [completed 1795]), and New Orleans provide the major examples of American urban ensemble planning before the 1893 fair. Of these, only Jackson Square in New Orleans (formerly the Place d'Armes), laid out by the French in 1720 and largely completed by 1815, was surrounded by a coordinated ensemble of public buildings.

16 The Palace of Fine Arts was originally the responsibility of Root, who gave it an airy Romanesque character (see Hoffman 1988). Atwood replaced this with the final design, an exercise in academic classicism that was composed with a freer plan than its counterparts in the Court of Honor.

17 Ruskin's *Stones of Venice* presented the Venetian Gothic style as an object lesson in the individual expression made possible by handicraft (and undermined by standardized industrial processes). See Ruskin 2003.

18 Sullivan famously claimed, in his *Autobiography of an Idea*, published over thirty years after the exposition, that it set the course of American architecture back "for half a century from its date, if not longer" (Sullivan 1956, p. 325).

19 This was due to the public nature and academic character of their work, rather than to its technical innovation. Richardson, the second American graduate of the École des Beaux-Arts and the first to synthesize its methods with a picturesque design tradition, was acknowledged as the foremost American architect during his lifetime (died 1886). The three main currents in American architecture at the time of his death all reflected his influence. Some architects continued to design in his Romanesque Revival style; some pursued his efforts to find proper expressions for new building types (primarily the tall office building); and some expanded the tenets of the École. The first group included Burnham and Root, the second Sullivan, and the third McKim and his partner, Stanford White, both of whom had worked for Richardson. The rise of academic classicism as a national style began with McKim's Boston Public Library of 1888 (see Hitchcock 1977, pp. 318–19).

20 The Ringstrasse in Vienna, begun in 1858, was the closest European precedent, but it was composed of individual buildings in multiple styles by multiple authors (see ibid., pp. 191–217).

21 This was undoubtedly the source of the sculptor Augustus Saint-Gaudens's comment that the fair's planning represented "the greatest meeting of artists since the fifteenth century" (Larkin 1966, p. 311).

22 The Galleria Vittorio Emanuele II was completed in Milan in 1877; the Galleria Umberto I in Naples was finished in 1890.

23 Nor were exuberant, uncoordinated expressions of new building technology out of place at the exposition. The first Ferris Wheel, riposte to the Eiffel Tower, stood on the Midway (see FIGURE 2.12, rear center).

24 Van Brunt 1969, pp. 232–33.

25 Ibid.

26 Critics explicitly warned against adapting the fair's lessons to urban planning. Montgomery Schuyler, perhaps the foremost contemporary critic of architecture, wrote, "To reproduce or to imitate the [fair's] buildings deprived of these irreproducible and inimitable advantages [unity, magnitude, and (primarily) illusion] would be an impossible task, and if it were possible it would not be desirable" (Schuyler 1961, p. 574).

27 Burnham, Bennett, and Moore 1909, p. 4.

CHAPTER 3

1   They were Post, Van Brunt, Peabody, and McKim (see aia.org/about/history/AIAS077478).

2   Olmsted wrote to his partners in 1893 of the Boston Parks that "they will be the seed of as good crops in suburban improvement as the Central Park has been in respect to public urban parks" (quoted in Roper 1973, p. 453). He considered the Back Bay Fens and the Muddy River Improvement to be sanitary engineering projects rather than parks (see Beveridge, Rochelau, and Larkin 1998, pp. 83–85).

3   On the capital's population growth, see Merriam 1901, p. 432. Rock Creek Park, a late manifestation of the parks movement, was established in 1890. For information on its development, see Bushong 1990.

4   Central Park was inserted into New York's existing street grid and was thus a later addition to its plan.

5   This is often called the McMillan Plan after him. On the political developments that supported the expanded initiative, see Peterson 2003, pp. 77–97.

6   The official title of the report submitted to McMillan's committee, Senate Report no. 166, was *The Improvement of the Park System of the District of Columbia* (see Moore 1902).

7   Saint-Gaudens proposed the colonnade screen at one end of the Court of Honor (see ch. 2, n. 21).

8   The Senate Committee on the District of Columbia appropriated funds for the preparation of the plan, but implementing it required full Congressional support.

9   Burnham, Bennett, and Moore 1909, p. 4 (see ch. 2, p. 28).

10 L'Enfant's 1791 manuscript plan referred to the Capitol as the Congress House and the White House as the President's House; the former is corrected on his copy. The President's House was referred to as the White House beginning in 1811; President Theodore Roosevelt officially changed its name to that in 1901 (see Seale 1992).

11 This is noted on the 1791 L'Enfant plan.

12 The canal was also supposed to supply a cascade from Capitol Hill into a basin at the head of the Mall. This feature of the plan was not executed.

13 Pennsylvania Avenue belonged to the diagonal web, the Mall to the orthogonal grid. In 1842 Charles Dickens wrote of Washington, "Spacious avenues, that begin in nothing, and lead nowhere; streets, mile-long, that only want houses, roads, and inhabitants; public buildings that need but a public to be complete; and ornaments of great thoroughfares, which only lack great thoroughfares to ornament—are its leading features" (Dickens 1868, p. 51).

14 L'Enfant's proposed street plan also bears some responsibility for the fitful realization of his overall plan. In 1791 the grid was already established as the primary system for organizing new cities, and Thomas Jefferson had suggested one as the basis for the capital's plan. A web of diagonal streets, however, was more responsive to topography and more conducive to monumental effect. By superimposing one system over the other, L'Enfant produced awkward intersections that interrupted traffic flow even along major axes and left triangular lots that were difficult to build on. Mumford suggested that this was a forced reconciliation (see Mumford 1955, p. 67). This raises a question about the extent to which L'Enfant envisioned Washington as urban. Were these irregular blocks meant to be filled in to their boundaries, or were the streets divisions in a landscape populated with objects? Christopher Wren's plan for rebuilding London after the 1666 fire reconciled a diagonal web with an orthogonal grid by confining them to adjacent zones.

15 Werner Hegemann and Elbert Peets showed that, left unimpeded, this axis would still have bypassed the White House as it was built (see Hegemann and Peets 1922, pp. 290–92).

16 See ch. 1, n. 17.

17 The Lincoln Memorial was designed by Henry Bacon and completed in 1922; the Jefferson Memorial was designed by John Russell Pope and completed in 1937. The latter was not designated for Jefferson in the 1901 plan.

18 The drawings and text of the report do not agree on this point (see Moore 1902, p. 49; and FIGURE 3.6).

19 The park commissioners designed the allée of linden trees on a slight angle to accommodate the obelisk's location south of the axis's centerline (see FIGURE 3.1).

20 The Pennsylvania Railroad acquired controlling interest in the Baltimore and Ohio Railroad in 1901 and with it this site. Even before then, Burnham pressed its president, Alexander Cassatt, to relocate an enlarged terminal off the Mall. His firm received the commission to design what became Union Station.

21 McKim, Mead, and White designed the memorial bridge, though it did not open until 1932.

22 See n. 6.

23 The park commissioners' efforts were not legally recognized until 1910, when Burnham, McKim, and Olmsted became charter members of the Commission of Fine Arts. Early efforts to impose the plan were largely confined to preventing new buildings and monuments, primarily the Lincoln Memorial and the Agriculture Building, from compromising it. The formation of the National Capital Park and Planning Commission in 1924 and the passage of the Capper-Cramton Act in 1930 provided for the purchase of suburban land for peripheral parks (see Bushong 1990, pp. 93–95).

24 See ch. 2, pp. 26–27, for a discussion of narrative planning at the World's Columbian Exposition.

25 In the elemental character of its buildings, their uniform white color, and their unified classical expression, the Mall explicitly recalled both the Court of Honor and the French Enlightenment designs of architects like Etienne-Louis Boullée. Its encyclopedic collection of elemental building forms—a domed capitol, an English Palladian villa, a Greek temple, a Roman rotunda, and an Egyptian obelisk—also aimed for the timeless and standard quality of Rome, which the park commissioners explicitly sought (see Moore 1929, p. 156).

CHAPTER 4

1 The boulevard systems proposed by Olmsted in Chicago (Riverside, South Park District), Brooklyn, and Buffalo are the common antecedents of later boulevard plans.

2 See Peterson 2003, pp. 151–72.

3 The Fairmount Parkway was completed in 1926 according to a 1917 design

by the French architect Jacques Gréber. The buildings lining it eventually included the Academy of Natural Sciences, the Philadelphia Free Library, the Cathedral of Saints Peter and Paul (all on Logan Square), and the Rodin Museum. City Hall and the Philadelphia Museum of Art, on the edge of Fairmount Park, occupied its ends. Fairmount Parkway was renamed the Benjamin Franklin Parkway in 1937 (see ibid., p. 154).

4 In 1903, though Chicago was the second-largest city in terms of population, it occupied the seventh place among American cities in total park acreage. In terms of the total length of its boulevard system (not included in park acreage), it occupied second place, after New York (see Perkins and Bradley 1905, p. 33). Compiled in 1904, the Perkins plan was published in 1905.

5 See Peterson 2003, pp. 151–72.

6 Bennett was an English graduate of the École des Beaux-Arts and the future coauthor of the *Plan of Chicago*. The *Report on a Plan for San Francisco* lists three related and familiar goals: to establish functionally distinct metropolitan centers, to improve and make public the surrounding landscape, and to connect these areas with a legible street plan. See Burnham, Bennett, and O'Day 1905, pp. 35–44.

7 The McMillan Plan utilized existing diagonal streets.

8 This inner circuit of streets was an armature for civic, cultural, and transportation programs developed around City Hall, which would complement but also dominate the existing centers of finance and manufacturing. Radial connections joined it to a boulevard that made a circuit of the surrounding hills, a peripheral version of the inner circuit of diagonal streets. In its language at least, the San Francisco plan was circumspect about cutting through existing city blocks, even for reasons of functional efficiency: "It is proposed to make a comprehensive plan of San Francisco, based on the present streets, parks and other public spaces and grounds, which shall interfere as little as possible with the rectangular street system of the city" (Burnham, Bennett, and O'Day 1905, p. 35).

9 In this context, the San Francisco earthquake, which occurred on Apr. 18, 1906, just before the plan's formal publication, can have had little to do with the city's ultimate failure to adopt its proposals.

10 See Smith 2006, pp. 64–70.

11 Burnham, Bennett, and Moore 1909, p. 33.

12 Ludwig Hilberseimer investigated the problem of congestion in radial cities when formulating his proposal for a linear city based on the automobile (see ch. 6).

13 See Cronon 1991, pp. 372–73.

14 See Delano 1906. Twelfth Street was renamed Roosevelt Road in 1919, after President Theodore Roosevelt.

15 See Arnold 1905.

16 The Tuileries axis was the specific precedent for the Mall armature.

17 On Paris's population between 1815 and 1848, see Jordan 1995, pp. 229–30.

18 See ch. 2, p. 21, for a comparison with the path to urban improvement in the United States.

19 Rasmussen ascribed the term *boulevard* to a corruption of the Nordic *bulvirke* (bulwark). See Rasmussen 1973, p. 109.

20 See Saalman 1971.

21 Napoleon III and Haussmann also provided Paris with a wider natural periphery. Two large parks, the Bois de Boulogne and the Bois de Vincennes, were the peripheral terminations of the urban boulevard systems. Like American peripheral parks, their romantic character evoked unspoiled nature (Olmsted met with their designer, Jean-Charles-Adolphe Alphand, when traveling through Europe in 1859). But in a planning approach that addressed housing in urban surroundings, these were distinct zones of escape and amusement for a residential population concentrated elsewhere. The metropolitan park systems in the United States, conceived with peripheral residents in mind, were the relevant precedents for peripheral planning in Chicago.

22 Multiuse buildings in the central city, such as Adler and Sullivan's Auditorium Building of 1889, belonged to another tradition of using office and hotel space to finance cultural program. Buildings that combined housing with other program were rare.

23 On the remaking of Chicago's central city, see ch. 1, pp. 9–10.

24 See ch. 12.

25 Burnham, Bennett, and Moore 1909, p. 32.

26 Ibid., pp. 33–34.

27 Ibid., p. 34.

28 Ibid., pp. 95–96.

29 Ibid.

30 Harbor facilities at the mouth of the Calumet River would also be linked to the freight-handling center. The plan projected that the ratio of rail to water transportation for freight would remain static, with water conveying five percent of the total freight (see ibid., p. 64).

31 Delano's 1904 plan for consolidating the railroad terminals included a widened public boulevard along Twelfth Street, a straightened Chicago River, and a program of office space for the railroads that was in essence a southern expansion of the Loop. Burnham's office made the drawings for this plan, and its proposals were incorporated and acknowledged in the 1909 plan. See ibid., p. 72; and Delano 1906.

32 Burnham and Bennett explicitly tied the street system to improved central-city circulation and peripheral park access. See Burnham, Bennett, and Moore 1909, p. 80: "The two prime considerations for every large city are, first, adequate means of circulation; and second, a sufficient park area to insure good health and good order."

33 Ibid., pp. 80 and 84.

34 Ibid., pp. 113–15.

35 Grant Park was named in 1896. The institutions that made up the cultural ensemble proposed by Burnham and Bennett were the Art Institute, the Field Museum, and the Crerar Library. Marshall Field pledged funds for constructing the Field Museum in 1894, at the close of the Columbian Exposition, and he increased this gift at his death in 1906. John Crerar pledged the Crerar Library to the city in 1894. However, only the Art Institute was actually in place in 1909.

36 Burnham, Bennett, and Moore 1909, p. 114.

37 The east-west section of Wacker Drive, between Michigan Avenue and Lake Street, was opened in 1926. It was named for Charles H. Wacker, the chairman of the Chicago Plan Commission from 1910 to 1926. A southern extension to Congress Parkway was completed in 1954, an eastward extension to Lake Shore Drive in 1975.

38 As a raised boulevard, it met the Michigan Avenue Bridge on grade (see FIGURE 4.20).

39 FIGURE 4.25 shows that some of the areas through which this boulevard would pass had already been divided into residential blocks in 1909.

40 Water transportation remained a viable means of moving raw materials for manufacturing. The establishment of Pullman in 1880, then beyond the periphery, foreshadowed this development, which the clustering of industry around the mouth of the Calumet River and the 1905 decision by U.S. Steel to create an industrial town on the Indiana lakefront confirmed. On the development and plan of Gary, see ch. 6, n. 11.

41 The highway planners, in the decades after World War II, found a way around this problem by separating highways by grade, limiting access, and breaking the orthogonal street grid. See ch. 8, p. 100.

42 On the orthogonal settlement pattern produced by the peripheral transportation network, see ch. 1, p. 10.

43 The first traffic light was invented in Chicago in 1910 by Ernest Sirine (see Sessions 1971, p. 24).

44 Pl. 91 in the printed plan is mislabeled. Proposed diagonal streets are in black, existing in red.

45 Real-estate interests caught in the financial panic of 1893 advocated height limits to discourage overbuilding; they were joined by citizens who felt that new buildings were too tall (see Willis 1995, p. 50).

46 See also pl. 74 in the plan for a diagram of the properties owned by the railroads in central Chicago at this time. The 260-foot limit imposed in 1902 was an increase from the 130-foot limit originally created in 1893 (see ibid., p. 52; and Fogelson 2001, pp. 141–44). The number of buildings constructed over that height after 1893 indicated the limit's ineffectiveness. A partial list of the buildings taller than 130 feet in 1901 includes the Home Insurance Building (1885) at 180 feet, the Rookery (1888) at 181 feet, the Reliance Building (1895) at 200 feet, the Marquette Building (1895) at 205 feet, the Auditorium Building (1889) at 238 feet, the Women's Temple Building (1892) at 262 feet, and the Masonic Temple Building (1892) at 302 feet. One North Dearborn, erected in 1905, was 322 feet tall. The Rookery, the Reliance Building, the Women's Temple Building, and the Masonic Temple Building were designed in Burnham's office.

47 The triangular blocks that would be created by new diagonal streets introduced a further impediment. Washington suffered from the same inorganic imposition of a diagonal web on an orthogonal grid, a problem that was therefore familiar to Burnham.

48 For the standard character of Chicago's commercial buildings, see ch. 1, p. 10.

49 See ch. 1, p. 7. The lakefront had in the past been treated as a building site primarily for the kind of cultural exhibition program the *Plan of Chicago* proposed. Ward's persistent and ultimately legally sanctioned efforts to enforce the charter suggest that, even if he was the lone steward of the public interest, that interest was real and it was best served by an open, natural lakefront (see Bachin 2004, pp. 176–82).

50 The *Plan of Chicago* addresses the problem in a cursory way; Burnham and Bennett limited their concerns largely to the public roles of commercial buildings along diagonal avenues and the spaces between houses and residential streets. See Burnham, Bennett, and Moore 1909, pp. 84–86.

51 South of the Chicago River, Michigan Avenue also includes access to underground parking garages.

52 The Michigan Avenue Bridge was ultimately responsible for the shift of the majority of Chicago's wealth from the South Side, where it was concentrated on Prairie Avenue, to the North Side, where it remains concentrated on the northern lakefront.

53 Additionally, a section of the Chicago River south of Roosevelt Road was straightened according to the plan's recommendation, based on Delano's earlier proposal (see n. 31). On the implementation of the Burnham and Bennett plan, see Smith 2006, pp. 130–50; and Condit 1973.

54 On the rise of the automobile in Chicago, see Mayer and Wade 1969, pp. 232–34.

55 Ford and Crowther 1922, pp. 72–73.

CHAPTER 5

1 See ch. 1, pp. 16–17, for a discussion of Riverside as a prototypical American suburb; and ch. 1, pp. 5 and 10, for a discussion of peripheral settlement patterns.

2 Competition entries were judged by a jury that included Chicago-area business interests and planning professionals. Its members were John C. Kennedy, formerly Secretary of the Housing Committee of the Chicago Association of Commerce; John W. Alvord, engineer and town planner; Jens Jensen, landscape architect; and George Maher and A. F. Woltersdorf, architects. These jurors specifically sought:

> The best methods of subdivision of residential land, the best disposition of space for parks and recreations centers, the most practical width and arrangement of roads, the most convenient location of stores and of public or semi-public grounds and buildings, the most desirable provisions for house yards and gardens and the proper density of population to be provided for (Yeomans 1916, pp. 1–2).

3 Ibid., p. 1.

4 A population density of 1,280 families per quarter section was considerably lower than the average residential population density of Chicago, which Hoyt calculated to be 16,000 people per quarter section in 1923 (1,000 people per acre multiplied by 160 acres, the number in a quarter section; see Hoyt 1933, p. 293). Young fixed the average family size in Chicago at 3.8 people in 1920, which makes the average density of a residential quarter section approximately 4,000 people (see Young 1932, p. 31). The peripheral location of the quarter-section site should be kept in mind when comparing this to the proposed density. Wright's quadruple-block plan included 32 homes on two square blocks, each on a lot approximately 60 x 65 feet, in the space typically occupied by a 36 houses on one rectangular block, each on a lot 33 x 125 feet. Together these comparisons give a general idea of the aims of the quarter-section competition with regard to typical existing conditions.

5 For the development of Bournville and Port Sunlight, see Newton 1971, pp. 447–63.

6 Block planning, ready transportation connections, and local public open space were also features of Pullman.

7 This plan was awarded the second prize by the City Club. See Yeomans 1916 for the keys to the plans.

8 The winning entry, by Wilhelm Bernhard of Chicago, was of this type.

9 Drummond's descriptions and drawings do not always correspond, and the latter should be understood as possible illustrations of a general strategy that might have varied in its execution.

10 Griffin was a Prairie school architect who planned Canberra, the capital of Australia. See p. 76.

11 The quadruple-block plan was based on two earlier plans: one that appeared in the *Ladies' Home Journal* in Feb. 1901; and a 1903 plan for the block between Chicago, Fair Oaks, Superior, and Ogden (now East) avenues in Oak Park (see Hitchcock and Kaufmann 1970, p. 113).

12 See ch. 1, pp. 11–16.

13 Quoted in Grese 1992, p. 80; and Jensen 1990, p. 85.

14 Wright 1943, p. 548.

15 This could not be overcome by Mahony Griffin's acceptance and incorporation of established zoning and transportation links. See Waldheim and Ray 2005, p. 152.

16 On the design of Canberra, see Zukowsky 1987, pp. 319–43.

17 See City Club of Chicago 1913.

18 The consolidated rail station that accommodated through traffic was also a legacy of the Burnham and Bennett plan.

19 On the dates of Jensen's work on a Greater West Park System, see Grese 1992, p. 87; and Jensen 1920, pp. 9–10.

20 Jensen 1990, p. 83.

21 Ibid., p. 89.

22 Grese 1992, p. 39.

23 Jensen was explicit, however, about the automobile's potentially damaging effects on urban life (see Jensen 1990, p. 91).

CHAPTER 6

1 This was the fate of H. H. Richardson's Marshall Field Warehouse. See Ochsner 1982, p. 330; and ch. 2, n. 19.

2 See Tunnard and Reed 1956, pp. 186–90, for a discussion of parking's effects on the central city.

3 Mies van der Rohe was the director of the Bauhaus from 1930 to 1933; Hilberseimer taught there from 1929 to 1933.

4 See Frampton 1980, pp. 123–29, for a discussion of how this curriculum evolved in Germany.

5 In their attention to detail, meticulous execution, and concern with problems of expression, the buildings of Mies van der Rohe, like the products of the Bauhaus more generally, exhibited a level of care more characteristic of traditional craft than industrial production. At the time, these products of art could not be produced through established industrial processes, though that may have been their goal.

6 See "The Chicago Frame" in Rowe 1995, pp. 89–118, for another comparison between a generalized European theory and an American practice rooted in the requirements of a specific place.

7 Increased through circulation was one aspect of the central-city program as Burnham and Bennett described it; increased building programs for commerce and culture were the others.

8 For a discussion of garden cities and nineteenth-century English town planning, see ch. 5, p. 70; for Broadacre City, see ch. 5, p. 76.

9 The academic conservatism of Le Corbusier's model distinguishes it from Burnham and Bennett's earlier plan for Chicago. Both plans divided the city into functional zones around a privileged central precinct where urban spaces shaped by adjacent buildings recalled historical models – references to the plan of Versailles, Michelangelo's idealized urban plan for St. Peter's Basilica, the Piazza del Popolo, and enclosed Parisian *places* can all be found in Le Corbusier's plan (these references occur, respectively, in the interlocking setback plans of the residential blocks, the plan of the transportation center in its rectangular precinct, the public plaza at the right angle of the central diamond, and the public squares along its sides). The distinct edge imagined by Le Corbusier, however, was an anachronism; traditionally, this had been maintained by a defensive wall. The elimination of city walls and the introduction of those transportation modes for which Le Corbusier was planning produced an urban pattern with an indistinct periphery. That regular geometric planning could accommodate such an indistinct edge was proven by Burnham and Bennett's plan. Le Corbusier's plan therefore lies more firmly in the Beaux-Arts tradition of hierarchically organized zones with discrete boundaries.

10 A five-kilometer stretch of the *ciudad lineal* was implemented beginning in 1894. See Collins 1959.

11 Beginning in 1906, Soria y Mata's planning model was effectively implemented in Chicago, where the functional efficiency and flexible expansion Hilberseimer sought for the city had been adopted by industrial planning as early as 1880, when Pullman was founded. In 1906 U.S. Steel founded Gary, Indiana, on the southern shore of Lake Michigan, as a linear city that coordinated the independent requirements of the railroad with those of the steel factory and a resident workforce. Whether Gary's planners looked to any kind of model is unclear in light of the obvious nature of their plan. Existing railroad lines that traversed the site divided an industrial zone on the lake from a gridded residential zone to the south; both could expand eastward or westward along the tracks. A trolley that ran perpendicular to the main railroad line connected them to one another. Gary expanded on Soria y Mata's model, enlarging its scale and using the city's main transportation line to separate different kinds of zones from one another; as an industrial undertaking, however, Gary did not have the linear city's urban pretensions – the railroad was simply a means for moving raw materials and finished products to and from the steel factories. Nevertheless, the city established industrial planning as the precursor to more-comprehensive urban models based on transportation requirements.

12 The quarter-section proposal of A. C. Tenney utilized these same methods (see Yeomans 1916, pp. 84–86).

13 Hilberseimer 1944, p. 140.

14 Hilberseimer arranged additional settlement units for heavy industry along concentric peripheral expressways; he gave these wedge-shaped plans that confined houses to a triangular zone of clear air, outside the circular area described by prevailing wind patterns, which was more likely to suffer from air pollution (see Hilberseimer 1955, pp. 216–18).

15 For proposed improvements to the Loop related to this plan, see ibid., p. 248; for proposed additions of high-rise housing to residential settlement units along the lakefront, see ibid., pp. 212–13 and 249–54.

CHAPTER 7

1 Montrose Point in the north and Promontory Point in the south.

2 Pommer, Spaeth, and Harrington credited Caldwell's thesis, "The City in the Landscape," as the basis for Hilberseimer's regional plans for Chicago (see Pommer, Spaeth, and Harrington 1988, p. 115; and Caldwell 1948).

3 See Cohen 1976.

CHAPTER 8

1 Subsequent plans fall into two categories: plans for parts of the city, and comprehensive plans that may include, but do not focus on, physical improvements. The 1958 *Development Plan for the Central Area of Chicago*, 1973 *Chicago 21* plan, 1983 *Central Area Plan*, and 2003 *Central Area Plan* belong to the first category. The 1966 *Comprehensive Plan of Chicago* and the 2001 *Chicago Metropolis 2020 Plan* belong to the second.

2 This sketch of Chicago's existing conditions is necessarily broad, though it also targets specific issues. For a more detailed analysis with a wider scope, see Berube and Prince 2003, and Johnson 2001.

3 In 1984 Los Angeles replaced Chicago as the country's second-largest city. See "Los Angeles Replaces Chicago as Second City," *New York Times*, Apr. 8, 1984, p. 27.

4 See Berube and Prince 2003, pp. 10–13.

5 This statistic comes from the Northeastern Illinois Planning Commission, whose 2030 population forecasts were most recently revised in 2006 (see www.nipc.org and Northeastern Illinois Planning Commission 2004).

6 Moody's Investors Service named Chicago the most diverse urban economy in the United States in 2003. See "Moody's: Chicago economy most balanced in U.S.," *Chicago Sun-Times*, June 23, 2003.

7 According to the United States Department of Labor, Bureau of Labor Statistics, *Chicago-Naperville-Joliet, IL: Economy at a Glance*, Aug. 2008–Jan. 2009.

8 According to the Illinois Department of Commerce and Economic Opportunity's *Report on Manufacturing in Illinois* for 2006 (United States Department of Commerce, Annual Survey of Manufacturers).

[9] See Leinbach and Capineri 2007, p. 127.

[10] See "The Top 50 Logistics Cities in the United States," *Logistics Today* 47, 10 (2006), pp. 37–41.

[11] Ibid.

[12] According to the Bureau of Economic Analysis, United States Department of Commerce; and the United States Census Bureau, *Survey of Current Business*, Oct. 2008. The difference between New York's and Los Angeles's shares of the national gross domestic product has remained constant since 2004 (Los Angeles's is sixty percent of New York's). The gap between Los Angeles's and Chicago's shares has widened during that same period, with Chicago's share dropping from seventy-four to seventy percent of Los Angeles's share. The gap between Chicago and Washington, D.C., has closed, the latter's share having risen from seventy-two to seventy-five percent of Chicago's (see Malagón, McInerney, and Panek 2008, p. 129, table 6).

[13] Richard Florida suggested that Chicago has already begun to consolidate midwestern commerce. See "How the Crash Will Reshape America," *The Atlantic Monthly* (Mar. 2009), pp. 44–55.

[14] According to the Bureau of Economic Analysis, United States Department of Commerce, *Percent Change in Real GDP by State*, 2007–08.

[15] Ibid.; and Perry 2001.

[16] They are important hubs for Federal Express and United Parcel Service, respectively. See John McPhee, "Out in the Sort: UPS and the Art of Moving Everything," *The New Yorker* (Apr. 18, 2005), pp. 160–73.

[17] Chicago ranked fourth on the Fortune 500 headquarters list for 2008, tying Dallas with twelve total headquarters. Atlanta ranked fifth with nine headquarters. New York was first with forty-three, while Houston was second with twenty-five.

[18] The *Freight Rail Bottom Line Report*, published in 2003 by the American Association of State Highway and Transportation Officials, discusses Chicago's historical rail inefficiencies. They are the very same problems that the *Plan of Chicago* proposed to redress (see American Association of State Highway and Transportation Officials 2002).

[19] The successful zoning of heavy industry—the only use in the industrial city that theoretically requires spatial segregation—is another factor in the more-elastic relationship between commerce and housing. On the persistent pattern of commercial suburbanization in Chicago, a factor in the current zoning pattern, see Breugman, "Schaumburg, Oak Brook, Rosemont, and the Recentering of the Chicago Metropolitan Area," in Zukowsky 1993, pp. 159–77.

[20] Burnham, Bennett, and Moore 1909, p. 91.

[21] See Wittman Hydro Planning Associates 2008.

[22] These were the results of a conference hosted by the Federal Reserve Bank of Chicago in Nov. 2008 (see Lombardi and Lavelle 2009).

[23] Burnham, Bennett, and Moore 1909, p. 94.

[24] See Chicago Metropolis 2020 2004.

[25] The Burlington Northern Santa Fe Railway also operates three other intermodal transit facilities in the Chicago area.

[26] The Eisenhower Expressway becomes the East-West Tollway at Hillside, just beyond Oak Park; it continues westward for ninety-six miles to its intersection with State Route 30 near Sterling/Rock Falls. This was renamed the Ronald Reagan Memorial Tollway in 2004.

[27] See Abalos, Herreros, and Ockman 2003, pp. 217–57.

CHAPTER 9

[1] The central city's northern boundary is more difficult to define, as north of the Chicago River, expansion follows both concentric and linear patterns. The high-density band of development along the north bank of the river's main branch is a peripheral expansion of the Loop; the perpendicular band along North Michigan Avenue is a linear spur. Both are serviced by conduits for through traffic along Ohio and Ontario streets.

[2] The blocks of the central city are based on a different division of the quarter section than those in the fabric, which measure 660 x 330 feet and divide each quarter section into thirty-two blocks. The blocks of the central city are contained within the original settlement of Chicago and its first additions, and they vary according to the order in which they were surveyed. See Hoyt 1933, pp. 427–29, for a concise account. A brief table is included here:

Settlement	Block Measurements	Street Measurements
Original settlement (bounded by State, Kinzie, Halsted, and Madison streets)	320 x 360 feet	80 feet
Kinzie Addition (bounded by Lake Michigan, Chicago Avenue, State Street, and the Chicago River)	218 x 300 feet	74 feet
Carpenter Addition (westward extension of original settlement to a line halfway between Racine [formerly Ann] and Elizabeth streets)	250 x 341 feet	66 feet

[3] This is the Floor Area Ratio (FAR). The FAR imposed for the central city was sixteen, meaning that a building's area could be sixteen times the area of its lot (see Willis 1995, p. 138).

[4] On the effects of building technology on the tall office building, see Willis 1995; and Ábalos, Herreros, and Ockman 2003.

[5] The building, on Wacker Drive between Wabash Avenue and State Street, was subsequently renamed the Pure Oil Building and is now called 35 East Wacker Drive. Its interior parking decks were converted to office use (see Willis 1995, pp. 117 and 196).

[6] Lang 2000, pp. 3–4. If satellite central cities (of which Chicago has, perhaps uniquely, few examples) are not considered, suburban office space in the United States in 1999 outweighed central-city office space.

[7] Ibid., pp. 5–6.

[8] Ibid., p. 6; and Chicago Department of Planning and Development, et al. 2003, pp. 15 and 19.

[9] Ibid., p. 15.

[10] Burnham, Bennett, and Moore 1909, p. 114.

[11] The Central Post Office was completed in 1932 and designed by Graham, Anderson, Probst, and White, the successor to D. H. Burnham and Company.

[12] *Hortus in Urbe*—"Garden in the City"—is the motto of the Chicago Park District. The city's motto is incorporated on its seal.

CHAPTER 10

[1] Hyde Park, annexed in 1889, was once an autonomous community as well.

[2] 2007 Population Distribution Map, City of Chicago, based on 2000 census figures (see City of Chicago 2007). For the quarter section as the basic module of the peripheral street grid, see ch. 5, p. 69.

[3] For the development of this pattern, see ch. 1, p. 10.

[4] The product of both 4 x 660 feet and 8 x 330 feet is 2,640 feet, or half a mile.

[5] Moving clockwise from the South Shore, the six regional parks are Jackson, Washington, Douglas, Garfield, Humboldt, and Lincoln. For their development, see ch. 1, pp. 11–16. For Columbus Park as a typical medium-size peripheral park, see ch. 5, pp. 74–75. Strictly local parks and playgrounds were integral to the park system proposed by Burnham and Bennett.

[6] See ch. 5, p. 69.

[7] See ch. 6, p. 81.

[8] See University of Chicago Library Map Collection 2001–06.

[9] This was not enough to offset overall population loss throughout the fabric. Mayer and Wade summarized the process of suburbanization and its effects on the fabric (1969, pp. 402–20).

[10] In general, mixed-income projects undertaken by institutions and private developers (Lake Meadows and Prairie Shores) were more successful than dedicated low-income housing undertaken by the government (Stateway Gardens and Robert Taylor Homes), where poor African American populations remained isolated and their social problems persisted (see Condit 1974, pp. 150–66 and 205–19).

[11] According to Mayer and Wade, the larger portion of Chicago's metropolitan

ENDNOTES

population lived beyond the city limits before the 1889 program of annexation that included the Village of Hyde Park, the Town of Lake, the City of Lakeview, and the Town of Jefferson. See FIGURE 1.8.

12 2030 Forecast Maps, Chicago Metropolitan Agency for Planning.

13 Ibid.

14 The rail line along the Eisenhower Expressway is not utilized for commuter trains; it connects Union Station with O'Hare International Airport. The Green line along Lake Street joins the Union Pacific West line of the Metra, which runs along Kinzie Avenue, at Lockwood Avenue.

15 The other, larger population was in Bronzeville on the South Side.

16 Ten Chicago neighborhood types are identified as part of a Census 2000 mapping exercise authored by Christopher Winters, Bibliographer for Anthropology, Geography, and Maps at the University of Chicago Library for the University of Chicago Library Map Collection, using multivariate analysis, also called social-area analysis (see University of Chicago Library Map Collection 2001–2006 and "Chicago, Census 2000 Maps," www.lib.uchicago.edu/e/su/maps/chi2000.html). Analysis is based on University of Chicago Library Map Collection, Census 2000 Maps.

17 For the development of Columbus Park, see ch. 5, pp. 74–75.

18 See n. 16.

19 Chicago already possesses several buildings that combine residential towers with platforms for parking. The Trump Tower presents a recent, well-integrated example; others along North Michigan Avenue incorporate townhouses above structured parking. On the architectural possibilities of buildings that remain contiguous with the urban fabric at street level and are set back above as discrete objects, see Rowe 1995, pp. 165–220.

20 The proposal shown here utilized blocks running north-south to preserve a clear relationship with the prototype plans of Jensen and Drummond.

21 The University of Chicago Library Census 2000 Maps indicate that this population emerged as a significant demographic group between 1990 and 2000.

CHAPTER 11

1 The Chicago-Gary-Kenosha Consolidated Metropolitan Statistical Area includes Cook, DuPage, McHenry, DeKalb, Lake, Kane, Kendall, Will, Grundee, and Kankakee counties in Illinois; Lake and Porter counties in Indiana; and Kenosha County in Wisconsin.

2 The Chicago Metropolitan Agency for Planning predicts that metropolitan population growth will be concentrated in the urban fabric and on the outermost periphery (see Northeastern Illinois Planning Commission 2004).

3 This configuration separates the on-ramps and off-ramps moving in either direction without increasing their number.

4 Larger intervals between one-mile nodes require either isolated pairs of neighborhood units or the extension of the access roads parallel to the expressway to neighborhood units without an exit of their own.

CHAPTER 12

1 On the division of responsibility for implementing the *Plan of Chicago*, see Burnham, Bennett, and Moore 1909, ch. 8.

2 Lake Shore Drive and the extension of the public lakefront undertaken after World War II are legacies, rather than direct progeny, of the 1909 plan. Congress Parkway's relationship to the plan's proposed Axis of Chicago is more tenuous.

3 See Burnham, Bennett, and Moore 1909, appendix, pp. 127–56.

4 Pinkney 1955, p. 133.

5 On public works as a means of improving urban conditions for the poor, see Jordan 1995, p. 228.

6 Ibid., p. 229.

7 Pinkney gave a value in equivalent 1955 dollars, which has here been converted using one of the available methods. Depending on the method of calculation, the actual number might be considerably higher (see Pinkney 1957, p. 45).

8 Jordan 1995, p. 234.

9 Pinkney 1957, p. 46.

10 Jordan 1995, p. 233.

11 Pinkney 1957, p. 52.

12 Jordan 1995, pp. 234–35; and Pinkney 1957, p. 52.

13 Jordan 1995, p. 234.

14 Ibid., p. 236.

15 Garvin 2002, p. 361.

16 Ibid., p. 363.

17 Olympia and York assumed payment of the bonds coming due in exchange for exclusive development of the office space (see Sudjic and Sayer 1992, p. 47).

18 It is interesting to note that both incorporated visually based design guidelines or directives.

19 See Fuchs 1992, p. 187.

20 In 2005, in Kelo v. City of New London, the United States Supreme Court upheld a municipal government's right to condemn private property for public improvement based on economic redevelopment. A private redevelopment corporation was involved in the New London redevelopment plan. Following this decision, several states passed laws that sought to restrict the use of eminent domain. On the significance of this decision, see Burke 2006.

21 On the character and effects of the Battery Park City design guidelines, see Wiseman 1998, p. 335.

ILLUSTRATION CREDITS

INTRODUCTION

Chicago History Museum, ICHi-03560.

CHAPTER 1

Figure 1.1 Chicago Park District Special Collections.
Figure 1.2 From Anderson Publishing Company 1917. Library of Congress.
Figure 1.3 Howe et al. 1956.
Figure 1.4 Chicago History Museum, ICHi-37310.
Figure 1.5 Chicago History Museum, ICHi-38124.
Figure 1.6 Chicago History Museum, ICHi-59963.
Figure 1.7 George A. Fuller Company 1910.
Figure 1.8 The Newberry Library.
Figure 1.9 Chicago History Museum, ICHi-37425.
Figure 1.10 From Andreas 1884-86, vol. 3. Courtesy Chicago History Museum, ICHi-61137.
Figures 1.11-1.12 Frederick Law Olmsted National Historic Site.
Figure 1.13 Art Institute of Chicago, Ryerson and Burnham Archives.
Figure 1.14 From *Harper's New Monthly Magazine*, Feb. 1885.
Figure 1.15 Library of Congress.

CHAPTER 2

Figure 2.1 Art Institute of Chicago, Ryerson and Burnham Archives.
Figure 2.2 From Hegemann and Peets 1922, p. 98. Courtesy Art Institute of Chicago, Ryerson and Burnham Libraries.
Figure 2.3 Library of Congress.
Figure 2.4 Library of Congress Prints and Photographs Division.
Figure 2.5 Library of Congress.
Figure 2.6 Chicago History Museum, ICHi-02524.
Figure 2.7 Chicago History Museum, ICHi-27750.
Figure 2.8 From McKim, Mead, and White 1914-15. Courtesy Art Institute of Chicago, Ryerson and Burnham Libraries.
Figure 2.9 Ryerson and Burnham Archives, Art Institute of Chicago.
Figure 2.10 Art Institute of Chicago, Ryerson and Burnham Archives.
Figures 2.11-2.12 Library of Congress Prints and Photographs Division.

CHAPTER 3

Figure 3.1 Courtesy U.S. Commission of Fine Arts.
Figure 3.2 Frederick Law Olmsted National Historic Site. Olmsted Lithograph Collection, Job # 00900 Boston Parks. City of Boston. Parks Dep.
Figures 3.3-3.4 Library of Congress Geography and Map Division.
Figure 3.5 From Hegemann and Peets 1922, p. 285. Courtesy Art Institute of Chicago, Ryerson and Burnham Libraries.
Figures 3.6-3.8 Courtesy U.S. Commission of Fine Arts.
Figure 3.9 Courtesy U.S. Commission of Fine Arts. Photo by Lee Stalworth.
Figures 3.10-3.11 Courtesy U.S. Commission of Fine Arts.
Figure 3.12 Courtesy U.S. Commission of Fine Arts. Photo by Lee Stalworth.

CHAPTER 4

Figure 4.1 Art Institute of Chicago.
Figure 4.2 Art Institute of Chicago, Ryerson and Burnham Archives.
Figure 4.3 Perkins and Bradley 1905, courtesy University of Illinois at Chicago Library.
Figures 4.4-4.5 David Rumsey Map Collection, www.davidrumsey.com.
Figure 4.6 Alphand 1873, courtesy Art Institute of Chicago, Ryerson and Burnham Libraries.
Figure 4.7 Art Institute of Chicago.
Figures 4.8-4.9 David Rumsey Map Collection, www.davidrumsey.com.
Figures 4.10-4.15 Art Institute of Chicago.
Figure 4.16 Chicago History Museum, ICHi-59759.
Figure 4.17 Chicago History Museum, ICHi-59728.
Figure 4.18 Chicago History Museum, ICHi-03547.
Figure 4.19 Art Institute of Chicago.
Figure 4.20 Art Institute of Chicago, Ryerson and Burnham Archives.
Figure 4.21 Art Institute of Chicago.
Figure 4.22 Chicago History Museum, ICHi-39070_3r.
Figure 4.23 Chicago History Museum, ICHi-39070_3w.
Figures 4.24-4.29 Art Institute of Chicago.

CHAPTER 5

Figure 5.1 Jensen Collection, Bentley Historical Library, University of Michigan.
Figure 5.2 Chicago History Museum, ICHi-06575.
Figure 5.3 From Yeomans 1916, p. 3.
Figure 5.4 Chicago History Museum, ICHi-61136.
Figure 5.5 Chicago History Museum, ICHi-59966a.
Figure 5.6 Chicago History Museum, ICHi-59967.
Figure 5.7 Chicago History Museum, ICHi-59965.
Figure 5.8 Chicago History Museum, ICHi-59970.
Figure 5.9 Chicago History Museum, ICHi-59969.
Figure 5.10 Chicago History Museum, ICHi-61050.
Figure 5.11 Chicago History Museum, ICHi-61049.
Figure 5.12 Chicago History Museum, ICHi-59971.
Figure 5.13 Jensen Collection, Bentley Historical Library, University of Michigan.
Figure 5.14 © 2009 The Frank Lloyd Wright Foundation.
Figures 5.15-5.16 Art Institute of Chicago, Ryerson and Burnham Archives.
Figure 5.17 Chicago History Museum, ICHi-59968.
Figure 5.18 Chicago History Museum, ICHi-59964.
Figures 5.19-5.20 Jensen Collection, Bentley Historical Library, University of Michigan.

CHAPTER 6

Figures 6.1-6.3 Art Institute of Chicago, Ryerson and Burnham Archives.
Figure 6.4 Fondation Le Corbusier, Photography FLC L3(20)1, © FLC/ARS, 2009.
Figure 6.5 Fondation Le Corbusier, Plan FLC 31006, © FLC/ARS, 2009.
Figure 6.6 Fondation Le Corbusier, Plan FLC 29712, © FLC/ARS, 2009.
Figure 6.7 © 2009 The Frank Lloyd Wright Foundation.
Figure 6.8 From Alonso Pereira 1998; originally published in the periodical *La Ciudad Lineal.*
Figures 6.9-6.17 Art Institute of Chicago, Ryerson and Burnham Archives.

CHAPTER 7

Figure 7.1 R. Samuel Roche.
Figure 7.2 Chicago Park District Special Collections.
Figure 7.3 © 2009 The Frank Lloyd Wright Foundation.
Figure 7.4 Chicago History Museum, HB-27273-J2, HB-27273-J2.

CHAPTER 8

Figures 8.1-8.3 Aric Lasher.

CHAPTER 9

Figure 9.1 Art Institute of Chicago.
Figure 9.2 Pictometry.
Figure 9.3 Michael Baumberger.
Figure 9.4 R. Samuel Roche and Michael Baumberger.
Figure 9.5 R. Samuel Roche; plan courtesy City of Chicago.
Figures 9.6-9.8 Aric Lasher.
Figure 9.9 R. Samuel Roche.
Figures 9.10-9.12 Museum of Finnish Architecture.
Figure 9.13 Art Institute of Chicago, Ryerson and Burnham Archives.
Figures 9.14-9.15 R. Samuel Roche and Michael Baumberger.
Figure 9.16 R. Samuel Roche.
Figures 9.17-9.19 Aric Lasher.

CHAPTER 10

Figure 10.1 Chicago History Museum, ICHi-61051.
Figure 10.2 R. Samuel Roche; plan courtesy City of Chicago.
Figure 10.3 Michael Baumberger.
Figure 10.4 R. Samuel Roche; plan courtesy City of Chicago.
Figures 10.5-10.7 Aric Lasher.

CHAPTER 11

Figure 11.1 Art Institute of Chicago, Ryerson and Burnham Archives.
Figure 11.2 Courtesy of Goettsch Partners.
Figure 11.3 Digital Image © The Museum of Modern Art / Licensed by SCALA / Art Resource, NY.
Figures 11.4-11.5 Okrent Associates.
Figures 11.6-11.8 Aric Lasher.

CHAPTER 12

Figure 12.1 Library of Congress Prints and Photographs Division.
Figure 12.2 Cooper, Robertson and Partners.

INDEX

COLOPHON

This book was composed in QuarkXPress 8.02
by the JNL graphic design, Chicago

Equipment used in the production
of this book included:
Apple Mac Pro / System 10.5.7
Apple Cinema Display monitor
Konica Minolta bizhub C300 printer for trial proofs
Epson 9800 printer for press proofs

Text: Luxo Art Silk 150 gsm
Endpaper: f-Color #855 Kardinalrot
Dust Jacket: Luxo Art Silk 150 gsm
Casewrap: Eratex, Were Leinen 002
Photographs: 300 line screen halftones and duotones
Printing: Offset lithography
Binding: Smyth sewn with 40oz caseboard
Edition: 5000

Typefaces:
The body of this book was set in Berthold
Baskerville Book, a typeface designed by Günter
Gerhard Lange and based on the original design
of John Baskerville, circa 1754. The Berthold version
of Baskerville was designed to work with
modern systems and materials while retaining the
delicacy of Baskerville's original forms. The sans
serif display face used in this book is Gotham,
designed by Hoefler & Frere-Jones, circa 2000.